Intercultural Communication:
From the Cultural Comparison Perspective

跨文化
王 君◎主编
中西交流

上海交通大学出版社
SHANGHAI JIAO TONG UNIVERSITY PRESS

图书在版编目(CIP)数据

跨文化中西交流/ 王君主编. —上海：上海交通
大学出版社,2018
ISBN 978 - 7 - 313 - 20551 - 3

Ⅰ.①跨… Ⅱ.①王… Ⅲ.①文化交流—研究—中国、
西方国家 Ⅳ.①G125

中国版本图书馆 CIP 数据核字(2018)第 276464 号

跨文化中西交流

主　编：王　君			
出版发行：上海交通大学出版社		地　　址：上海市番禺路 951 号
邮政编码：200030		电　　话：021 - 64071208
出版人：谈　毅		
印　制：上海春秋印刷厂		经　　销：全国新华书店
开　本：710 mm×1000 mm　1/ 16		印　　张：13.5
字　数：319 千字		
版　次：2018 年 12 月第 1 版		印　　次：2018 年 12 月第 1 次印刷
书　号：ISBN 978 - 7 - 313 - 20551 - 3/ G		
定　价：49.00 元		

前　言

　　在政治、经济、文化全球化的新时期,中国英语学习者在出国留学,国外生活,与来自不同民族、种族、肤色和不同语言文化的人进行交往等情景中,难免会因为中西方在社会制度、地理环境、民族传统习俗、价值观念、生活方式、思维方式、语言和非语言符号等方面存在的差异而产生隔膜、误解甚至冲突。人们需要通过跨文化交流促进中西文化沟通,减少文化误解和冲突。因此,培养跨文化交流意识和增强跨文化交流能力对于中国英语学习者在今后的工作中更有效地学习世界经验、传播中国文化至关重要。

　　为了满足新时期跨文化交流能力培养的需求,编者针对我国高校英语学习者的实际情况,在多年课堂教学实践的基础上,编写了《跨文化中西交流》这本教材,旨在通过阐述和分析中西方文化异同,剖析其中蕴含的文化根源,提高学生的跨文化交流意识,培养他们的跨文化交流能力。本教材由八个单元组成,每个单元有五个模块:Warming Up、Basic Knowledge、Knowledge Expansion、Knowledge Application 和 Knowledge Practice。本教材力求体现理论联系实际的原则,从多角度、多视角为学生介绍和分析跨文化中西交流的主要内容和重要问题,为学生提供多样化的学习材料、知识应用练习题目。每单元的 Warming Up 模块为学生提供了体验真实的跨文化交流案例的电影片段,能有效激发学生的学习兴趣;Knowledge Expansion 模块为学有余力的学生提供深入了解跨文化交流知识的阅读材料;Knowledge Application 模块有助于学生巩固和应用在 Basic Knowledge 模块所汲取的跨文化中西交流基本知识;Knowledge Practice 模块可供学生课外进一步讨论探究重要的跨文化问题。希望学生通过这些多角度、多视角、多样化的跨文化交流现象体验、知识学习、知识巩固应用及问题讨论探究,将跨文化交流知识转化为交流技能,达到增强跨文化交流意识和能力的目的。

　　在本教材编写、修改过程中,得到了同事、朋友、家人的指点与帮助,在这里衷心感谢他们。还要感谢洪庆福教授在教材编写过程中给予的宝贵建议。

　　由于受水平和条件的限制,教材中难免会有不足之处,恳请读者提出宝贵意见,以便在重印时及时修订完善。

编　者

2018 年 6 月

Contents

Unit 1

Intercultural Communication

● **Learning Objectives**

By the end of this unit, you should be able to:
1. Understand the definition of intercultural communication;
2. Explain the forms of intercultural communication;
3. Describe the development of intercultural communication study;
4. Understand the importance of intercultural communication;
5. Know the potential challenges in intercultural communication.

Part One Warming Up

Watch the following movie clip from *Rush Hour 1* and then answer the questions below the script.

Questions for discussion:
1. Why doesn't Lee reply to Carter in English when Carter meets him at the airport?
2. Why does Lee replies to the taxi driver in English?
3. What cultural differences between China and the U.S. cause the communication conflict between Carter and Lee?

Part Two   Basic Knowledge of Intercultural Communication

1. Definition of Intercultural Communication

Intercultural Communication is the term first used by Edward T. Hall in 1959 and is simply defined as interpersonal communication between members of different cultures. For Samovar et al.（2000：48），"Intercultural communication is communication between people whose cultural perceptions and symbol systems are distinct enough to alter the communication event."

The Chinese scholar Jia Yuxin（1997）defines intercultural communication as the communication between people from different cultural backgrounds. According to Robinson，intercultural communication is regarded as complicated communication full of excitement and frustration. (L.A. Samovar & R.E. Porter，2007)

According to Byram，the term "Intercultural communication" has two senses：its narrow sense and broad sense. And his definition in the narrow sense is widely accepted，but his definition in the broad sense has been criticized because similar studies had been carried out previously，using the same methods. His definition in the narrow sense is that intercultural communication refers to a peculiar communication situation：the various language and discourse strategies people from different cultural backgrounds use in direct，face-to-face situations（Yu Weihua，2006）. As this term became more popular，it was also used to refer to studies in translation，in contrastive linguistics，in foreign literature reading or in comparative analysis of cultural meanings. Furthermore，research and its applications in the narrow sense of the term developed into specific fields of interest，namely the discourse analysis of communicative events，where people from different cultural backgrounds engage in face-to-face communication. More often，people use the term cross-cultural communication with a focus on the comparison and analysis of the differences between cultures when referring to communication between people from different cultures.

Based on the above mentioned definitions，we hold that intercultural communication refers to the communication between people from different cultural backgrounds，who may come from different countries on the other side of the earth or from the same country.

2. Forms of Intercultural Communication

According to Samovar et al.（2000），there are three forms of intercultural communication.

2.1　Interracial Communication

Interracial Communication occurs when the sender and the receiver exchanging messages are from different races that pertain to different physical characteristics. The major difficulty encountered in interracial communication is racial prejudice, a problem that can often be traced to ethnocentrism. Strong prejudice leads to stereotyping and suspicion, both of which prevent meaningful interaction. Another barrier to interracial communication is the use of power by the dominant culture to control the degree to which racial groups are accepted into the main stream.

2.2　Interethnic Communication

Interethnic communication refers to communication between people of the same race but different ethnic backgrounds. Ethnic minorities usually form their own communities in a country or culture. Chinese living in San Francisco, Cubans in Miami, Mexicans in San Diego might all be citizens of the United States, but they have quite different backgrounds, perspectives, goals and languages.

2.3　Intracultural Communication

Intracultural communication is defined as communication between members of the same culture, including racial, ethnic and other co-cultures. Generally, people, who are of the same race, political persuasion and religion or who share the same interest, communicate intraculturally. Although the term can define the exchange of messages between members of the dominant culture, it is usually applied to communication in which one or both of the participants hold dual membership. In these cases, factors like racial, ethnic, or something else also come into playing a role in them.

3. The Development of Intercultural Communication

Although the phenomenon of intercultural communication enjoys the same history with human society, the study of intercultural communication as an academic discipline is relatively new, and originated in the United States in the 1950s. And then the study in this field spread to other countries including China.

3.1　The Development of Intercultural Communication Studies in America

3.1.1　Earlier Period (1950—1960)

Edward Hall is considered as the father of the field of intercultural communication study. His book, *The Silent Language*, which was published in 1959, marked the beginning of intercultural communication studies. During the 1950s when Edward Hall worked for the State Department of the United States teaching intercultural skills to foreign service personnel, he developed concepts like "high-context culture" and "low-context culture", and he also wrote several popular practical books on dealing with intercultural issues. In *The Silent Language*，Hall (1959) defined culture as a form of communication which is governed by hidden rules involving both speech and actions. He coined the term "polychromic" to describe those with the ability to attend multiple events simultaneously，as opposed to "monochromic" used to describe those who tend to handle events sequentially. Hall also introduced other terms such as "intercultural tensions" and "intercultural problems".

The beginning of Intercultural communication studies was for application rather than for theoretical considerations：training was the main issue. The first target audience was American diplomats and development personnel whose intercultural skills required improvement.

3.1.2　Development Period (1960—1980)

Hall's influence on the study of intercultural communication is far-reaching. His research has attracted numerous scholars to the study of intercultural communication. Two representative books in the 1960s are Oliver's *Culture and Communication* (1962) and Smith's *Communication and Culture* (1966). Oliver's study focuses on Asian philosophy and communication behaviors，especially from a rhetorical perspective. His book establishes a model for comparative study of communication behavior between cultures. In Smith's book，essays on human communication covering thirteen types of communication studies are collected.

The first intercultural communication training actually started in the 1960s with Peace Corp members，who required training in cultural awareness before they were sent to their missions overseas. The first college class in this field was taught in 1966 at the University of Pittsburgh in the United States.

The 1970s witnessed rapid development in the field of intercultural communication. The major achievements in the study may include：

(1) In 1970 and 1971，intercultural communication was recognized by the Intercultural Communication Association (ICA) and the National Communication Association (NCA) respectively.

(2) SIETAR-International (the International Society for Intercultural Education，Training and Research) began in 1975，and is now probably the largest international organization engaged in intercultural communication.

(3) In 1977，an academic journal titled *International Journal of Intercultural Relations* was first published under the editorship of Dan Landis，which influenced research in the field of intercultural communication in the years that followed.

3.1.3　Establishment of the Theoretical Framework (1981-the present time)

Scholars who received formal academic training in intercultural communication in the late 1960s and the 1970s began to make contributions in research and teaching in the

1980s. Theory building and methodological refinement characterized intercultural communication study during this decade. The book titled *Theories in Intercultural Communication* by Kim and Gudykunst （1988） features two approaches to theory building.

In the United States, intercultural communication has now become an important academic discipline. The ICA has over 5,000 members and the NCA has over 7,500. In addition, the Speech Communication Association （SCA）, the International and Intercultural Communication Annual (IICA) have also helped determine the direction for the study of intercultural communication from the 1970s to the present time.

As Hart （1996） summarized, the study of intercultural communication gained acceptance through training and testing practice in the 1960s and the 1970s, and formed its basic framework of the intercultural communication in the late 1970s and has made great achievements in the theory building ever since the 1980s both inside and outside the United States. Today intercultural communication has become one of the main academic disciplines in the United States, and is also widely acknowledged and researched in all parts of the world.

3.2   The Development of Intercultural Communication Studies in China

Intercultural communication studies in China began in the early 1980s. Although it has a much shorter history than that in the United States and Europe, there has been widespread interest in it. According to Hu Wenzhong （2004）, this short history of Intercultural Communication Studies in China can be divided into three distinct periods.

3.2.1   Earlier Period （1980—1990）

Intercultural communication was first introduced into China during the early 1980s by teachers of English who took an interest in it for the purpose of changing training and teaching methodology into communicative approach. Professor Xu Guozhang was one of those investigators who first wrote articles on the cultural loading of words or the meanings of words. Professor Hu Wenzhong, He Daokuan and others paved the way for the development of intercultural communication studies in China. They focused on the problem of how language and culture interact with each other.

3.2.2   Establishment Period （1991—2000）

In this period, scholars began to engage in intercultural communication research, and some of them introduced western intercultural communication achievements to China, which laid foundation for the studies in China. In this aspect, we can find powerful American influence. In 1995, "the 5th International Conference on Cross-cultural Communication: East and West" was held in China. During this conference the China Association for Intercultural Communication was established. Besides, intercultural communication research spread into journalism and communication studies.

3.2.3 Development Period (2001—present)

With the further development of globalization, intercultural communication studies have proved to be more and more important in China. Numerous articles were written and then were followed by books. Their study grew from academic interest to theoretical research and practical application. Many universities have developed courses in intercultural communication for both graduate and undergraduate students. Intercultural training and teaching is gaining popularity in some more developed cities in China.

Today, scholars engaging in intercultural communication research mainly come from two different fields: one is foreign language teaching, the other is communication. The former is interested in the core problem of linguistic and cultural difference, and the relevant issues such as pragmatic transfer, intercultural competence, cultural value orientation, identity and translation. The latter is interested in the core problem of how ideas are transmitted by media, and the relevant issues such as the role of power, communication ethics, national image and the impact of globalization.

As we move further into the 21st century and become more globalized, the importance of intercultural communication as a major field of study will definitely be recognized and numerous linguists, language teachers and scholars are engaged in research in this field, laying a solid foundation for a deeper understanding of different cultures.

4. The Importance of Intercultural Communication

In today's world, no nation, group, or culture can remain alone or autonomous. International developments have made intercultural contact pervasive.

4.1 Changes in the World Population

Changes in population migration have contributed to the development of increasing intercultural contact. People from all over the world leave their own countries for one reason or another to find peace, seek jobs, receive better education or to start a new life. Countries such as the United Sates, Australia, Canada, the U. K, China and so on have become the destinations of choice for such people.

In the United States, people are now redefining and rethinking the meaning of the word "American". It can no longer be used to describe a somewhat homogeneous group of people sharing a European heritage. As Ben J. Wattenberg (1989) tells us, America has become the first universal nation, a truly multi-cultural society marked by unparalleled diversity (Samovar, Porter, McDaniel, 2007). This multiethnic composition calls for an understanding of the dynamic of the communication among people from different nations and ethnic groups.

4.2 Technological Development

The development of new transportation and information technologies makes it much easier for people from different cultural backgrounds to get together and communicate in the modern world. New technologies of transportation systems have accelerated intercultural contact. Trips once taking days, weeks, or even months are now measured in hours. Transcontinental aviation now makes it possible for tourists, business executives, or government officials to enjoy breakfast in San Francisco and dinner in Paris on the same day. Innovative communication systems have also encouraged cultural interaction. Communication satellites, sophisticated television transmission equipment, and digital switching networks now allow people throughout the world to share information and ideas instantaneously. As a consequence, we have to adjust to this rapidly changing communication styles.

4.3　Economic Globalization

Globalization of the world economy has contributed to the rapid increase of intercultural communication. As a result of conducting business internationally, international businesses have become an important economic force for many countries. For example, according to Harris and Moran (1996), there are now more than 37,000 transnational corporations with 207,000 foreign affiliates. This expansion in globalization has resulted in multinational corporations participating in various international business arrangements such as joint ventures and licensing agreements. These economic ties and countless others mean that it would not be unusual for someone to work for an organization that does business in many countries. In fact, when managers and employees are working for foreign-owned companies or in their dealings with foreign suppliers, customs, and co-workers, they do business in an intercultural environment. In any case, the globalization of the world's economy will challenge virtually all businesspersons to become internationally aware and interculturally competent.

5. The Potential Challenges in Intercultural Communication

When a person arrives in a new country, his/her cultural and personal background will influence his/her behaviors, words and decisions. Most of the people he/she will meet in the new country are no exception. Their behaviors, words and decisions will be influenced by their own backgrounds culturally, personally and socially. If he or she ignores the sensitivity of cultural differences, he or she may have difficulties in communicating with people from other cultures, and even fail in intercultural communication. It is generally agreed that problems like lacking the sensitivities of cultural differences, stereotyping and discrimination are the common potential challenges in intercultural communication. Therefore, to learn intercultural communication well, it's very important to learn about the potential challenges in intercultural communication.

5.1　Lacking the Sensitivities of Cultural Differences

In intercultural communication, most people take it for granted that those who share the common outlooks, habits, etc. with them may have the similar culture background with theirs'. But it may not be the case, because those who have the common outlooks and habits may have a history different from their own. It is the differences that separate them from those people. Therefore, lacking the sensitivities of cultural differences is a big difficulty which needs to be solved in intercultural communication. Take the following case for example. Yang Hong is a Chinese visiting scholar at a British university. He stays with a British family. One day, the hostess's father-in-law, Mr. Green, flew from London to York to visit his son's family in York. He is a nice man in his 70s. After his son's introduction, Mr. Green and Mr. Yang began the following conversation.

Mr. Green: I didn't know you are so handsome, Hong.

Mr. Yang: Thank you! Mr. Green. My English name is Peter.

Mr. Green: Please call me Bob.

Mr. Yang: But you are as old as my dad, I can't call you by you first name.

Mr. Green: Nobody calls me Mr. Green, I'm not used to it, Hong.

When they said good night to each other, they both felt quite uncomfortable about the way they were addressed. The reason behind the uncomfortable feelings of them lies in their lack of the awareness of the differences between their addressing cultures. In Chinese culture, it is impolite to call an elderly man by his first name, so it's really difficult for Yang Hong to call his hostess's father-in-law by his first name. While in western culture, it is unacceptable to call an ordinary man by Mr. instead of his first name.

5.2 Stereotyping

Stereotyping takes place when people have false assumptions about characteristics of people from other cultures. Stereotyping hampers intercultural communication, because people with stereotyping behavior always make a distinct line between people by taking some people as their in-group members and other people as out-groups. Besides, people with stereotyping behavior always oversimplify or overgeneralize or exaggerate characteristics of those they consider as out-groups. Take the following case for example. A young man named Mohamad came back to his homeland Kuwait. Before he went to a college in the United States to further his study, he had a false assumption that Americans discriminate people from the Middle East and their religion. However, when he arrived in America, and studied there, he understood that not all Americans discriminate people from the Middle East and dislike their religion. In fact, he met a lot of Americans who are interested to know about his country and culture.

Glossary

1. **perception**   *n*. the ability to see, hear, or become aware of something through the

senses 感知能力；认识能力

2. **symbol** *n*. a thing that represents or stands for something else，especially a material object representing something abstract 象征

3. **distinct** *adj*. recognizably different in nature from something else of a similar type 可辨别的，有区别的，不同的

4. **alter** *vt*. make or become different；change in character，appearance，etc. 改变，更改；修改

5. **scholar** *n*. a specialist in a particular branch of study，especially the humanities；a distinguished academic （尤指人文学科的）学者

6. **define** *vt*. state or describe exactly the nature，scope，or meaning of sth. 下定义；确切地说明（或解释）

7. **frustration** *n*. the feeling of being upset or annoyed，especially because of inability to change or achieve something （尤指因无能为力而引起的）痛苦；恼怒

8. **sense** *n*. a faculty by which the body perceives an external stimulus；one of the faculties of sight，smell，hearing，taste，and touch 官能；感觉

9. **broad** *adj*. having a distance larger than usual from side to side；wide 宽的，广的

10. **criticize** *vt*. indicate the faults of（someone or something）in a disapproving way 批评；责备

11. **previously** *adj*. existing or occurring before in time or order 以前的，先前的

12. **refer** *vi*. mention or allude to 提到，谈到；指

13. **peculiar** *adj*. strange or odd；unusual 奇怪的，古怪的；不寻常的

14. **discourse** *n*. written or spoken communication or debate （口头或书面的）交谈；辩论

15. **strategy** *n*. a plan of action or policy designed to achieve a major or overall aim 战略

16. **contrast** *n*. the action of calling attention to notable differences. 对比，对照

17. **linguistics** *n*. the scientific study of language and its structure，including the study of grammar，syntax，and phonetics. Specific branches of linguistics include sociolinguistics，dialectology，psycholinguistics，computational linguistics，comparative linguistics，and structural linguistics 语言学

18. **literature** *n*. written works，especially those considered of superior or lasting artistic merit 文学作品

19. **comparative** *adj*. measured or judged by estimating the similarity or dissimilarity between one thing and another；relative 比较而言的；相对而言的

20. **analysis** *n*. detailed examination of the elements or structure of something，typically as a basis for discussion or interpretation 分析

21. **engage** *vt*. occupy，attract，or involve（someone's interest or attention） 引起（某

人的兴趣或注意),吸引

22. **cross-cultural**　*adj*. of or relating to different cultures or comparison between them　(与)交叉文化(有关)的,(与)涉及多种(不同)文化(有关)的,(与)跨文化(有关)的

23. **comparison**　*n*. a consideration or estimate of the similarities or dissimilarities between two things or people　比较;对照

24. **occur**　*vi*. happen; take place　发生

25. **pertain**　*vi*. be appropriate, related, or applicable　适合,符合;有关,涉及;适用

26. **characteristic**　*adj*. typical of a particular person, place, or thing　特有的,独特的

27. **encounter**　*vt*. unexpectedly experience or be faced with (something difficult or hostile)　遇到(困难或不利的事),碰到;面临

28. **racial**　*adj*. of or relating to race　人种的,种族的;民族的

29. **trace**　*vt*. find or discover by investigation　(通过调查)找到,发现

30. **ethnocentrism**　*n*. belief in the superiority of one's own ethnic group　种族(民族)中心主义,种族(民族、集团)优越感

31. **prejudice**　*n*. preconceived opinion that is not based on reason or actual experience　先入之见,成见

32. **stereotype**　*n*. a widely held but fixed and oversimplified image or idea of a particular type of person or thing　陈规,老套,旧框框
　　vt. view or represent as a stereotype　使成为老一套,使成为陈规;对……有成见

33. **suspicion**　*n*. a feeling or thought that something is possible, likely, or true　怀疑

34. **barrier**　*n*. a fence or other obstacle that prevents movement or access　屏障;障碍物

35. **dominant**　*adj*. most important, powerful, or influential　(最)重要的;(最)强大的;(最)有影响的

36. **stream**　*n*. a mass of people or things moving continuously in the same direction.　(人,东西)流动,涌动

37. **ethnic**　*adj*. of or relating to a population subgroup (within a larger or dominant national or cultural group) with a common national or cultural tradition　(与)种族(有关)的;(与)民族(有关)的

38. **perspective**　*n*. the appearance of viewed objects with regard to their relative position, distance from the viewer, etc.　(被观察物的相对位置及与观察者之间的距离等因素造成的)视觉;外观

39. **dual**　*adj*. consisting of two parts, elements, or aspects　双的,两的;两体的;二元的

40. **academic**　*adj*. of or relating to education and scholarship　(与)教育和学问(有关)的;学术的

41. **discipline**　*n*. branch of knowledge; subject of instruction　学科;科目

42. **coin** *v*. invent or devise (a new word or phrase) 创造(新词、短语),杜撰

43. **polychromy** *n*. the art of painting in several colours, especially as applied to ancient pottery, sculpture, and architecture (尤指应用于古陶器、雕塑和建筑上的)彩绘艺术

44. **polychromic** *adj*. 彩饰的

45. **multiple** *adj*. having or involving several parts, elements, or members 多个的,多成分的,多成员的

46. **simultaneously** *adj*. occurring, operating, or done at the same time 同时出现的,同时操作的,同时进行的,同步的

47. **monochrome** *n*. a photograph or picture developed or executed in black and white or in varying tones of only one colour 黑白照片,单色照片,单色画,单色图片

48. **monochromic** *adj*. 单色的

49. **sequentially** *adj*. forming or following in a logical order or sequence 连续的;有序的

50. **rhetorical** *adj*. ① of, relating to, or concerned with the art of rhetoric (与)修辞(有关)的 ② expressed in terms intended to persuade or impress. 虚夸的;空洞华丽的

51. **methodology** *n*. a system of methods used in a particular area of study or activity 方法学;方法论;系统方法

52. **refinement** cultured elegance in behaviour or manner (举止)高雅,优雅;有教养

53. **pave** *v*. (常作 be paved with) cover (a piece of ground) with flat stones or bricks; lay paving over 用石(或砖)铺(路);铺砌,铺筑

54. **pragmatic** *adj*. dealing with things sensibly and realistically in a way that is based on practical rather than theoretical considerations 讲究实际的,讲求实效的,实用的

55. **orientation** *n*. the determination of the relative position of something or someone (especially oneself) (尤指自身)定向,定位;确定方向

56. **pervasive** *adj*. (especially of an unwelcome influence or physical effect) spreading widely throughout an area or a group of people (尤指令人讨厌的影响或身体感受)弥漫性的,渗透性的;遍布的,流行的

57. **homogeneous** *adj*. of the same kind; alike 同种的;相似的

58. **unparalleled** *adj*. having no parallel or equal; exceptional 独特的;无比的

59. **multiethnic** *adj*. of, relating to, or constituting several ethnic groups 涉及不同种族的

60. **instantaneous** *adj*. occurring or done in an instant or instantly 瞬间发生的,瞬间完成的

61. **affiliate** *vt*. officially attach or connect (a subsidiary group or a person) to an organization [as affiliated] 使(下属集团、个人)隶属,加入

62. **license** *vt*. grant a licence (to someone or something) to permit the use of

something or to allow an activity to take place 颁发许可证(或执照),批准,许可

63. **multicultural** *adj*. of，relating to，or constituting several cultural or ethnic groups within a society （与)多种文化(有关)的,融合多种文化的

64. **discrimination** *n*. the unjust or prejudicial treatment of different categories of people or things, especially on the grounds of race，age，or sex 区别对待;歧视

65. **mosaic** *n*. a picture or pattern produced by arranging together small variously coloured pieces of hard material, such as stone，tile，or glass 马赛克,(小块杂色硬质材料如石头、瓷砖、玻璃等的)镶嵌图案

66. **assimilate** *vt*. take in and understand fully（information，ideas，or culture） 吸收,领会(信息、思想或文化)

67. **contemporary** *adj*. living or occurring at the same time 生活在同时代(或时期)的;同时代(或时期)发生的

68. **polyculture** *n*. the simultaneous cultivation or exploitation of several crops or kinds of animals (多种庄稼或动物)同时培育,同时利用

● Comprehension Check

I. Decide whether the following statements are true (T) or false (F).

1.（ ）As a phenomenon, intercultural communication has existed for thousands of years. However，as a discipline，its history is only about fifty years.

2.（ ）Intercultural Communication as a discipline first started in Europe.

3.（ ）Satellite transmission of telephone，radio and television signals is one of the reason for the increase of intercultural communication.

4.（ ）International computer networks such as the Internet don't play a role in the growth of people's intercultural interaction.

5.（ ）Increased speed and availability of air travel has contributed to the globalization.

6.（ ）International economic relationships such as multi-national corporations and foreign trade are an important reason for the growth of intercultural communication.

7.（ ）Economic cooperation through organizations such as the European Union，the Association of Southeast Asian Nations and Asia-Pacific Economic Cooperation haven't played a role in the rapid increase of intercultural communication.

8.（ ）Globalization of the world economy has contributed to the rapid increase of intercultural communication.

9.（ ）Stereotyping makes up a big challenge in intercultural communication.

10.（ ）The sensitivities of cultural differences may not affect intercultural communication.

II. What do the following acronyms stand for?

1. ICA

2. NCA

3. SCA

4. IICA

III. Please define the following terms.

1. international communication

2. interethnic communication

3. intracultural communication

4. intercultural communication

IV. Questions for group discussion.

1. Please give specific examples to illustrate international, interethnic, intracultural communication.

2. Please try to come up with at least 3 cases in your daily life to illustrate the intercultural communication phenomenon.

3. How was the study of intercultural communication developed both in America and in China?

4. Can you give one crucial development for the rapid increase of intercultural communication and explain it with your personal experience.

5. Please give more examples about potential challenges in intercultural communication.

V. Fill in each of the blanks in the following passage with an appropriate word from those listed below.

A. establish   B. communication   C. material   D. environment

E. extent   F. express   G. messages   H. similar

I. influence   J. symbols

Communication is central to our existence. It is through __1__ that we learn who we are, and what the world around us is like. To a large __2__, our identity as both individual and cultural being is shaped through communication. Through this, we explore the world around us, and __3__ bonds, networks, and relationships with other people. Communication permits us to __4__ our thoughts and feelings to others, and to satisfy our emotional and __5__ needs as we learn to communicate better, we begin to achieve some measure of control over events that affect us and those around us. There are three basic aspects of communication: our individual personality, the culture we operate in, and the physical __6__ that surrounds us. Each of these aspects has a (n) __7__ on what and how we communicate.

Communication is transactional. Each person encodes and sends messages, and in turn receives and decodes __8__. The coding and decoding process is primarily culture-based and involves a diverse set of elements, including words, gestures, __9__, values, etc. Whether a communication is successful or not depends greatly on the circumstances. The key is whether the participants have some __10__ cultural background, knowledge and experiences. In cross-cultural situations, this shared area may be very small. (Hu Chao, 2006)

Part Three Knowledge Expansion

Reading 1

Multiculturalism: One Imperative Factor Influencing Intercultural Communication

Multiculturalism is the appreciation, acceptance or promotion of multiple cultures. By making the broadest range of human differences acceptable to the largest number of people, multiculturalism seeks to overcome racism, sexism and other forms of discrimination. The term is applied to distinct cultures of immigrant groups in developed countries.

Multiculturalism is seen by its supporters as a fairer system that allows people to truly express who they are within a society, that is more tolerant and that adapts better to social issues (Lerman, 2010). They argue that culture is not one definable thing based on one race or religion, but rather the result of multiple factors that change as the world changes.

The development of multiculturalism in the Western English-speaking countries:

(1) Canada

Multiculturalism was adopted as the official policy of the Canadian government during the premiership of Pierre Elliot Trudeau in the 1970s and the 1980s. The Canadian government has often been described as the instigator of multicultural ideology because of its public emphasis on the social importance of immigration. Multiculturalism is reflected in the law through the Canadian Multiculturalism Act and Section 27 of the Canadian Charter of Rights and Freedoms. In 2001, approximately 250,640 people immigrated to Canada. The newcomers settle mostly in the major urban areas of Toronto, Vancouver and Montreal. By the 1990s and the 2000s, the largest component of Canada's immigrants came from Asia, including the Middle East, South Asia, South-East Asia and East Asia. Canadian society is often depicted as being very progressive, diverse, and multicultural. Accusing a person of racism in Canada is usually considered a serious slur.

(2) Australia

The next country to adopt an official policy of multiculturalism after Canada was Australia, with many similar policies, for example, the formation of the Special Broadcasting Service. According to the 2006 census, more than one fifth of the population were born overseas. Furthermore, almost 50% of the population were either born overseas or had one or both parents born overseas.

(3) The United States

In the United States, multiculturalism is not clearly established in policy at the federal level. Instead, it has been an issue primarily through the school system, with the rise of ethnic studies programs in higher education and with attempts to make the grade school curricula more inclusive of the history and contributions of non-white peoples. It has also become an issue for businesses as they address how to meet the needs of a workforce that is increasingly more diverse but not that does not always understand the differences that occur between cultures.

In the United States, continuous mass immigration had been a feature of economy and society since the first half of the 19th century. The absorption of the stream of immigrations became, in itself, a prominent feature of America's national myth. The idea that the melting pot is a metaphor implies that all the immigrant cultures are mixed and amalgamated without state intervention.

Multiculturalism affects the educational process because it affects the cultural dynamics of the classroom. The educational approach to multiculturalism has since spread to the grade school system in the U.S. as school's system try to rework its curricula to introduce students to diversity earlier — often on the grounds that it is important for minority students to see themselves represented in the classroom. For instance, history classes can spend more time making students aware of the presence and struggles of ethnic minorities, and literature classes can use texts by ethnic minority authors.

(4) The United Kingdom

Multicultural policies were adopted by local administrations from the 1970s and the 1980s onwards, in particular by the Labour Government of Tony Blair. Most of the immigrants of the last decades came from the Indian subcontinent or the Caribbean. In 2004 the number of people who became British citizens rose to a record 140,795 — a rose of 12% on the previous year. This number had risen dramatically since 2000. The overwhelming majority of new citizens were born in Africa (30%) and Asia (40%), the largest three groups being people from Pakistan, India and Somalia.

The development of multiculturalism in the Eastern countries:

In Asian countries like Indonesia, Malaysia, the Philippines, Singapore, etc., there are more than three living languages spoken in one nation which lead to the multiculturalism in those countries. In Indonesia there are 700 living languages spoken which articulate that diversity shapes the country. In Malaysia, 52% of the population in the country are Malays who make up the majority, about 30% of the population are Malaysians of Chinese descent, Malaysians of Indian descent comprise about 8% of the population. The Philippines is the

8th most multiethnic nation in the world. In Singapore, besides English, three other languages are recognized, namely Chinese Mandrin, Tamil and Malay, as its official languages, with Malay being the national language. Besides being a multilingual country, Singapore also acknowledges festivals celebrated by these three ethnic communities.

And the trend of multiculturalism is spreading to more Asian countries, for instance, Republic of Korea is among the world's most ethnically homogeneous nations. However, the word "multiculturalism" is increasingly heard in Republic of Korea.

With this trend of multiculturalism in the world, the pattern of intercultural communication will surely be affected. People in the world should learn the appropriate ways of interacting so as to deal with frictions in the multicultural communication environment, and adjust to new cultural realities smoothly.

（Cheng Wenjuan & Yan Xiaofeng, 2012: 25-29）

● Comprehension Check

I. Answer the following questions.

1. Please give examples to explain what multiculturalism is.
2. How is multiculturalism policies carried out in Western countries?
3. What is the multiculturalism like in Eastern countries?
4. How should people in the world do to deal with frictions caused by the multicultural environment?

II. Translate into Chinese the following passage in the above text.

Multiculturalism is the appreciation, acceptance or promotion of multiple cultures. By making the broadest range of human differences acceptable to the largest number of people, multiculturalism seeks to overcome racism, sexism and other forms of discrimination. The term is applied to distinct cultures of immigrant groups in developed countries.

Multiculturalism is seen by its supporters as a fairer system that allows people to truly express who they are within a society, that is more tolerant and that adapts better to social issues. They argue that culture is not one definable thing based on one race or religion, but rather the result of multiple factors that change as the world changes.

Reading 2

Technology Makes People All Over the World Connected

How is technology important to the development of a metacultural layer of behavior? The answer is obvious to us in the 21st century: the explosion of technology has led to increased and frequent contact between and among cultures, regardless of time, geographical or political boundaries. Being in constant contact allows people to learn about one another both directly and indirectly. Marshall McLuhan envisioned such a scenario in his notion of the global village. Remember, the global village is the idea that people are connected to one another via technology, no matter how remote or isolated their culture generally is.

One way to portray just what this means is to compare the following statistics of cultural usage of the internet. Now for some of us, usage of the internet is just as much a part of our lives as eating and drinking. In fact, as Fig.2.3 indicates, we have the ability to access immediate information right in the palm of one hand. However, this has not always been the case around the globe. Clearly the increase of internet usage has been most importantly felt in non-Western cultures over the last few years. One study conducted in December of 2009 reports that while internet usage in North America increased by 140% and the EU growth increased by 240% over the course of the study, the Middle East showed a surge of 1,675%, and the African continent came in at a whopping 1,810%!

Furthermore, the advances of technology have radically changed the domains of medicine, scientific research, space programs, telecommunications, the entertainment industry, etc.. The development of technology simply makes life easier for many people. DNA testing, forensic science, biometrics (the science of digitalizing information), banking, financing, advances in alternative forms of fuel, and various advances in fiber optics are some of the many examples where we can see how technology has changed the way we live — not only in a specific culture, but globally. In other words, we now have the world right at our fingertips!

The whole process is rather circular. Technological advances have allowed the spread of globalization. In turn, globalization has more widely distributed new technologies.

Of course, there are disadvantages to globalized technology, as well as presuppositions and dangers, and we shall address these issues later on. For now, let's turn our attention to some of the more evident ways in which technology has connected us.

Our Wireless World

Advances in technology have done much to change the way we live and communicate over the past quarter-century, but no breakthrough has revolutionized life as much as the advent of the "wireless world," according to a panel of experts assembled by CNN to pick the top 25 ('top technological advances').

We are mesmerized, it seems, by screens. The media plays one of the single most important roles in both spreading and advancing technology. Information is now available instantly, not just quickly, and most regions of our planet are connected via the Internet. One area that technology and the media have transformed is with news and newscasters. No longer are we dependent on a certain hour for television headlines and news to retrieve important information. In fact, a new form of journalism has taken shape even in the last few years: participatory journalism. This type of reporting is not subject to the same constraints that traditional news media might have been. For example, traditional broadcast media was based on a few reporting to many listeners/watchers. Now, individuals can instantly film, photograph, or record important global events and upload these immediately onto the Internet, so that we have many reporting to many, and in almost real-time parameters.

In addition to reporting and news availability, technology has had an enormous effect on spreading cultural information and norms through advertising, education, and of course, entertainment. Whether Hollywood, Bollywood, or Dollywood, the entertainment industry is broadcast globally and has affected cultural trends worldwide. Information is not only accessible; it can be frozen in time to repeat over and over, which enhances the educational effects. First videos, then DVD's, and now BluRay ® provide ways to maintain information over the constraints of space and time.

Technological advances have thus provided us with very real ways of spreading cultural information and norms in major segments. Music, fashion, religion, politics, various lifestyles, and of course language are all examples of cultural elements that are shared or available in most parts of the world.

Dynamic Nature of the Metaculture

Technological advances highlight the dynamic nature of a metaculture. Fashion, music, movies, political policies, business practices, etc. are constantly changing or adapting to generational preferences. This means that the surface metacultural level of shared norms will also change. What people choose to do or value can fluctuate depending on what is the newest, up-to-date, or currently popular social behavior. For example, consider the top ten lists in the entertainment industry. Movies and music shape both behavior as well as fashion, and we can see how the metacultural level of shared norms is directly tied to what's on a current top ten list.

World events are also a force for the dynamic or changing nature of a metaculture. Recent emphasis on terror networks and the fight against them have radically changed how we experience travel. Security norms have evolved dramatically over the last decade, and passengers are far more used to stringent checks and searches than they were before. No matter which airport you find yourself in, for example, you expect to be closely examined from head to toe by the security personnel before being allowed on a flight.

In sum, the explosion of technology has indeed created a global village. Contact created as a result of such a virtual village has greatly helped the spread and change of a surface-level of cultural behavior. These shared patterns constitute a real, dynamic level of culture that is noticeable globally. (Melanie Moll, 2012: 19 - 24)

Comprehension Check

I. Answer the following questions.

1. How does the development of technology makes the world like a global village?
2. How do the advances of technology influence people's life?
3. How do the advances in technology have changed the way people communicate over the past quarter-century?
4. How has technology effected the spread of cultural information and norms?
5. What is the dynamic nature of the metaculture?

II. Translate into Chinese the following passage in the essay.

Technological advances highlight the dynamic nature of a metaculture. Fashion, music, movies, political policies, business practices, etc. are constantly changing or adapting to generational preferences. This means that the surface metacultural level of shared norms will also change. What people choose to do or value can fluctuate depending on what is the newest, up-to-date, or currently popular social behavior. For example, consider the top ten lists in the entertainment industry. Movies and music shape both behavior as well as fashion, and we can see how the metacultural level of shared norms is directly tied to what's on a current top ten list.

Part Four   Knowledge Application

Case Analysis

I. Case 1

A Failure Sale

An American team called Canwall, which is a wallpaper printing equipment manufacturer, went to Jiangsu to negotiate a sale with a new Chinese wallpaper production company. In the first two days when the representatives from the American company arrived in China, they were showed around some places for relaxation by the representatives from the Chinese company. In the third day, the negotiation meeting began. But actually, the Chinese company spent a lot of time talking about some issues unrelated to the sale. The American representatives didn't know why the Chinese company talked about so many things unrelated to business.

Analysis:

This case is an example of communication failure. The Chinese company preferred to spend much time on establishing relationship, whereas the American company tended to discuss the sale issues at the beginning of a negotiation. The Chinese company tended to establish a good relationship at the cost of time. The American company tended to achieve the goal of a task despite rather than spent a long time establishing relationship. This shows that the lack of sensation and knowledge of culture differences is the big problem standing in the way of intercultural communication.

II. Case 2

First Name or Last Name?

Two men meet on a plane from Tokyo to Hong Kong. Zhang Yong-hui is a Hong Kong exporter who is returning from a business trip to Japan. Andrew Richardson is an American buyer on his first business trip to Hong Kong. It is a convenient meeting for them because Mr. Zhang's company sells some of the products Mr. Richardson has come to Hong Kong to buy. After a bit of conversation they introduce themselves to each other.

Mr. Richardson: By the way, I'm Andrew Richardson. My friends call me Andy. This is my business card.

Mr. Zhang: I'm Peter Zhang. Pleased to meet you, Mr. Richard. This is my card.

Mr. Richardson: No, no. Call me Andy. I think we'll be doing a lot of business together.

Mr. Zhang: Yes, I hope so.

Mr. Richardson (reading Mr. Zhang's card): "Zhang Yong-hui." Yong-hui, I'll give you a call tomorrow as soon as I get settled at my hotel.

Mr. Zhang (smiling): Yes. I'll expect your call.

When these two men separate, they leave each other with divergent impressions of the situation. Mr. Richardson is very pleased to have made the acquaintance of Mr. Zhang and feels they have gotten off to a very good start. They have established their relationship on a first-name basis and Mr. Zhang's smile seems to indicate that he will be friendly and easy to do business with. Mr. Richardson is particularly pleased that he has treated Mr. Zhang with respect for his Chinese background by calling him Yong-hui rather than using his western name, Peter, which seemed to him an unnecessary imposition of western culture.

In contrast, Mr. Zhang feels quite uncomfortable with Mr. Richardson. He feels it will be difficult to work with him, and that Mr. Richardson might be rather insensitive to cultural differences. He is particularly bothered that Mr. Richardson used his given name,

Yong-hui, instead of either Peter or Mr. Zhang. It was this embarrassment which caused him to smile.

Analysis:

The communication between Mr. Zhang from Hong Kong and Mr. Richardson from America is not smooth. The different cultural backgrounds are the main reason. To be specific, in American business circles, people tend to prefer close, friendly, egalitarian (平等的) relationships in business engagements. This system of symmetrical solidarity (一致) is often expressed in the use of given (or "first") names in business encounters. Mr. Richardson feels most comfortable in being called Andy, and he would like to call Mr. Zhang by his first name. At the same time, he wishes to show consideration of the cultural differences between them by avoiding Mr. Zhang's western name, Peter. His solution to this cultural difference is to address Mr. Zhang by the given name he sees on the business card, Yong-hui.

Mr. Zhang, on the other hand, prefers an initial business relationship of symmetrical deference (尊敬). He would feel more comfortable if they called each other Mr. Zhang and Mr. Richardson. Nevertheless, when he was away at school in North America he learned that Americans feel uncomfortable calling people Mr. for an extended period of time. His solution was to adopt a western name. He chose Peter for use in such situations.

When Mr. Richardson uses Mr. Zhang's Chinese given name, Yong-hui, Mr. Zhang feels uncomfortable. The name is rarely used by anyone, in fact. What Mr. Richardson does not know is that Chinese have a rather complex structure of names which depends upon situations and relationships, which includes school names, intimate and family baby names, and even western names, each of which is used just by the people with whom a person has a certain relationship. Isolating just the given name, Yong-hui, is relatively unusual and to hear himself called this by a stranger makes Mr. Zhang feel quite uncomfortable. His reaction, which is also culturally conditioned, is to smile.

Unfortunately, Mr. Richardson is not aware that one means of expressing acute embarrassment for Mr. Zhang is to smile. While within North American culture there is consciousness of what might be called "nervous laughter", there is a general expectation that a smile can be taken as a direct expression of pleasure or satisfaction. Mr. Richardson misinterprets Mr. Zhang's embarrassment as agreement or even pleasure at their first encounter, and as a result, he goes away from the encounter unaware of the extent to which he has complicated their initial introduction. In conclusion, it is the culture differences that mainly cause the misunderstanding between the two persons from different cultures on how to address a stranger correctly. So culture influences the effect of intercultural communication.

Part Five Knowledge Practice

Translation

I. Translate the following passage into Chinese.

In conversations with people who know each other, however, customs in English speaking countries demand that there should be eye contact. This applies to both the speaker and the listener. For either one not to look at the other person could imply a number of things, among which are fear, contempt, uneasiness, guilt, indifference. Even in public speaking there should be plenty of eye contact. It would be regarded as inconsiderate and disrespectful for a speaker to "bury his nose in his manuscript" to read a speech instead of looking at and talking to his audience.

II. Translate the following passage into English.

拱手礼也叫作揖礼。这个礼既能表达施礼者对别人的感谢和尊敬,也是中华民族传统的见面礼仪,有着浓浓的中国特色和人情味儿。

拱手礼已经有两三千年的历史了,从西周起就开始在同辈人见面、交往时采用了。古人通过程式化的礼仪,以自谦的方式表达对他人的敬意。中国人是讲究以人和人之间的距离来表现出"敬"的,而不像西方人那样喜欢身体亲近。这种距离不仅散发着典雅气息,也比较符合现代卫生的要求。所以很多礼学专家都认为,拱手礼不仅是最能体现中国人文精神的见面礼节,而且也是最恰当的一种交往礼仪。

Case Study

I. Case 1

Feeling Starving

When Wang Xing, a Chinese professor, was a visiting scholar in the U.S., she stayed in an American home. She found Americans usually had very simple breakfast or lunch, and sometimes they even skipped breakfast or lunch. Americans usually have a cup of coffee, an apple, a banana, or a pancake for breakfast. Americans don't cook lunch at home, or have lunch break at school. They just have some chips, soft drinks, or a sandwich for lunch. Americans only cook dinner. When they cook dinner, they usually cook only two dishes for a family with four or five members. Eating with her host

American families, Wang Xing always felt starving.

Questions for discussion:

1. Why did Wang Xing always feel starving when eating with her host American families?
2. What are the differences between American eating culture and Chinese eating culture?
3. What do you think should Wang Xing do to avoid being starving?

II. Case 2

Being in a Dilemma

When Liu Xiao was studying in Britain, he stayed in a British home. He liked the hosts, and was interested in Bible study as his major was foreign literature. But his hosts wanted him to be Christian. His host family members would ask him to join them on church activities like Sunday service or religious holidays. He thought that he was really in a dilemma.

Questions for discussion:

1. Why was Liu Xiao in a dilemma?
2. What do you think Liu Xiao should do to get away from the dilemma?
3. Please point out briefly the main differences between Chinese religious culture and British religious culture showed in the above case.

Unit 2
Communication and Culture

By the end of this unit, you should be able to:
1. Understand the definitions of communication and culture;
2. Understand the functions of communication and culture;
3. Explain the components of communication and culture;
4. Describe the types of communication and the levels of culture;
5. Describe the characteristics of communication and culture;
6. Be aware of the influence of culture on communication.

Part One   Warming Up

Watch the selected scene "Carter and the Chinese Master at the Kung-fu Studio" from the movie *Rush Hour 3* and answer the questions below the script.

Questions for discussion:
1. Is there an effective communication between Carter and the Master?
2. What caused the conflicts between them and how to avoid such conflicts?

Part Two   Basic Knowledge of Communication and Culture

To better understand intercultural communication, we need to know the basic theories of the two concepts in the definition of communication and culture. As Hall (1977) pointed out, "Communication is culture, and culture is communication".

How we communicate and what is "said" through our communication helps define what "our culture" is, just as Smith stated: In modern society different people communicate in different ways, as do people in different societies around the world; and the way people communicate is the way they live. It is their culture. Who talks with them? How? And about what? These are questions of communication and culture ... Communication and culture are inseparable. (as cited in Samovar, Potter & Stefani, 2000: 34)

Since communication and culture are significantly related to each other, in the following part, basics of communication and culture will be reviewed respectively.

1. Communication

Living in society everyone has to play a variety of roles in different groups by communicating with many different people either in face-to-face encounters or through letters, telephones, or the Internet. Communication occurs not only between members of one culture, but across the boundary of two cultures. Even within a single culture, there are still different cultural groups contrasted to the dominant culture. Interaction and communication are integral to the daily life of every individual.

1.1　Definition of Communication

According to Dance and Larson's (1972) literature review on communication, there are more than 126 definitions of communication. However, there is a basic assumption that communication is a form of human behavior derived from a need to connect and interact with other human beings. Therefore, communication can simply refer to the act and process of sending and receiving messages among people.

1.2　Functions of Communication

To summarize, people communicate with each other for a number of reasons: to meet their practical needs, to fulfill their social needs, to make better decisions, and to promote personal growth, etc.

1.2.1　Practical Functions

As human beings, we are all limited in our knowledge and experience, so even in our daily life, we have to find information we need from people near and far. For example, we may ask strangers in the street about the location of a hospital, consult our friends about buying furniture, find out a phone number or the departure time of a flight through a phone service, or search the Internet for information about certain goods at low prices. Such communication is often brief and right to the point which immediately serves our purpose, brings us convenience and saves us a lot of time (Dou Weilin, 2007).

1.2.2　Social Functions

We communicate with other people like family, friends or strangers to enjoy the pleasure of communication, maintain friendship, establish ties and develop intimate relationship. In the modern time of booming information and widespread cooperation, we need to contact others, understand and cooperate with each other, so communication plays an indispensable and even decisive role in our social life.

1.2.3　Decision Making Functions

In our daily life, we have to make a lot of important decisions about life, and communication can help us to make decisions. Generally speaking, the more information we receive, the better the decisions we make. For example, if we plan to take the bus, we need to find out the time when a bus leaves; if we want to know about other people, events and places in the world, we need to read the news as much as possible.

1.2.4　Personal Growth Functions

We are not born with a special talent to communicate well with others, but have to acquire this ability within our culture as well as across different cultures. We learn communication skills consciously and unconsciously in very much the same way we learn our culture. We are taught by our parents and teachers to communicate with others in certain ways. We also observe people around us and imitate them. Constant interaction with others defines and confirms our identity, offers us a sense of belongings, increases our knowledge and experience, and endows us with abilities to meet new challenges and proves our special values. Therefore, communication plays an indispensable role in our intellectual, social and psychological growths (Dou Weilin,2007).

1.3　Types of Communication

Communication is exchanging information in the form of messages, symbols, and signs. There are many different types of communication, depending on the medium used, the way in which information is exchanged, or the number of persons involved.

(1) Based on the channels used for communicating, the process of communication can be broadly divided into verbal communication and nonverbal communication.

A. Verbal communication refers to the use of sounds and language to send a message. It serves as a vehicle for expressing desires, ideas and concepts and is vital to the processes of learning and teaching. Verbal communication can be used to inform, inquire, argue and discuss topics of all kinds. It can be further divided into written and oral communications.

B. Nonverbal communication is usually understood as the process of communication through sending and receiving wordless messages, such as through gestures and touches, by body language or posture, by facial expression and eye contact, etc..

(2) Based on the style of communication, there are formal and informal communications that have their own set of features.

A. Formal communication refers to the presentation or written piece that strictly adheres to rules, conventions, and ceremony without colloquial expressions. The different forms of formal communication include: departmental meetings, conferences, telephone calls, company news bulletins, special interviews and special purpose publications. Communication through these formal channels greatly hinders the free and uninterrupted flow of communication. It is generally time-consuming and possibly leads to a good deal of distortion and misunderstanding.

B. Informal communication is the opposite of formal communication. It happens when you have a face-to-face conversation with a friend or relative. In an organization or a company, informal communication is also known as grapevine. Normally, such communication is oral, but there can be written emails and memos in the informal style. Informal communication is implicit, spontaneous and diverse.

(3) Based on the social levels, communication can be classified into interpersonal communication, organizational communication and mass communication.

A. Inter personal communication can be either face-to-face communication like talking, chatting or asking questions or communication without seeing each other but through such means as telephone, telex, fax, wireless phone, computer communication, etc.

B. Organizational communication refers to communication that maintains the normal operation of organization, unit, department or enterprise.

C. Mass communication means to publicize to the public by means of books, newspapers, publications, movies, broadcast television, video recordings, computer software, CDs, the Internet, as well as new media like blog, Twitter, etc.

1.4　Components of Communication

Communication is a process of exchanging verbal and nonverbal messages. It is a continuous process. Scholars identify eight key components of communication within the framework of intentional communication: message, sender, receiver, channel, noise, feedback, encoding and decoding. Each of them plays an important role in the process of communication.

(1) Message: Whether verbal or nonverbal, it is the content of communication and ideas from one person to another.

(2) Sender: the person who sends the message.

(3) Receiver: the person who receives the message.

(4) Channel or medium: the ways of sending and receiving messages.

(5) Noise refers to the disturbances along the communication process, which may result in unintended meaning perceived by the receiver.

(6) Feedback refers to reaction from the message receiver to the message sender. It could be negative or positive, and internal or external.

(7) Encoding is understood as the process of sending and interpreting the message into signal.

(8) Decoding is understood as the process of receiver interpreting the signal from the sender.

Among these eight components, encoding and decoding are of special significance because communication is achieved only when the message decoded is identical to the message encoded. What is worth our attention is that noise along the channel may interfere with or even distort the receiver's interpreting of the signal from the sender.

1.5 Characteristics of Communication

The eight ingredients of communication make up only a partial list of factors that function during a communication event. In addition to these components, when we conceive of communication as a process, getting familiar with several characteristics will help us understand how communication actually works.

1.5.1 Dynamic

Communication is an ongoing and ever-changing activity, so whatever a person has said or done cannot be retrieved since it is bound to create certain effects upon others (Samovar et al. 2000). Later words and behaviors inevitably replace the previous ones and throughout a communication both parties experience constant changes in their body and mind, sometimes very subtle and sometimes very obvious. Besides, all the components of a communication constantly interact with each other. The specific time, place, occasion and the number of people with their particular rules, values, norms, traditions, customs and taboos testify to the fact that communication undergoes continual change and is a complex system.

1.5.2 Symbolic

The very means enabling culture to be transmitted from generation to generation is symbolic. Cultural symbols can be in a host of forms, including gestures, clothes, books, picture, religious totems, and the like. Among all these, language can be regarded as the most important symbolic one. Although all cultures use symbols, they usually assign their own meanings to the symbols. In other words, the same symbol can bear different meanings in different cultures.

1.5.3　Self-reflective

Just like we use symbols to reflect on what goes on outside of us, we also use them to reflect on ourselves. This unique ability enables us to be participant and observer simultaneously: we can watch, evaluate, and alter our performance as a communicator at the very instant we are engaged in the act. Self-reflection is a basis for human identity, but there is an intercultural dimension in our capacity to be self-reflective.

1.5.4　Interactive

Communication takes place between at least two individuals. Each party in a communication event will be affected to a certain degree by the other and these physical or psychological consequences immediately help modify or alter one's responses either in words, tones, gestures, facial expressions or postures, or even in silence, whose implications and connotations are culturally based.

1.5.5　Learned

We learn the language, gestures, and customs of the culture in which we are raised. Consequently, communication is "culture bound." Since most communication is learned, we can learn effective and new ways of communicating.

2. Culture

2.1　Definition of Culture

As is the case with communication, it is really difficult to define culture. The following definitions are just some of the better known ones.

Culture is man's medium; there is not one aspect of human life that is not touched and altered by culture. This means personality, how people express themselves, including shows of emotion, the way they think, how they move, how problems are solved, how their cities are planned and laid out, how transportation systems function and are organized, as well as how economic and government systems are put together and function. (Edward T. Hall, 1959)

Culture is the collective programming of the mind which distinguishes the members of one group or society from those of another. (G. Hofstede, 1997: 5)

Culture is a mental set of windows through which all of life is viewed. It varies from individual to individual within a society, but it shares important characteristics with members of a society. (L. Beamer & I. Varner, 2003)

Culture is the combination of beliefs, customs, values, behaviors, institutions and communication patterns that are shared, learned and passed down through the generations in an identifiable group of people. (Linell Davis, 2004: 24)

These and other definitions all point to the fact that culture is all pervasive, including customs and habits, ideas and beliefs and the houses built by humans as well.

2.2　Functions of Culture

According to Dressler and Carns (1969), culture has the following functions:

(1) Culture enables us to communicate with others through a language that we have learned and that we share in common.

(2) Culture makes it possible to anticipate how others in our society are likely to respond to our actions.

(3) Culture gives us standards for distinguishing between what is considered right or wrong, beautiful or ugly, reasonable or unreasonable, tragic or humorous, safe or dangerous.

(4) Culture provides the knowledge and skill necessary for meeting sustenance needs.

(5) Culture enables us to identify with — that is, include ourselves in the same category with — other people of similar background.

2.3　Components of Culture

Components of culture are simply parts (items, pieces and features) that make up culture. Cultures vary from one another and can be broken down into components in several ways as bellow.

A. Communication aspect: language and symbols

B. Environment aspect: geography, climate and places in the country

C. Science and technology aspect: math, physics, inventions, roads, railways

D. Economic system: money, finance, trade

E. Spiritual aspect: religion, mythology

F. Cognitive aspect: values, belief

G. Artistic aspect: art, literature, architecture

H. Behavioral aspect: laws, rituals

I. Daily life aspect: family, education, entertainment, dress, food, transportation, house

J. Social structure: social classes, ethnicity

2.4　Levels of Culture

Larry A. Samovar (2000: 58) said that "the value of culture may not be the value of all individuals within the culture." How you view the world and how you communicate in that world are influenced by factors as divergent as age, gender, status, occupation, politics, group, and co-culture affiliations. Samovar's view parallels Greert Hofstede's idea of levels of culture. Hofstede (1997: 10) classifies culture into the following different levels:

A. A national level: according to one's country (or countries for people who migrated during their lifetime)

B. A regional level (or ethnic, or religious, or linguistic level): because most nations composed of culturally different regions and ethnic/religious/language groups

C. A gender level: according to whether a person was born as a girl or as a boy

D. A generation level, which separates grandparents from parents from children

E. A social class level, which is associated with educational opportunities and with a person's occupation or profession

Hofseted thinks that almost everyone belongs to a number of different groups and categories of people at the same time, so people inevitably carry several levels of mental programming within themselves, corresponding to different levels of culture. He further points out that these various levels are not necessarily in harmony. For example, one's religious values may conflict with generation values. (Hofsted, 1997: 10)

2.5 Characteristics of Culture

Samovar et.al (2000: 38-48) concluded seven characteristics of culture, and Jia Yuxin (1997: 17-20) concluded ten of them. In this book, we list six most prominent characteristics of culture.

2.5.1 Culture Is Learned

"Culture is learned, not inherited. It derives from one's social environment, not from one's genes." (Hofstede, 1997: 5) This is not to say we can talk objectively about our own culture, but we acquire and are taught through symbols. We learn our culture in many ways and from a variety of sources. We learn our culture from folk tales, legends and myths; we also learn our culture through art and mass media, etc.. All of this learning occurs as conscious or unconscious conditioning that leads one toward competence in a particular culture. This activity is frequently called enculturation, in which one learns his/her culture.

If one particular culture can be learned, then other cultures must also be learnable. This notion has important implications for intercultural communication, because the learned nature of culture serves as a reminder that since we have mastered our own culture through the process of learning, it is possible for us to learn other culture as well.

2.5.2 Culture Is Transmitted from Generation to Generation

If a culture is to exist and endure, it must ensure that its crucial messages and elements are passed on from generation to generation. This idea supports our assertion that culture and communication are linked: it is communication that makes culture a continuous process, for once cultural habits, principles, values, attitudes, and the like are "formulated", they are communicated to each individual.

It is worth noting that some elements of a culture to be passed on are universal, but some are unique. For example, Chinese tell each generation to look back to the past for guidance and strength. But Americans tell each generation to always look forward, that competition is of great significance. For Mexicans and Native Americans, the message is that cooperation is more important than contest. Americans tell each generation to value youth. In Korea, the message is to respect and treasure the elderly. As Keesing (1965: 28) pointed out, "Any break in the learning chain would lead to a culture's disappearance." So if there is a break in the passing, a certain aspect or maybe the whole culture will get lost. For instance, In America, many American Indians could not write their language because they are not taught the language. Similarly, many African tribes are facing the same problem. Therefore a point can be made that the content of culture is what gets transferred from generation to generation.

2.5.3 Culture Is Shared

A culture is shared by a society. Members of the society agree about the meanings of things, and the reasons. Since we learn our culture from our old family members, teachers, spiritual leaders, peers, representatives of legal, political, and educational institutions as well, we will interpret life experience in ways that validate our own culture views.

Members of a culture share a set of ideas, values, and standards of behavior, and this set of shared ideas is what gives meaning to their lives, and what bounds them together as a culture. Groups are motivated by common views, which are a dynamic force in enabling groups to achieve social goals.

2.5.4 Culture Is Dynamic

Culture is motional and changeable. Changes in cultures are more drastic today because of globalization. Culture changes mainly through three mechanisms, namely innovation, diffusion, and acculturation (Samovar et.al, 2000: 45).

Besides, history abounds with examples of how cultures have changed because of environmental changes, wars, disasters, shifts in values, influx of migrants. In addition, economic change can lead to significant change in social organization, and advancement in technology also proves to be an important factor changing the pattern of a culture.

Culture changes, but most changes affect only the surface of the culture. The deep structure of a culture resists major alterations. Values associated with such things as ethics and morals, work and leisure, definitions of freedom, the importance of the past, religious practices, the pace of life, and attitudes toward gender and age are so deeply embedded in a culture that they persist generation after generation. That's what Hall told us after his experiences with the Navajo after the Great Depression: "Culture is more than mere custom that can be shed or changed like a suit of clothes." (Hall, 1990a: 23)

2.5.5 Culture Is Ethnocentric

Samovar et al. (2000: 46) stated, "ethnocentrism is the view of things in which one's own group is the center of everything, and all others are scaled and rated with reference to it." Like culture, we learn ethnocentrism early in our life and it has come to settle primarily in our subconsciousness when we grow up, so every culture is characterized by ethnocentrism.

There is a tendency to assume that the elements of one's own culture are logical and make good sense. If other cultures are different from theirs, those differences are often viewed to be negative, and illogical. People tend to consider the different as wrong.

Awareness of our own ethnocentrism may never eliminate it but will enable us to minimize its negative effects. We should try to understand other people by thinking from the stand of their unique cultural background.

2.5.6 Culture Is Integrated

All aspects of culture must be reasonably well integrated in order to function properly. As Hall said, "You touch a culture in one place and everything else is affected." (Hall, 1976: 13-14)

A complex example of the interconnectedness of cultural elements is the civil right movement in the United States. This movement has caused noticeable changes in housing patterns, discrimination practices, educational opportunities, the legal system, career opportunities, and even communication. So this one aspect of culture has changed American attitudes, values and behavior.

If we can view cultures as integrated, we can see how particular culture traits fit into the integrated whole, and understand well how people in a particular cultural context perceive the world and behave in a particular way.

2.6 Metaphors for Culture

To better understand the abstract concept of culture and the characteristics of culture, the metaphors of culture are offered as follows.

2.6.1 Culture Is like an Iceberg

Culture is like an iceberg which has a visible section above the waterline and a large invisible section below the waterline, i.e. culture has some aspects that are observable and others that can only be imagined. Also like an iceberg, the part of culture that is visible (observable behavior) is only a small part of a much bigger whole, but a big part of culture is invisible.

Culture above the waterline means the aspects of culture that are visible, and can be taught. This includes how we behave, what we eat, what clothes we wear, how we speak, what words we use, etc.. They can be understood easily when observed. It is said only 10 percent of culture is visible. But 90 percent of it is below the waterline (hidden under the water) that is invisible, and is not taught directly. This part includes habits, concepts of beauty, values, judgements, body languages and so on.

2.6.2 Culture Is like an Onion

As Geert states, culture consists of the following four levels which embody the total concept of culture just like an onion has four layers: symbols, heroes, rituals, and values. These have been depicted like the skins of onion, in which symbols represent the most superficial and easiest to be perceived and understood immediately, such as the way people are dressed, the language they speak, the cars they drive, the food they eat, the houses they live in, the hairstyle they wear, etc.. The second layer, like the skin of onion, is heroes, which refer to the kind of people you worship. Wukong (the monkey king) in China and batman in the U.S. can serve as cultural heroes. The third layer is rituals. Rituals are those activities that are considered socially important within a culture, it can be done by groups of people or individuals. For instance, greeting is a very common ritual, and sporting events are rituals. Symbols, heroes, and rituals have been included in the category of practice. Practice means what people do. They are visible and easy for an outsider to observe. They are determined by the core of culture — values, which are the deepest part of culture and the most difficult for an outsider to understand and which is the goal of studying culture.

3. The Relationship Between Culture and Communication

Understanding the intertwined relationship between culture and communication is crucial to intercultural communication. On the other hand, culture conditions communication. First of all culture is the foundation of communication. Without the sharing and understanding between speakers, no communication is possible. Secondly, culture dictates every stage of the communication process. We communicate the way we do because we are raised in a particular culture and learn its language, rules and norms. What we say, what gestures we use, with whom we talk, when and how to talk are all determined by our culture. On the other hand, communication had made the development of human culture possible and it is through communication that culture is transmitted from one generation to another. At the same time, culture is learned through communication. We acquire our membership of culture mainly through socialization with other members of our culture and this socialization is realized by interacting with different social groups: families, friends, neighbors, teachers, colleagues, etc.. Without socialization through communication, the learning of culture is totally impossible.

Culture and communication are said to be like Siamese twins, one is inseparable from the other; the understanding of one demands the understanding of the other and the changes to one will cause changes in the other. If a culture is different, the communicative patterns in that culture will be different too. The major task of intercultural communicators is to find out how culture and communication condition and transform one another so that real understanding can be achieved among intercultural interactions.

Glossary

1. **inseparable** *adj.* unable to be separated or treated separately   不可分的;不可区别对待的

2. **boundary**   *n.* a line which marks the limits of an area; a dividing line   分界线,边界;界限

3. **integral**   *adj.* necessary to make a whole complete; essential or fundamental   必需的;必要的;基本的,基础的

4. **etymologically**   *adv.* 词源上地

5. **derive**   *vt.* obtain something from (a specified source)   从……中获得(或取得)

6. **summarize**   *vt.* give a brief statement of the main points of (something)   总结,概括

7. **consult**   *vt.* seek information or advice from (someone with expertise in a particular area)   请教,求教;向(专家)咨询

8. **furniture**   *n.* large movable equipment, such as tables and chairs, that are used to make a house, office, or other space suitable for living or working   家具

9. **departure**   *n.* the action of leaving, typically to start a journey   出发,启程;离开

10. **intimate**   *adj.* closely acquainted; familiar, close   熟悉的,亲密的,亲切的

11. **booming**   *adj.* having a period of great prosperity or rapid economic growth 飞速发展的

12. **indispensable**   *adj.* absolutely necessary   不可或缺的,必需的

13. **consciously**   *adj.* aware of and responding to one's surroundings; awake   清醒的;感到的

14. **endow**   *vt.* give or bequeath an income or property to (a person or institution)   向(人、机构)捐赠;资助

15. **medium**   *n.* an agency or means of doing something   媒介;途径,方法,手段

16. **adhere**   *vi.* stick fast to (a surface or substance)   粘在(表面、物质)上

17. **convention**   *n.* a way in which something is usually done, especially within a particular area or activity   (尤指特定地区或特别事件的)行为规则;惯例

18. **colloquial**   *adj.* used in ordinary or familiar conversation; not formal or literary   (语言)用于日常交谈的,口语的;非正式的,非文学的

19. **bulletin**   *n.* a short official statement or broadcast summary of news   公报

20. **hinder**   *vt.* create difficulties for (someone or something), resulting in delay or obstruction   阻碍,打扰

21. **time-consuming**   *adj.* taking a lot of or too much time 耗费时间的;旷日持久的

22. **distort**   *vt.* pull or twist out of shape   扭曲;使变形

23. **grapevine**　*n*. vine native to both Eurasia and North America，especially one bearing fruit（grapes）used for eating or winemaking. Numerous cultivars and hybrids have been developed for the winemaking industry　葡萄藤（产于欧亚和北美的藤本植物，尤指所产葡萄可食用或酿葡萄酒的；人们因葡萄酒酿造业的需要已经培育出众多的栽培品种和杂交品种）

24. **memo**　*n*.（informal）a written message，especially in business　（非正式）（尤指商业上的）备忘录，备忘便条

25. **implicit**　*adj*. implied though not plainly expressed　含蓄的，不言明的

26. **spontaneous**　*adj*. performed or occurring as a result of a sudden inner impulse or inclination and without premeditation or external stimulus　自发的，不由自主的

27. **classify**　*vt*. arrange（a group of people or things）in classes or categories according to shared qualities or characteristics　把……分类

28. **enterprise**　*n*. a project or undertaking，typically one that is difficult or requires effort　（艰巨的）计划，事业

29. **blog**　*n*. a weblog　网络日志，博客

30. **Twitter**　*n*. an American online news and social networking service　推特

31. **component**　*n*. a part or element of a larger whole，especially a part of a machine or vehicle　（尤指机械或车辆的）部件，零件；（构成整体的）组成部分，成分

32. **framework**　*n*. a basic structure underlying a system，concept，or text　（系统、概念或文章的）结构，构造

33. **perceive**　*vt*. become aware or conscious of（something）；come to realize or understand　认识到，意识到；理解

34. **feedback**　*n*. information about reactions to a product，a person's performance of a task，etc. which is used as a basis for improvement　反馈信息

35. **internal**　*adj*. of or situated on the inside　内的，内部的

36. **external**　*adj*. belonging to or forming the outer surface or structure of something　外面的，外部的

37. **ingredient**　*n*. a component part or element of something　成分，因素

38. **conceive**　*vt*. form or devise（a plan，idea，or work）in the mind　想出，构思，设想（计划、主意、作品）

39. **retrieve**　*vt*. get（something）back；regain possession of　收回，找回；重新得到

40. **subtle**　*adj*. so delicate or precise as to be difficult to analyse or describe　（尤指变化或差别）微妙的，细微的，难以描述的，难以分析的

41. **testify**　*vi*. give evidence as a witness in a law court　作证

42. **undergo**　*vt*. experience or be subjected to（something，typically something unpleasant，painful，or arduous）　经受，遭受，忍受

43. **totem**　*n*. a natural object or animal that is believed by a particular society to have

spiritual significance and that is adopted by it as an emblem　图腾(被特定社会认为具有精神意义,并以之为标志的物体或动物)

44. **evaluate**　*vt.* form an idea of the amount, number, or value of; assess　估算,估价,评价

45. **self-reflection**　*n.* meditation or serious thought about one's character, actions, and motives　反思,省察

46. **dimension**　*n.* an aspect or feature of a situation, problem, or thing　(局势、问题、事物的)方面,特征

47. **connotation**　*n.* an idea or feeling which a word invokes for a person in addition to its literal or primary meaning　含义,含意

48. **bind**　*vt.* tie or fasten (something) tightly together　系紧,拴紧,固定

49. **distinguish**　*vt.* recognize or treat (someone or something) as different　识别,区分

50. **mental**　*adj.* of or relating to the mind　精神的,心理的,智力的

51. **tragic**　*adj.* causing or characterized by extreme distress or sorrow　悲惨的,可悲的

52. **spiritual**　*adj.* of, relating to, or affecting the human spirit or soul as opposed to material or physical things　(与)精神上(有关)的,心灵的

53. **mythology**　*n.* a collection of myths, especially one belonging to a particular religious or cultural tradition　[总称](尤指属于特定宗教或文化传统的)神话

54. **cognitive**　*adj.* of or relating to cognition　(与)认识(有关)的,(与)认知(有关)的

55. **ritual**　*n.* a religious or solemn ceremony consisting of a series of actions performed according to a prescribed order　(宗教等)庄严仪式

56. **ethnicity**　*n.* the fact or state of belonging to a social group that has a common national or cultural tradition　种族属性,民族属性

57. **divergent**　*adj.* tending to be different or develop in different directions　不同的;有分歧的

58. **affiliation**　*n.* the state or process of affiliating or being affiliated　隶属,从属

59. **gender**　*n.* the state of being male or female (typically used with reference to social and cultural differences rather than biological ones)　(多指与社会或文化方面而非生理上的差异有关的)性别状态

60. **prominent**　*adj.* important; famous　重要的;卓越的,著名的

61. **inherit**　*vt.* receive (money, property, or a title) as an heir at the death of the previous holder　继承(金钱、财产、头衔)

62. **enculturation**　*n.* the gradual acquisition of the characteristics and norms of a culture or group by a person of another culture　对某种文化的适应

63. **notion**　*n.* a conception of or belief about something　概念;观念;看法,见解

64. **assertion** *n.* a confident and forceful statement of fact or belief 断言，语气肯定的话

65. **validate** *vt.* check or prove the validity or accuracy of（something） 证实，验证

66. **dynamic** *adj.* characterized by constant change，activity，or progress（过程、系统）动态的；不断变化的

67. **drastic** *adj.* likely to have a strong or far-reaching effect；radical and extreme 猛烈的，激烈的；激进的，极端的

68. **diffusion** *n.* the spreading of something more widely 扩散，散播

69. **acculturate** *v.* be assimilated or cause to be assimilated by a different culture，typically the dominant one （使）适应新文化（尤指主流文化），（使）同化

70. **acculturation** *n.* 文化传入，文化适应

71. **influx** *n.* an arrival or entry of large numbers of people or things （人、物的）涌进，汇集

72. **embed** *vt.* fix firmly and deeply in a surrounding mass 把（物体）牢牢嵌入

73. **ethnocentrism** *n.* 民族优越感；种族（民族）中心主义，种族（民族、集团）优越感

74. **eliminate** *vt.* completely remove or get rid of（something） 消除，根除，除去

75. **iceberg** *n.* a large floating mass of ice detached from a glacier or ice sheet and carried out to sea 冰山

76. **waterline** *n.* the level reached by the sea or a river visible as a line on a rock face，beach，or riverbank 水位；海岸线

77. **depict** *vt.* show or represent by a drawing，painting，or other art form （用绘画或其他艺术形式）表现，描绘

78. **superficial** *adj.* existing or occurring at or on the surface 表面的

79. **worship** *n.* the feeling or expression of reverence and adoration for a deity 敬神，拜神

80. **intertwine** *v.* twist or twine together 缠结，缠绕

81. **dictate** *vt.* lay down authoritatively；prescribe 命令，规定

82. **socialization** *n.* 社会化

83. **pattern** *n.* an arrangement or sequence regularly found in comparable objects or events. 样式，模式

84. **transform** *vt.* make a thorough or dramatic change in the form，appearance，or character of 彻底改变，使发生巨变，使改观，变革

● Comprehension Check

I. Decide whether the following statements are true (T) or false (F).

1. （ ）Cultural is a static entity while communication is a dynamic process.

2. (   ) Culture can be seen as shared knowledge that people need to know in order to behave acceptably in a given culture.

3. (   ) In intercultural communication, we should separate one's individual character from cultural generalization.

4. (   ) All people of the same nationality will have the same culture.

5. (   ) One's actions are totally independent of his or her culture.

6. (   ) Culture cannot be known without a study of communication, and communication can only be understood with the understanding of the culture it supports.

7. (   ) Culture is all men's medium; there is no aspect of human life that is not touched and altered by culture.

8. (   ) The culture shown in an onion consists of two levels: a level of norms and values, or an invisible level, and a visible level of human behavior.

9. (   ) Without the sharing and understanding between speakers, communication is possible.

10. (   ) Culture and communication are said to be like twins, one is inseparable from the other.

II. Answer the following questions.

1. What are the needs and purpose for human communication?
2. What are the components in the process of communication?
3. Can you explain the characteristics of communication with examples?
4. What is common to the various definitions of culture?
5. Can you explain the characteristics of culture?
6. Can you explain with examples from Chinese society the various ways that cultures change?

III. Fill in each of the blanks in the following passage with an appropriate word from those listed below.

A. current   B. capital   C. generation   D. goods

E. interconnected   F. arguments   G. tangible   H. culture

I. reasons   J. benefits

Throsby first introduced the idea of cultural capital in economics. Cultural capital, in an economic sense, can provide a means of representing __1__ which enables both tangible and intangible manifestation of culture to be articulated as long-lasting stores of value and providers of __2__ for individuals and groups. Like Klamer, he separates economic from cultural capital, but emphasizes that cultural capital can give rise to both economic value and cultural value. This distinction is an important one when it comes to valuing cultural __3__, there would be expected to be zero substitutability between cultural and physical capital in respect of its cultural output.

The recognition of cultural capital as an economic value can thus produce a whole new set of __4__ for the public funding of culture. Throsby draws a parallel between the preservation of natural capital and cultural capital, which generates the kinds of moral arguments that have been used in the case of the preservation of natural __5__ for years. For example, if the present stock of cultural capital is allowed to decline through lack of investment, one could argue that future generations will be deprived of its benefits, since their interests are not reflected in the current market. Throsby agrees with Klamer that the __6__ economic preoccupation with efficiency may be undermining the notion of fairness, that is, the rights of the present __7__ to fairness in access to cultural resources and to the benefits flowing from cultural capital, viewed across social classes, income groups, locational categories and so on.

Like the arguments for maintaining natural capital, __8__ for maintaining the diversity of cultural capital can also be made, since new capital formation can be shown in both cases to depend crucially on the existing capital stock. Even more compelling is the argument that, as in the natural world, no system is isolated, but all are __9__ and the long term sustainability of our existence depends on the maintenance of all these systems, including natural ecosystems and cultural capital.

Unlike Klamer, who argues for a complete break away from measuring the outcomes of culture in traditional economic terms, Throsby still sees the link as important: It is becoming clearer that cultural 'ecosystems' support the operation of the real economy, affecting the way people behave and the choices they make. Neglect of cultural capital by allowing heritage to deteriorate, by failing to sustain the cultural values that provide people with a sense of identity and by not undertaking the investment needed to maintain and increase the stock of both __10__ and intangible cultural capital, will likewise place cultural systems in jeopardy and may cause them to break down, with consequent loss of welfare and economic output.

(Jeanette D. Snowball, 2008: 20 - 21)

Part Three Knowledge Expansion

Reading 1

Considering the Context in Intercultural Communication

From culture to culture the proportion of nonverbal behavioral communication varies relative to the verbal communication that is used. Communication styles that focus relatively more on words to communicate and less on behavior and the context in which the words are used are said to be in low-context. In High-context cultures, in contrast, rely relatively more on nonverbal context or behaviors than they rely on abstract, verbal symbols of meaning. The difference in style is similar to that of time being conveyed to the second by the precise, numeric display of a digital watch, as compared to telling time by the halting movement of the hands of an analog grandfather clock. This dissimilarity in communication styles between low-context and high-context cultures creates frequent, significant obstacles to intercultural communication.

A high-context message is one in which more of the information is contained in the physical context or internalized in the person receiving it, and less in the coded, explicit, transmitted verbal part of the message. A low-context communication is just the opposite. The focus is on vesting more of the information in the explicit verbal code. Low-context communication can be compared to interfacing with a computer. It is a system of explicit prompt and response exchanges. If the computer does not read an inaccurate response's programming, then it does not compute. North Americans have a low-context communication style and intend to transmit their messages primarily in words spoken, which are applied or overridden relatively less than in many other cultures by nonverbal signals such as gestures, silence, eye contact, or ritual.

Thus a low-context person consciously focuses on words to communicate, but a high-context person is acculturated from birth to send and receive a large proportion of messages through behavioral context, both consciously and unconsciously. When this high-context person receives a verbal message from a low-context person, misunderstanding is necessarily created when the high-context person erroneously attributes meaning to nonverbal context when such meaning is not intended. This same high-context person will then, in turn, communicate much by context along with a verbal message. The low-context person may not apprehend, much less understand, much of the contextual nonverbal message that is being expressed. The low-context person relies primarily on words themselves for meaning when, in fact, the context probably contains the real message.

The distinction between high-and low-context cultures does not mean that context is meaningless in low-context cultures. It means that culture dictates a large variation in degree of importance of the context to communicative meaning.

In many societies with a high-context communication style, such as Japan or Mexico, it is considered impolite to respond with "no" to a request. The courteous response of "may be" or "I will try" is clearly understood as "no" to a person familiar with that culture and contextual ritual. A person from a low-context culture will typically ignore the ritual (context) because he is accustomed to focusing on the words. He takes the words spoken literally and treats them as being information specific. This low-context person is then incensed or offended when he does not get what he expects. If he protests, the high-context person cannot understand why the low-context person wants to force a rude response, or why the low-context person is being rude by insisting. When an Occidental moves to French Polynesia, she may be frustrated at receiving what appears to be no response at all when asking a question of a Polynesian. It may be days or months (or never) before she realizes that the person addressed has just responded "yes" by an almost imperceptible raising of the eyebrows. Though she would understand the nodding of the head that by convention signals assent in many Western cultures, she relies on words and does not even see the subtle, unfamiliar nonverbal reply. Moreover, before she becomes familiar with Polynesian culture, she would not know how to interpret the answer correctly if she did notice it. In Greece, for example, the same eyebrow flash means no. Even so, some nonverbal messages are obvious. Clearly a different message is sent and received by the delivery of a bouquet of roses than by the delivery of a person's severed ear.

One cannot rely on the similarity of communication styles between two Western cultures, nor even on the similarity of styles between two Spanish-speaking countries. There are, for example, many differences between Colombian and Venezuelan cultures. Colombia is very formal; hierarchy (class) is paramount. In comparison, Venezuela is more informal. Venezuelans make a point of being equal to persons in high or important positions. They more commonly use the familiar tu form to address each other than do many other Spanish-speakers. This difference may have evolved because of Venezuela's oil production, which raised living standards and afforded more public education, making the general public here less class conscious than that in Colombia. (Novinger, Tracy, 2011)

Comprehension Check

I. Answer the following questions.

1. How can you differ the differences between high-context culture and low-context culture?
2. What are the characteristics of high-context communication style?
3. What are the characteristics of low-context communication style?
4. Please give examples to show the high-context communication style and the low-context style communication style

II. Translate into Chinese the following passage in the essay.

From culture to culture the proportion of nonverbal behavioral communication varies relative to the verbal communication that is used. (Communication styles that focus relatively more on words to communicate and less on behavior and the context in which the words are used are said to be in low-context.) High-context cultures, in contrast, rely relatively more on nonverbal context or behaviors than they rely on abstract, verbal symbols of meaning. The difference in style is similar to that of time being conveyed to the second by the precise, numeric display of a digital watch, as compared to telling time by the halting movement of the hands of an analog grandfather clock. This dissimilarity in communication styles between low-and high-context cultures creates frequent, significant obstacles to intercultural communication.

Reading 2

What is Material Culture?

Material culture refers to the objectification of human culture, inclusive of activities of material character and their products.

In practice, people give form to their knowledge, wishes, beliefs, skills, and aesthetics by converting the natural form of resources into products such as tools, clothing, food, wares, and architectures. In this way, object itself is humanized and becomes a part of cultural phenomena. In other words, essentially, material culture is about the material process and products which encapsulate, demonstrate, and embody the way people live, exist, think, and feel.

Material culture is the most ubiquitous and explicit cultural form. Its colorful representations fall into two categories: utensil culture and economic culture.

1. Utensil Culture

Consider clothing, a common phenomenon of material culture, as an example. The formation of human civilization is associated with the moment when man started to dress himself. In both Chinese and Western mythologies and legends, the act of putting on clothes represents the moment when man acquired self-consciousness and viewed himself apart from mere beasts. Those who teach people how to dress, say, the legendary figure Emperor Huang (who, allegedly, taught people tailoring) and Lei Zu (who is said to have taught people silkworm breeding and silk producing), are worshiped as "the Ancestors." Hence forth, people have taken an interest in what to wear. What to wear and how to wear, for reflecting people's production and the development of life, have taken on a rich and complicated social significance.

Since ancient times, dress serves as a concrete representation of the lifestyle and social relations within an ethnicity or certain group. It is a comprehensive demonstration of people's cultural characters like morality, religion, and aesthetics. People of different social status or professions or of different nationalities or ages dress distinctively. The "stately dress code" requiring officials to wear "high hat and loose robe" represents a royal civilization (one being tamed by manners and etiquettes); that is why the act of wearing robes of minor ethnic groups in the north and west of the country was revolutionary in its own right. Distinctive ethical clothing also reflect different life styles and historical evolvement: the Arabian turban, veil, and robe are always associated with mosques, Kuran, camels, ancient Arabian medicine, mathematics, and folklore in daily life and Arabian religion. We have got a taste of the mystery and wisdom of Arabian culture through these clothes. Suits, evolving from ancient European clothes, bear heavy relation with commercialized life experience and thus present an image that looks both serious and smart; while jeans shows a practical style that befits the work of laborers. Modern clothing, more open to variety, have even given birth to a cultural industry that focuses on clothes — the fashion industry. In this industry, clothes are designed, created, and worn by models. It is viewed as a rising field of art, where people do not wear for practical ends.

Architecture provides another good example. Housing and transportation constitute an indispensable part of human civilization in the same way as eating and dressing. Imagine types of architecture you have encountered: buildings, roads, bridges, factories, reservoirs, parks, amusement parks. The increase in architectural variety reflects the expanding needs and contents of human life, and the enhanced ability of human being to exploit and transform nature. Also, the advancement in architectural material such as earth and stone, brick and stud, concrete, steel, plastic, alloy and so on has enlarged their creative potential.

On some level, architecture is the objectification of human being. The architecture built by different people of different times has heavy bearings with their living environments and conditions, especially the enhancement of their ability to change the world. It also tells the history of progress of different ethnicity in different regions. Chinese architecture, primarily built in brick-and-stud structure, speaks the distinctive aesthetic culture held by ancient Chinese — an emphasis on harmony, nature, and soulfulness. Classical gardens in regions on the southern side of the Yangtze River, with its exquisite, elegant, zigzagging layout, exude local colour all over the place. While royal architecture in the north emphasizes on a proper demonstration of social status and political symbols, the architectural section in Imperial Palace, for instance, oozes a sense of orderly gravity brought by its grand and solemn style and balanced layout. Viewers of architecture of this kind might feel compelled to hush their voices down and genuflect spontaneously out of a sheer sense of awe. What the gothic architecture in Europe creates is a totally different feeling — a desire to embrace sublimity and transcend reality aroused by its sky-pointing, cloud-shrouding towers which conjure up the image of holy God and the heavenly state. Generally speaking, we see in architecture the essence of humanities and human history. Just like what a poet has said: a beautifully designed building is "a piece of frozen poem," while a combination of new and old buildings constitutes "a frozen book of history."

There is literally no end to the list of the branches of utensil culture, such as the culture of cuisine, the culture of transportation, the culture of clocks and watches, of road lamps, of chopsticks.

2. Economic Culture

A broader and more important aspect of material culture lies in economic life — how people produce and live. Economy is the process of people's using social material sources (including production sources and living sources) to produce, exchange, redistribute, and circulate; it also concerns consumptions made by people in daily life. Presumably, economic life, too, constitutes a certain cultural pattern: it is not only a primary form of material culture, but also a deep structure of human culture.

Economic life ranks as the primary form of human existence and development. We change the nature, appearance, and function of nature through production and labor, humanizing it to render it exploitable; we produce material sources and create spiritual culture based on labor and through social relations. All of these activities constitute economy. Economy is a fundamental way for man to humanize the world and civilize himself. Without economic life, there will be no basic social relations, no society … there will be no "us." According to the view of "culture as humanization", one thing can be said for sure that human production is based on labor, namely material production; it is a human relation linked by the bond of material. It humanizes the material and civilizes mankind. Economy itself comes as the first form of material culture.

Economic activities constitute a specific cultural pattern — economic culture. Economy is inclusive of not only plentiful unique objects (sources, tools, energy resources, products, etc.), but also material and physical input and output, thoughts and movements, cooperation and interaction between each other, and so on. It is distinguished from political, moral, and military culture for being featured by the forms and functions of objects. Economic culture entails the production, exchange, distribution, circulation, application, and consumption of material life resources, together with related conceptualized and systemized patterns. In economic culture, a relatively independent and complete system with its innate procedure and logic is formed through the interlock and influence of property relations, exchange channels, distribution systems, circulation procedures, and consumption characteristics, etc.. For example, in primitive economy, labor is done collectively and with simple tools, its products later fairly distributed. While agricultural economy, based on land rental system, shows heavy reliance on labor and weather, in industrial and commercial economy, interests, profits, and efficiencies are heavily emphasized, with commodities exchanged at equal values to sustain, to a certain degree, mechanism for cooperation and orderly competition. Each type of economy provides a basic way of living for human existence and development, thus acquiring certain cultural signification in a deeper sense.

The rich essence of economic culture establishes its significant place in the cultural realm. Economic activities as a whole have reflected the relations between man and nature, individual and society, material aspect, and spiritual aspect of human life, thus telling a true story of man's development and image. Economic operation, though relying on man's participation, has a set of mechanism and logic of its own, hence is not subject to man's arbitrary manoeuverings. From here, we can observe some objective necessities about humanization and civilization. Man's living pattern, conditions for development and goals are sure to be enclosed in economy, which shows his will to live and develop, his wisdom and intelligence, his moralities and feelings, his aesthetics, and his national spirits. All the aforementioned essences of utensil culture are to be acquired solely through such an act. Utensil culture springs from economic culture: the latter being the cause, the former bearing its fruit. (Deshun Li, 2016: 31 - 34)

● Comprehension Check

I. Answer the following questions.

1. What is the definition of material culture?
2. What does the form of material culture constitute?
3. What is utensil culture? Please give examples to explain utensil culture.
4. How does architecture reflect material culture?
5. Please explain economic culture by giving examples.
6. How economic activities reflect economic culture?

II. Translate into Chinese the following passage in the essay.

The rich essence of economic culture establishes its significant place in the cultural realm. Economic activities as a whole have reflected the relations between man and nature, individual and society, material aspect, and spiritual aspect of human life, thus telling a true story of man's development and image. Economic operation, though relying on man's participation, has a set of mechanism and logic of its own, hence is not subject to man's arbitrary manoeuverings. From here, we can observe some objective necessities about humanization and civilization. Man's living pattern, conditions for development and goals are sure to be enclosed in economy, which shows his will to live and develop, his wisdom and intelligence, his moralities and feelings, his aesthetics, and his national spirits. All the aforementioned essences of utensil culture are to be acquired solely through such an act. Utensil culture springs from economic culture: the later being the cause, the former bearing its fruit.

Part Four   Knowledge Application

Case Analysis

Case 1

A Puzzling Question

An English professor named Wang Hong at Zhejiang University went to the United States as an exchange scholar. She was invited to stay at an American professor's home. The host was enthusiastic and prepared a reception party for Wang Hong. More than thirty guests were invited, including the host, the dean, the chair of the English Department, some English professors, and the Chinese-American professors at the University. Wang Hong felt grateful to the host for this special occasion. All the guests were very nice to Wang Hong. Some even brought her gifts and cards. She was very much impressed. She had a very good time except for one thing which puzzled her. During the party, all the guests would go over to Wang Hong and talk with her for a few minutes. One lady whose name was Mary began with praising Wang Hong's good English before asking her some personal questions:

Mary: Do you have your home back in China?

Wang Hong: Yes.

Mary: I mean "Are you married?"

Wang Hong: Yes, and I have a daughter.

Mary: How old is your daughter?

Wang Hong: She's ten.

Mary: But you look so young.

Wang Hong: Thank you! I'm not as young as you thought.

After the party Wang Hong thought about this conversation and was confused by Mary's question. As an English teacher, she knows that it is impolite to ask about people's marital status in American culture. But why did Mary ask her this question. She wondered whether Mary was rude or she really looked very young. But later on several other occasions some more women asked her about her marital status. She was more confused. She didn't understand it until her old friend who had been staying in the U.S. for more than fifteen years told her that the reason was just because she didn't wear her wedding ring.

Analysis:

In the West, it is a social tradition and convention that a married person should wear the wedding ring which symbolizes the person's state of marriage. The ring, whose shape is a circle with no beginning or end, is viewed as a symbol of eternity. In the West, it is the custom to exchange the wedding ring. However, in China, there's no such tradition and convention. It doesn't count whether a married person wears the wedding ring or not. It's just people's personal habits. Wang Hong was not aware of this difference in wearing wedding rings until her own experience in the United States.

In this case, Wang Hong has some knowledge of American culture, but she didn't realize the importance of knowing the nature and characteristics of culture and communication. According to Hall, culture, which is based on symbols, is communication. So the wedding ring, a symbol of the American culture, is a message. Those who asked Wang Hong about her marital status were not being impolite. It's true that in the United States, one is not supposed to ask others about their ages or marital status. However, communication is a systematic process. It always occurs in context, and the nature of communication depends largely on this context. The setting and environment help one to determine the words and actions he or she generates and the meanings he or she gives to the symbols that are produced by other people. So the language, topic selection, and something like that are all adapted to context depending on variables namely location, occasion, time, and number of people. In Wang Hong's case, the location, the occasion, and the individual determine the nature of the communication in a reception party held at her host's home. It's a casual occasion, not a formal one. And those who asked about her marital status were women, and they were speaking to her with a lot of other people around.

II. Case 2

Being Confused about Friendship in America

Peter and Ranser first met in their chemistry class at an American university. Ranser was an international student from Jordan. He was excited to know an American, and because he wanted to learn more about American culture, Ranser hoped that he and Peter would become good friends.

At first, Peter seemed very friendly. He always greeted Ranser warmly before class. Sometimes he offered to study with Ranser. He even invited Ranser to have lunch with him. But after the semester was over, Peter seemed more distant. The two former classmates didn't see each other very much at school. One day Ranser decided to call Peter. Peter didn't seem very interested in talking to him. Ranser was hurt by Peter's change of attitude. "Peter said we were friends," Ranser complained. "And I said friends were friends forever." (Xu Lisheng, 2004)

Analysis:

In the above case, both Peter and Ranser should not be blamed for their troubled relationship. The reason why Ranser felt puzzled is that he is a layman to American culture. He doesn't understand how Americans consider friendship. "Friend" has very general meanings to Americans. Americans may use "friends" to call either casual acquaintances or close companions. Americans make up "friends" usually based on instrumental purpose. Once their goal achieved or their shared activities end, the friendship among them may fade. For example, in order to finish a task or an activity successfully, Americans may make up friends in school, in workplace, in sports field, in neighborhood, and they have school friends, work friends, sports friends and neighborhood friends. However, once their shared goal achieved, their shared activities end, their friendship may disappear. Likewise, although Peter and Ranser once were classmates and also friends, now they are no longer classmates, so their friendship has changed, and Peter no longer views Ranser as his friend.

In some cultures, friendship means a strong life-long bond between two people. In these cultures, friendships develop slowly and once the friendships are built, the friendships may last forever. However, American society is one of rapid change, and studies show that one out of every five American families moves from one place to another place every year. American friendships develop quickly, and the friendships may end quickly just as it develops.

People from the United States may seem friendly at their first meeting with others. Americans often chat easily with strangers. They can exchange information with strangers about families, hobbies and work. They may smile warmly towards each other and say, "Have a nice day!" or "See you later." Schoolmates may say to each other, "Let's get together sometimes." However, friendliness is not always an offer of true friendship in America.

People like Ranser shouldn't give up trying to make up friends with Americans. Americans do value strong life-long friendship, with Americans and non-Americans. When making friends, it helps to view friendship with Americans correctly so as to have a good cross-cultural understanding.

Part Five　Knowledge Practice

⬤ Translation

I. Translate the following passage into Chinese.

Talking about problem-solving or decision-making within a national environment indicates studying many complex cultural elements. It means trying to measure the impact of these factors on modern life，and also coming to catch changes now taking place.

The difference of management in business between Western countries and Eastern countries is that Western style decision-making proceeds mostly from top management and often does not consult middle management or the worker while in Eastern countries，ideas can be created at the lowest levels，travel upward through an organization and have an impact on the final decision. This is the management style of being from the bottom to the up.

II. Translate the following passage into English.

中国传统文化是中华文明经过演变而汇集成的一种反映民族特质和风貌的民族文化,是民族历史上各种思想文化、观念形态的总体表现,是指居住在中国地域内的中华民族及其祖先所创造的、为中华民族世世代代所继承发展的、具有鲜明民族特色的、历史悠久、内涵博大精深、传统优良的文化。它是中华民族几千年文明的结晶,除了儒家文化这个核心内容外,还包含有其他文化形态,如道家文化、佛教文化,等等。

⬤ Case Study

I. Case 1

Low vs. High Context Culture

(1) When President George Bush went to Japan accompanied by leading American businessmen，he made direct demands on Japanese leaders，which violated Japanese etiquette. To the Japanese，it is rude and a sign of ignorance to make direct demands. Some analysts believe that it damaged the negotiation and made the Japanese confirmed that Americans are barbarians.

(2) A Japanese manager working in an American company was told to give critical feedback to a subordinate during a performance evaluation. It took the manager five tries

to make the American subordinate understand because the Japanese are used to high context language and feel uncomfortable with giving direct feedback to others.

Questions for discussion:

1. Why did the Japanese think Americans are barbarians?
2. Why was it so difficult for the Japanese to tell his subordinate about his poor performance?

II. Case 2

In or Out

In a language institute in Beijing, there were overseas students studying English and Chinese who came from Europe, America, Africa and Asian countries. In 1989, a Japanese student, named Hashida, came to the institute after he completed his two year studies in Australia. His English was good enough to communicate, and his Chinese was fairly good. One day, he met a girl on the campus from Holland, who introduced herself as Mary. She was studying Chinese here. Both of them could communicate in English, of course. Hashida greeted her in Chinese, and Mary responded with a sweet smile and they began their talk in not so good Chinese. As they were sitting on a bench, Mary turned her body towards Hashida and seemed to be quite happy to meet this Japanese boy. As agreed, they met in Mary's apartment the following day, continuing their talk.

Seeing that Mary was standing and sitting very close to him and looking at him with a sweet smile, Hashida instantly knew she liked him very much, so he made his first approach to her by putting his arm around the back of the girl. But to his disappointment, Mary gave him a push and stopped him from doing that. Hashida thought she was shy, so he maneuvered a second approach by trying to hug her, but Mary gave him a second push and let him out of her apartment. Hashida was quite puzzled and didn't know why.

(Adapted from Wang Fuxiang and Ma Dengge, 1999)

Questions for Discussion:

1. Why was Hashida puzzled?
2. Why was Mary so angry at Hashida?
3. What advice would you give Mary and Hashida if you were their friend?

Unit 3

Verbal Communication and Culture

Learning Objectives

By the end of this unit, you should be able to:

1. Understand what is verbal communication;
2. Understand how language is closely related with culture;
3. Analyze culturally-loaded words in both English and Chinese;
4. Explain cultural reflections on proverbs and sayings in both English and Chinese;
5. Explain the different verbal styles between English and Chinese.

Part One Warming Up

Watch the following movie clip from *Meet the Parents* and then answer the questions below the script.

Questions for discussion:

1. Why did Jack think what Grey said when praying interesting? What are the differences in cultures between Jewish religion and Christian religion concerning praying words?
2. Can you point out the differences in cultures between Budda religion and Christian religion concerning praying words?

3. Can you identify people's religion by his or her praying words?

| Part Two | Basic Knowledge of Verbal Communication and Culture |

1. Verbal Communication

Verbal communication refers to the communication that is carried out either in oral or in written form with the use of words. (Xu, Lisheng, 2004) Verbal communication is the transferring of thoughts between individuals via spoken or written messages. (Du, Ruiqing, Tian Dexin & Li Bnexian, 2004)

Verbal communication occurs when people are chatting with their friends, discussing an issue in a group, making a public speech, etc.. Skillful and effective verbal communication involves careful choice of language that takes into account logical and emotional effects, contextual factors, and the needs of the message sender and receiver, especially when they come from different cultural backgrounds. For example, if you want to be an effective communicator, you have to adapt your words, manner to the person/persons with whom you are talking, and find out what interests the person/persons you are talking to.

In verbal communication, culture factors need to be considered. A word may have rich culturally-created connotative meaning in one language, while it is seldom used with the same meaning in another. Lions in English culture are the symbol of courage, danger and power. They are considered the king of animals. But lions do not have such a connotative meaning in Chinese culture. In Chinese culture, it is tigers that convey similar messages.

1.1　The Relationship Between Language and Culture

Chaika states, "Language and society are so intertwined that it is impossible to understand one without the other. There is no human society that does not depend on, is not shaped by, and does not itself shape language."(Chaika, 1989: 2) What Chaika said makes clear the relationship between language and culture. That is, a close relationship exists between language and culture.

1.1.1　Language Reflects the Environment

Language reflects the environment in which we live. We label things that are around us. For example, People who live in an environment where it snows during most time of the year may have much more different words for snow. The Eskimos' complex classification of types of snow is a classic example. There is one word for each category of snow to express "falling snow", "fallen snow", "flaky snow", "crusty snow", and "powdery snow". The Eskimos make categories of snow because their survival needs a precise knowledge of snow conditions. In the Amazon and certain African areas in the equatorial forests people do not have a word for snow because snow is not part of the environment. It simply does not exist.

1.1.2　Language Reflects Cultural Values

In addition to the environment，language expressions reflect cultural values. Edward T. Hall points out that the Navajos（纳瓦霍人：美国最大的印第安部落）do not have a word for "late". Time does not play a role in Navajo life. There is a time to do everything，a natural time rather than the artificial clock time that industries use. As a result，the Navajos do not have the differentiated vocabulary connected with time and clocks that Americans have. Time and the passing of time are things one can't control；therefore，one should not worry about wasting time and setting schedules. There is no Japanese or Arabic word for "privacy" because both cultures prefer crowding. Greeks have many words to express gratitude.

1.1.3　Language Affects People's Way of Thinking

People who speak different languages have different ways of thought patterns. Some scholars even argue that language not only transmits but also shapes our thinking，attitudes，and beliefs. They say the language people speak determines the way they perceive the world and determines culture. That is "language determinism（语用决定论）". It's based on a hypothesis put forward by Sapir and Whorf；their studies result in what is called today the Sapir-Whorf Hypothesis. According to Sapir，language is the medium of expression for human society，and it conditions our thinking about social problems and processes. He believes that language influences or even determines what people think and how people think.

No language can exist without the context of culture；and no culture can exist without the structure of natural language. Culture influences language at various levels. Five different but interrelated sets of rules combine to comprise linguistic study：phonology，morphology，syntax，semantics，and pragmatics. Each part emphasizes a different aspect of the way language works. Culture has an impact on language at all these levels. However，phonemic and syntactical variation are often taken for granted. At the lexical，pragmatic and discourse level，there are a lot worth studying as for intercultural communication.

2. Culturally Loaded Words

Vocabulary is the basic element of a language and it reveals the corresponding culture.

2.1   Same Words or Terms in Both Languages with Different Meanings

There are some words or terms in one language which have equivalent words or terms in another language. But the meanings of equivalent words are not always the same in both languages.

There exist differences between the meanings of some equivalent words in both Chinese and English. Although the Chinese for "dragon" is "龙" in all English-Chinese dictionaries；the same with "知识分子" for "intellectual"，the associations of them in Chinese are different from those in English.

In Chinese culture，"龙" is a totem with many royal associations，such as "龙颜""龙袍""龙心大喜". However，the associations of "dragon" to Westerners are horrible monsters. Likewise，in China，the term "知识分子"generally refers to those people who have had a college education，they include college teachers，college students，middle school teachers，and such people as doctors，engineers，interpreters. However，in the U.S. and Europe，"intellectual" includes only those people with high academic status such as college professors，not including college students. So the term in English covers a much smaller range of people. Apart from the difference，"intellectual" is not always a positive term in the U.S.. And sometimes it is used in a derogatory sense.

2.2   Words or Terms without Counterparts in the Other Language

There are many examples of an object or concept that exists in one culture but not in another. The Chinese expression "干部" is mostly interpreted as "cadre" in English. But "cadre" is not the same as "干部". Actually "cadre" is not commonly used in English，and many English-speaking people do not know the meaning of "cadre". No wonder the following terms have been suggested as substitutes：official，administrator，etc.. But none of these has exactly the same meaning as "干部".

The term "social sciences" deserves people's attention. The equivalent term of "social sciences" is "社会科学"，but they are not really the same，and both terms cover different fields. According to contemporary Chinese usage，"社会科学"covers all the fields except the ones in natural sciences and applied sciences. It would be the same with the English term 'the humanities' which includes language，literature，philosophy，etc. and the branches of learning that mainly deal with the cultural aspects of civilization. However，the English term "social sciences" covers a smaller area of learning. It includes political science，economics，history and sociology and the branches of learning that study human society，especially its organization and relationship of individual members to it.

2.3   Same Things or Concepts Are Represented by Different Terms in Two Languages

Things or concepts are represented by one or perhaps two terms in one language，but by many more terms in the other language.

For example，in English，the meaning of taking something is expressed by "carry", but in Chinese，there are a lot of words represent the concept，such as "带""背""扛""提""挑""挎". Similarly，"uncle" in English could be expressed by "叔""伯""姑父""舅""姨夫".

On the other hand，in Chinese，we only have one expression for "副"，but in English we have "vice，associate，deputy，assistant，under" to express the concept with different collocations，like in "vice-chairman，associate professor，deputy director，assistant secretary，undersecretary（副国务卿）".

3. Cultural Reflections on Proverbs and Sayings

Proverbs may provide glimpses or clues to a people's geography，history，social organization，and social views. People who live along areas of sea coasts and whose livelihood is dependent on the sea will have proverbs about sailing，about braving the weather and about fish and fishing. Nomadic people like the Arabs will have sayings about the desert or pasture-land，about sheep，horses，or camels，and about wolves and jackals. In cultures where old age is respected and admired，there will be proverbs about the wisdom of the elders. And in societies where women's status is low，there will be a number of sayings that make them feel demeaned.

Human experiences and observations of the world are similar in many respects. So，despite the dissimilar cultural backgrounds of the Chinese and the English-speaking peoples，the number of proverbs or sayings in the two languages that are equivalent or close approximates is surprising. Consider the following：

Strike while the iron is hot.	趁热打铁
Out of sight，out of mind	眼不见，心不烦
Many hands make light work.	人多好办事
Look before you leap	三思而后行
Where there's a will there's a way.	有志者事竟成
Where there's smoke there's fire.	无风不起浪
All good things must come to an end.	天下没有不散的筵席

Since culture plays an important role in giving a language its characteristics，the dissimilarities are naturally more apparent. Compared with English proverbs，Chinese proverbs have certain distinctive features. First of all，their number is immense. Chinese seems to have a proverb or saying for almost every situation including human-nature situations and human-human relations. Secondly，many of the sayings show distinctive Chinese quality. "挂羊头，卖狗肉" is typical. It refers to a Chinese butcher's shop with items that would be shocking to many westerners. Thirdly，many of the proverbs reflect social inequalities and the feelings of those deprived and oppressed. "只许州官放火，不许

百姓点灯"is a case in point. Fourthly, many of the proverbs or sayings show the influence of Buddhism on Chinese customs and thinking, as in "平时不烧香，临时抱佛脚", while English proverbs reflect the influence of Christianity. Another feature is that many of the proverbs or sayings reflect what might be called social harmony, or brotherhood, or "doing good", such as "前人栽树，后人乘凉。一人得道，鸡犬升天". Chinese proverbs which lack commonly-known English equivalents are numerous.

There are also some common English proverbs that do not have exact Chinese equivalents. The following are some examples：

Absence makes the heart grow fonder.	越是不见越想见。
You can't have your cake and eat it too.	鱼和熊掌不可兼得。
Let sleeping dogs lie.	莫惹是非。
You can't teach an old dog new tricks.	年逾花甲不堪教。

The points of differences that are mentioned above are not intended to be exhaustive, but aimed to give the reader some idea of the differences in cultures between Chinese proverbs or sayings and English ones.

4. Cultural Reflections on the Language Usage: Direct Versus Indirect Language Usage Styles

When people want to assert themselves as unique (individualism), they must be direct so that they can be understood where they stand. When describing themselves to others, individualists must be direct. Indirect communication, however, often is used in close relationships (e.g., to express emotions). If people's goal is to maintain harmony in the group (collectivism), they cannot be direct because they might offend another member of the group. In order to maintain harmony, collectivists must be cautious and indirect. Therefore, indirect communication predominates in collectivistic cultures whenever maintaining harmony is considered important. Collectivists, however, often use direct communication when maintaining harmony is not considered a primary concern.

Language usage reflects the patterns of thinking which vary within and among cultures depending on the situation. Particular patterns predominate in different cultures. Analytic thinking tends to predominate in the United States, while synthetic thinking tends to predominate in China. Analytic thinking focuses on looking at parts, rather than the whole. In contrast, synthetic thinking tries to grasp things in their totality. Low-context message construction requires analytic thinking, and high-context message construction needs synthetic thinking. Analytic thinking leads to the fact that people use the pattern of linear reasoning when talking or writing because they need to specify how the parts are related to each other. Synthetic thinking leads to the fact that people use the pattern of a more ambiguous or implicit logic.

The direct and indirect forms of communication which are adopted in the United States and Japan can reflect the differences of culture.

When it comes to the value of precision, Americans tend to use words explicitly, which is the most notable feature in their communicative style. They are more likely to use such categorical words as "absolutely", "certainly", and "positively" ... The English syntax requires that the absolute "I" be placed at the beginning of the sentence in most cases, forming the subject-predicate relation in an ordinary sentence. On the contrary, the culture advocating interdependence and harmony dictates Japanese speakers' tendency to use implicit and even ambiguous words. They like to depend more frequently on qualifiers such as "maybe", "perhaps", "probably", and "somewhat" to avoid leaving an assertive impression. The qualifier predicate is the predominant form of sentence construction for Japanese syntax, which does not always require the use of a subject in a sentence.

Even when Japanese speak in English and U.S. Americans speak in Japanese, these differences mentioned above are still obvious.

There's no denying that indirectness also occurs in individualistic cultures like the United States. However, the reasons for indirectness in individualistic cultures like the United States seem to be different from those in collectivistic cultures. According to a professional interpreter in Japan, U.S. Americans can be just as indirect as the Japanese, but they are indirect about different things, and being indirect bears a different meaning. U.S. Americans are usually indirect when discussing something sensitive or when they are nervous about how the other person's reaction. Whenever U.S. Americans are indirect, the interpreter, "I can sense that something is going on!"

Japanese indirectness is not always because they are such kind and considerate people that they worry about other's reactions. In most cases, it is just that they know their own fates and fortunes are closely related with others. I think you can value directness when you value individualism, or when you are with people you know and trust completely.

At times, Americans are indirect and Japanese also are direct, especially with close friends.

(William B. Gudykunst: 1998)

Glossary

1. **connote** *vt.* (of a word) imply or suggest (an idea or feeling) in addition to the literal or primary meaning （词）意味着,有……的含意
2. **connotative** *adj.* 隐含的,内涵的
3. **convey** *vt.* transport or carry to a place 载送,输送
4. **equatorial** *adj.* of, at, or near the equator （在）赤道（附近）的

5. **artificial**   *adj*. made or produced by human beings rather than occurring naturally, especially as a copy of something natural   人工的,人造的

6. **differentiate**   *vt*. recognize or ascertain what makes（someone or something）different   区别,区分

7. **determinism**   *n*. the doctrine that all events, including human actions, are ultimately determined by causes regarded as external to the will. Some philosophers have taken determinism to imply that individual human beings have no free will and cannot be held morally responsible for their actions   （哲）决定论

8. **hypothesis**   *n*. a supposition or proposed explanation made on the basis of limited evidence as a starting point for further investigation   假设

9. **comprise**   *vt*. ① consist of，be made up of   由……组成,由……构成；② make up; constitute. 组成,构成

10. **phonology**   *n*. the system of contrastive relationships among the speech sounds that constitute the fundamental components of a language   音位系统

11. **morphology**   *n*.（linguistics）the study of the forms of words，in particular inflected forms.   （语言学）形态学

12. **syntax**   *n*. the arrangement of words and phrases to create well-formed sentences in a language   句法

13. **semantics**   *n*. the branch of linguistics and logic concerned with meaning. The two main areas are logical semantics，concerned with matters such as sense and reference and presupposition and implication，and lexical semantics，concerned with the analysis of word meanings and relations between them，such as synonymy and antonymy   语义学

14. **phonemic**   *n*.（phonetics）any of the perceptually distinct units of sound in a specified language that distinguish one word from another，for example p, b, d, and t in the English words pad, pat，bad，and bat   （语音）音位

15. **lexical**   *adj*. of or relating to the words or vocabulary of a language   （与）词汇（有关）的

16. **reveal**   *vt*. make（previously unknown or secret information）known to others   先前未知或秘密信息）透露,暴露,泄露,揭露

17. **equivalent**   *adj*. equal in value, amount, function, meaning, etc.   （价值、数量、功能、意义等）相等的,相同的,等同的

18. **royal**   *adj*. having the status of a king or queen or a member of their family   国王的,女王的；王室的,王族的

19. **intellectual**   *adj*. of or relating to the intellect   智力的,才智的

20. **status**   *n*. the relative social, professional, or other standing of someone or something   （人或物的）相对社会地位,相对身份

21. **derogatory**   *adj*. showing a critical or disrespectful attitude   持批评态度的,贬低的,不敬的

22. **philosophy**　*n*. the study of the fundamental nature of knowledge, reality, and existence, especially when considered as an academic discipline　哲学

23. **collocation**　*n*. (Linguistics) the habitual juxtaposition of a particular word with another word or words with a frequency greater than chance　（语言学）（词的）习惯搭配，组合

24. **deputy**　*n*. a person whose immediate superior is a senior figure within an organization and who acts for this superior in their absence　副手；代理人

25. **undersecretary**　*n*. a subordinate official, in particular (in the UK) a junior minister or senior civil servant, or (in the U.S.) the principal assistant to a member of the cabinet　副部长；次长；副国务卿

26. **proverb**　*n*. a short pithy saying in general use, stating a general truth or piece of advice　谚语，俗语，常言

27. **glimpse**　*n*. a momentary or partial view　一瞥，一看

28. **pasture-land**　*n*. land used as pasture　牧草地，牧场

29. **jackal**　*n*. a slender long-legged wild dog that feeds on carrion, game, and fruit and often hunts cooperatively, found in Africa and southern Asia　豺，胡狼

30. **approximate**　*adj*. close to the actual, but not completely accurate or exact　近似的，接近但不完全正确的

31. **deprive**　*vt*. deny (a person or place) the possession or use of something　剥夺（人、地方）对某物的所有（或使用）

32. **oppress**　*vt*. keep (someone) in subjection and hardship, especially by the unjust exercise of authority　压迫，虐待

33. **Buddhism**　*n*. a widespread Asian religion or philosophy, founded by Siddartha Gautama in NE India in the 5th century BC　佛教

34. **Christianity**　*n*. the religion based on the person and teachings of Jesus of Nazareth, or its beliefs and practices　基督教

35. **assert**　*v*. state a fact or belief confidently and forcefully　断言，坚称，肯定有力地说出事实（看法）

36. **predominate**　*vi*. be the strongest or main element; be greater in number or amount　（数量上）占优势，占绝大多数

37. **analytic**　*adj*. (linguistics) (of a language) tending not to alter the form of its words but to use word order to express grammatical structure. Chinese and English are examples of analytic languages　（语言学）（语言）分析性的

38. **synthetic**　*adj*. (of a substance) made by chemical synthesis, especially to imitate a natural product　（物质）合成的；人造的

39. **ambiguous**　*adj*. (of language) open to more than one interpretation; having a double meaning　（语言）可作多种解释的；有歧义的

40. **implicit**   *adj.* implied though not plainly expressed   含蓄的,不言明的

41. **stepping-stone**   *n.* 踏脚石;手段,方法

42. **explicit**   *adj.* stated clearly and in detail,leaving no room for confusion or doubt   详述的;明晰的,明确的

43. **involve**   *vt.* (of a situation or event) include (something) as a necessary part or result   (情况或事件)包括,包含;牵涉,卷入

44. **contextual**   *n.* the circumstances that form the setting for an event,statement,or idea,and in terms of which it can be fully understood and assessed   (事件、声明或观念的)环境;背景;来龙去脉

● Comprehension Check

I. Decide whether the following statements are true (T) or false (F).

1. (   ) Verbal communication is the transferring of thoughts between individuals only via spoken message.

2. (   ) Verbal communication is not as clarified and efficient as other ways of communication,e.g. written communication.

3. (   ) "Dragon" means the same to the Westerners "龙"to the Chinese.

4. (   ) The Chinese phrase "知识分子" has the same meaning as "intellectual".

5. (   ) A term in one language may not have a counterpart in another language.

6. (   ) The following six English words:"vice", "associate", "assistant", "deputy", and "under" can all mean "副"in Chinese language.

7. (   ) There are as many similarities as dissimilarities between English proverbs and Chinese proverbs.

8. (   ) Patterns of thought vary with culture.

9. (   ) Particular patterns predominate in different cultures.

10. (   ) Analytic thinking tends to predominate in the China,while synthetic thinking tends to predominate in the United States.

II. Answer the following questions.

1. Can you think of specific examples that illustrate the link between culture and language?

2. Can you explain the cultural differences in direct and indirect forms of communication by comparing the United States with China?

3. What is your understanding of translating the language or translating the meaning?

4. What is the difference between analytic thinking and synthetic thinking?

III. Fill in each of the blanks in the following passage with an appropriate word from those listed below.

A. behaviors   B. information   C. borders   D. intercultural

E. dynamics   F. patterns   G. communication   H. described
I. global   J. provided

Just as quickly as current events shape and are shaped by our societies, so we too must adapt our understanding of how cultures are developing. In 1967, Martin McLuhan famously ___1___ a world in which technology would connect even the most remote areas of the planet. He called this phenomenon the ___2___ village. Today, we can definitely see how we are united to other people via our technology. This of course leads to more intercultural contact and exchange. In fact, it has also given rise to more modern forms of ___3___, such as email, discussion boards, texting, twittering, etc.. You can communicate individually with people you have never met face-to-face. Social researchers note that the Internet itself has ___4___ an enormous venue for increased interpersonal communication, regardless of geographic and political ___5___.

There are several consequences to such ___6___ in communication. First, more contact and exchanges means we are able to receive more ___7___ about cultures that were previously less known or discussed. Also, it is possible to observe various common global ___8___ which make up what we will call the metaculture. Because of increased contact due to globalization, we can identify a supra-level of mutual global behaviors across cultures. Most of our world shares at least one lingua franca, or a shared code of meaning — at the moment this is English. However, we also share certain symbols, ___9___, and practices. For example, consider the enormous social networking effects of Facebook (Fig.1.3). Using a medium such as Facebook allows us to talk to one another in real-time, create groups, organize social causes, market products. Such elements as Facebook are crucial contributors to increased ___10___ communication, and to the resulting increase of shared practices and norms. We will examine how globalization has shaped, and in turn is being shaped by, this surface level we call metaculture. (Melanie Moll, 2012: 10)

IV. Give the Chinese equivalents of the following expressions.

1. Justice has long arms
2. Diamond cut diamond
3. golden saying
4. fat office
5. You will cross the bridge when you get to it
6. Better be the head of a dog than the tail of lion
7. drink like a fish
8. Tread upon eggs

Part Three　Knowledge Expansion

Reading 1

The Confucian Concepts of *Jen* and *Li*

Of the four principles of Confucianism (*jen*, *i*, *li*, and *chih*), *jen*, humanism, is the cardinal principle. In understanding East Asian patterns of communication, it is vital to understand *jen* in conjunction with *li*, propriety, or proper etiquette and ritual behavior. The author's earlier article proposed that Asian interpersonal relationships differ from the North American ones by their particularistic orientation, emphasis on long-term and asymmetrical reciprocity, sharp distinction between in-group and out-group members, frequent use of informal intermediaries and overlap between personal and public relationships. Of these five distinctions, the particularistic orientation received special attention. In East Asia, particular rules and interaction patterns are applied depending upon the relationship and context (particularistic orientation). In North America, general and objective rules tend to be applied across diverse relationship and contexts (universalistic orientation). In Riding the Waves of Culture, a Dutch business consultant, Trompenaars, suggested that the "universalist" versus "particularist" schism is one of the fundamental premises that comprise human culture. His distinction between universalism and particularism is very similar to my own description: Americans and Canadians are at the extreme end of universalism while people in Republic of Korea and China are at the other extreme end of particularism.

The particularistic orientation in interpersonal relationships is translated into communication patterns of "differentiated linguistic codes" in which different linguistic codes are used depending upon what persons are involved and in what situations. Extensive rules, rituals, and etiquettes mark East Asian communication patterns. East Asian languages are very complex and differentiated according to social status, degree of intimacy, age, sex, and level of formality. These differentiations are manifested not only in referential terms, but also in verbs, pronouns, and nouns. For example, the simple noun, cooked rice, has three variations in Korean depending upon the level of deference that one expects to exhibit to those present. There are also minutely differentiated and extensive kinship terms. The term children use for their father's elder sister differs from the term they use for his younger sister, for their mother's elder sister or younger sister, and so forth. In social settings, it is imperative to use proper titles when addressing another person. One's first name is rarely used. Because of such sociolinguistic rules, East Asian languages are considered to be especially difficult for Westerners to master.

Such strict adherence to communication rules can be understood by examining the Confucian principles of *jen* and *li*. *Jen* is the most important teaching of Confucianism as manifested by the fact that it is the most frequently mentioned concept in the Analects. "*Jen* appears 105 times, and 58 out of 482 chapters in the Analects are directly concerned with its meaning, function or practice". Oddly, Confucius never explicitly defined its meaning. The ideographic Chinese character for *jen* (仁) consists of the sign for person (人) and the sign for two (二). Literally, then it means the relationship formed between two people. But beyond this, it also means the warm human feelings between people, and humanism in general. *Jen* is like a seed from which springs all the qualities that make up the ideal human being. *Jen* refers to the possession of all of these qualities to a high degree. *Jen* is love for fellow human beings in the narrow sense, but more importantly it is an all-encompassing ethical ideal. *Jen* is the main thread running through the whole system of Confucianism and in its core, it embodies integration of one's self with others.

Confucius mentions three ways of practicing *jen*. The first is to have absolute sincerity in dealing with others; the second is not to do to others what you yourself do not like, and the third is to cultivate one's own virtues so that one never complains of others, either in affairs of state or at home. To Confucius, *jen* cannot exist without the other person. In the Analects, he says, "One who wishes to establish one's own position must first establish the position of others; one who wishes to be prominent oneself must first help others to be prominent." In Confucianism, humanism starts with cultivating oneself (overcoming ones own shortcomings) and continues with affection and reverence toward one's parents and brotherly and sisterly love to one's siblings, then circles outward to treat others as one's own parents or siblings.

Li originally referred to rites of sacrifice, but expanded over time to a much broader concept and norm that govern polite behavior. As an objective criterion of social order, *li* was perceived as the rule of the universe and the fundamental regulatory etiquette of human behavior. Confucius said that *li* follows from *jen*, that is, from being considerate of others and expressing one's reverence toward the occasion. Confucianism provides elaborate rules in dealing with various occasions as well as in dealing with different relationships such as rulers and subjects, fathers and sons, the elder and the younger, husbands and wives, and between friends. There are two interpretations regarding Confucius' conception of the relation between *jen* and *li*: the instrumentalist and the definitionalist interpretations. According instrumentalist interpretation, the observance of *li* is a means to cultivating and expressing *jen*. It is through *li* that a person who achieved high level of *jen* ideal expresses his/her emotional dispositions and attitudes constituting the ideal. *Li* can be instrumental for a person who has not yet achieved *jen* as well because diligent participation in *li* would lead him or her to a deeper appreciation of humanity. In other words, if one were engaged in respectful and sincere patterns of interaction with the other person, one would develop a sincere human feeling toward the person. This idea is somewhat similar to the Western psychological principle that when one is engaged in behaviors that go against one's attitude (forced compliance), one's attitudes changes following the overt behavior.

Definitionalist interpretations maintain that *li* is intrinsically important independent of *jen*. "It is the observance of *li* which has ultimate value, from which the value of being the kind of person who generally observes *li* is derived". Scholars such as Mencius often listed it with other virtues such as humanity, filial piety, and sincerity. Both instrumentalist and definitinalist approaches point to the importance of li in understanding the East Asian emphasis on proper communication. The important point is that the inner feelings (*jen*) and outer expressions (*li*) are in harmony whichever comes first.

One of the criticisms of Confucianism in East Asia is that it is too formalistic. The strict ritualism that gained prominence in the Sung dynasty in China and Lee dynasty in Korea was blamed for the stagnation of Confucianism as well as for reduced creativity. However, *li*, instead of being strict rules, is open for modification depending upon time and situations. Confucius himself suggests that certain rites are open for modification. Xunzi who is known for his theorizing of *li* goes as far as to assert that norms governing the most basic relations should be continually refined as long as harmony is not disturbed.

Li are defined as those meaning-invested roles, relationships, and institutions which facilitate communication, and which foster a sense of community. They are a social grammar that provides each member with a defined place and status within the family, community, and polity. They further suggest that what makes rituals profoundly different from law or rule is that each person needs to personalize them. Studies show that ritualization will not work as social control if it is perceived as not amenable to some degree of individual adjustment. (June Ock Yum, 2007)

Comprehension Check

I. Answer the following questions.

1. What is the content of Confucian Concept of *Jen*?
2. What is the content of Confucian Concept of *Li*?
3. What is the relationship between Confucian Concept of *Jen* and Confucian Concept of *Li*?

4. What do Confucian Concept of *Jen* and Confucian Concept of *Li* influence East Asian culture?

II. Translate into Chinese the following passage in the essay.

Confucius mentions three ways of practicing *jen*. The first is to have absolute sincerity in dealing with others, the second is not to do to others what you yourself do not like, and the third is to cultivate one's own virtues so that one never complains of others, either in affairs of state or at home. To Confucius, *jen* cannot exist without the other person. In the Analects, he says, "One who wishes to establish one's own position must first establish the position of others; one who wishes to be prominent oneself must first help others to be prominent." In Confucianism, humanism starts with cultivating oneself (overcoming ones own shortcomings) and continues with affection and reverence toward one's parents and brotherly and sisterly love to one's siblings, then circles outward to treat others as one's own parents or siblings.

Reading 2

Corporate Cultural Modernization in a New Global Economy

In order to understand the concept of corporate cultural modernization one has to primarily grasp the dynamics of the current transformation of economic relations. No matter which terms we apply to describe these changes, be it informational economy, knowledge-based society or service economy, it is all about a new economic order that integrates a series of technical and cultural, social and political developments in the economic action repertoire without violating its rational criteria and requiring a stronger state. Lash observes a process of change in economic life as a result of "a new framework of what might be called 'reflexive accumulation'". He argues that the reflexive nature of the current economic system is based on the fact that the old "structural, capital accumulation is possible only on the condition that agency [firm] can free itself from rule-bound 'Fordist' structures". This means that for the process of capital accumulation to be possible "firms and workers in firms must innovate that much more quickly". According to Lash, the new accumulation regime shifts the center of gravity in the production process from the "material labor process" towards a "knowledge intensive 'design process'". Following his argument that "knowledge intensity necessarily involves reflexivity", the modernization of traditional Fordist corporate cultural values is necessary in order to transform heteronomous workers into self-monitoring workers. Successful self-management requires an absolutely new and unprecedented qualification from everyone, namely, "to think and act like an executive manager". This requires firms to reformulate and transform their basic principles and assumptions in order to achieve a continuous process of innovation. Although the theoretical framework is not designed to discuss these issues at length, a brief insight of the main directions of corporate cultural modernization are nevertheless necessary.

1. Transformation of Labor and Employment

Traditional corporate cultural values and practices are increasingly undermined by the transformation of labor processes and employment aspects as one of the most direct expressions of systemic change. The nature of this systemic change is simply described in the shift from live to work to work to live. This changing paradigm alters the fundamental logic of the industrial society as modernization compromises between labor as institution and capital markets may create new relationships between wealth and labor, enterprise and knowledge, vital flexibility and methodical lifestyle. This ultimate revolution of labor is accurately decoded by Anthony Giddens who holds the view that the drive to push the constant accumulation has become weakened or disappeared. Indeed the transformation of value systems in the post-scarcity order is a consequence of the fact that persons actively rebuild their working lives, revalue their things than their economic prosperity. The search for a new corporate cultural system is underscored by the changing character of compulsiveness to work and the relationship to the phenomenon of life-time paid work, a fact that is becoming very generation specific as such that people have to detach themselves from the idea that a person works for 40 years in one company. On the other hand it is a good feeling to work 40 years for one company as it provides job security. One cannot dismiss someone as easily after 40 years as they can after two years. The young people have a completely different culture in terms of dealing with the employer and their work.

The traditional value system has been dramatically destabilized by the abandonment of the lifetime formula where the workplace is an office or shop floor. Castells concludes that "the traditional form of work which is based on full-time employment, clear-cut occupational assignments, and a career pattern over the lifecycle is slowly but surely fading away". He argues that as networking and flexibility become characteristic of the new industrial organization, and as the new technologies make it possible for small business to find market niches, a resurgence of self-employment and mixed employment status arises. This implies the emergence of new forms of employment as flexi-time, multi-tasking, networkers, outsourcers, job-rotators, non-careerists and many others. A German company in Russia may have employees at more than 12,000 km and nine time zones away from their headquarters. The general manager will therefore never see this employee, who must still perform and fulfill the required task and remain motivated. One of the central questions of the post-industrial corporate cultural logic is thus: how to build a value bridge to this employee? What words motivate this person and make him feel part of the team? The changing trident relationship between job, family and lifestyle towards new stabile patterns requires therefore a redefinition of corporate values, if they are to fulfill their primal functions of coordination, motivation and organization. In addition, the worldwide war for talents will radically alter the message of corporate values. Firms attempting to become an employer of choice must rethink the methods how to increase the company attractiveness and reflect the life-style attitude to work and employment. The need to modernize the traditional corporate culture of the industrial society and adapt it to the conditions of the informational and knowledge-based society is certainly thus one of the most difficult management challenges of the future.

2. Internationalization of Companies and Management of Global Cultural Diversity

The process of internationalization represents the phenomenon of an encounter with non-Western shaped capitalism. The ethnic heterogeneity of company staff requires that the globally operating enterprises manage the cultural diversity of their subsidiaries around the world. Organizations that pursue the globality path have been further forced to interrogate their own traditional corporate values as such that management of globality has become a multicultural field of discourse about values. Global activity has confronted management with the challenge of developing value orientations that would bridge the gap between global standards and local adaptation. Practitioners understand this duality with their favorite slogan think globally, act locally. Efforts to adapt to local conditions have unleashed in turn a general tendency to redefine the traditional assumptions and develop corporate cultural profiles that meets the new realities of a culturally borderless network enterprise. In other words, the need for corporate cultural modernization must observe the global-local dichotomy and create valid and universal values on all meridians.

3. Transformation to Innovative Knowledge Organizations

Another direction of cultural modernization emerges from the transition of manufacturing companies of the industrial society to innovative knowledge-based organizations of the information society. Studies show that long ago, a new means of production is reshaping the capitalist mode of accumulation in a unique and dramatic way. This new means of production would no longer be capital, natural resources or labor. But it is and will be knowledge.

Study shows that value is now created by productivity and innovation. In order to achieve these added values the role of knowledge workers is essential. In a knowledge: based economy and society, top performance becomes possible only through the increased productivity of existing employees. Therefore, the main challenge of the new economic order is to make average employees achieve extraordinary results. This in turn implies a fundamental transformation of corporate values and norms oriented towards a completely new understanding of performance and efficiency principles, job responsibility and task fulfillment, motivation and trust (Ghenadie Anghel, 2012: 24-27).

Comprehension Check

I. Answer the following questions.

1. How do you understand the concept of corporate cultural modernization?
2. How are Labor and Employment transformed in a new global economy?
3. Please explain the internationalization of companies and the management of global cultural diversity.
4. Why should traditional knowledge armed workers be transformed to innovative knowledge armed workers?

II. Translate into Chinese the following passage in the essay.

The process of internationalization represents the phenomenon of an encounter with non-Western shaped capitalism. The ethnic heterogenization of company staff requires that the globally operating enterprises manage the cultural diversity of their subsidiaries around the world. Organizations that pursue the globality path have been further forced to interrogate their own traditional corporate values as such that management of globality has become a multicultural field of discourse about values. Global activity has confronted management with the challenge of developing value orientations that would bridge the gap between global standards and local adaptation. Practitioners understand this duality with their favorite slogan think globally, act locally. Efforts to adapt to local conditions have unleashed in turn a general tendency to redefine the traditional assumptions and develop corporate cultural profiles that meets the new realities of a culturally borderless network enterprise. In other words, the need for corporate cultural modernization must observe the global-local dichotomy and create valid and universal values on all meridians.

Part Four   Knowledge Application

Case Analysis

I. Case 1

Was She Not Honest?

Ms Liu was a baby-minder in a German family living in China. She got on well with the whole family at the beginning though her English was very limited. Ms Liu was a good cook and the whole family was very pleased with her delicious food. However, before the dinner, she always said to them: "I am sorry that I am a poor cook. Please try the dishes cooked by me. If they are bad, please forgive my fault." The German couple was surprised to hear what she said for the first time, because the dishes were unexpectedly very delicious. However, she repeated it as a rule whenever she put the dishes on the table. The couple's confusion finally led to the belief that Ms Liu was hollow-hearted. They could not understand why she was lying.

Analysis:

In China, modesty is shown in various ways such as self-belittling which is regarded as a virtue in daily life. Boasting or even fact-based positive remarks about oneself is interpreted as bad manner and not encouraged in social settings. Thus Ms Liu's self-evaluation well fits in the Chinese culture context but definitely not the German one. In Germany, people normally make judgments based on facts, otherwise they might regard it as a lie or dishonesty as Ms Liu's remark indicates. Both of them need to learn what guides their behaviors and how the judgments are made in their cultures respectively. Ms Liu should follow the same social rules as the host culture has in order to well adapt to the new culture.

II. Case 2

Is It an Acceptable Thing to Talk about?

Janet lives in a Canadian city with her two-year-old adopted Chinese daughter Huang. Janet is a busy professional woman and a single parent who wants her daughter to speak Chinese and know the culture she was born into. For this reason Janet invites new Chinese immigrants to live in a spare bedroom in her house. She always interviews prospective housemates before they move in. She wants to avoid any misunderstandings by making her expectations clear, and she wants everyone who lives in the house to benefit. Among other things, she wants to see how Huang likes any new person who might live with them. She expects a new resident in her home to agree to share housework and to speak Chinese to Huang. In exchange Janet agrees to help with English and any other problems the newly arrived immigrant might face in adapting to life in Canada.

Janet liked 32-year-old Deng, an engineer from northeast China, immediately when she came for her interview, and so did Huang. Deng thought this would be an ideal place to spend the six months she had to wait until her husband and 4-year-old son could join her. They lived with Deng's parents where she and her husband had lived since they married. She had never lived apart from her parents except when she lived in a university dormitory, so she was pleased to be able to live with a family. She readily agreed to everything Janet said during the interview.

After a few weeks Janet noticed that Deng seldom did any housework. She did not even clean up after herself, so Janet had more housework than before Deng moved in. Janet helped Deng with English and job applications, and practiced job interviews with her. At the same time Deng did not seem to spend more time with Huang.

Janet gave Deng some lighthearted reminders such as joking about how she hates housework or saying, "Huang, tell me what you and Deng did this afternoon."

This did not produce any positive results, so Janet decided to discuss the problem directly. One evening at the kitchen table Janet said, "I think we have some crossed lines of communication. I understood that we had a certain agreement between us, but you obviously understood something different. Can we talk about it?"

Deng was silent and stared at the table.

Janet tried again, "I hoped you would spend more time with Huang. You two got along so well at first. She likes you and is disappointed that you don't play with her."

Deng did not say anything. She did not look at Janet. Her body stiffened, her face turned red, and she stared at the floor.

Janet tried again. "I'm not angry, just confused, tell me what you're thinking, I want to understand your point of view."

More silence.

Finally Janet could not tolerate Deng's silence any longer. She was angry when she said, "You know, in this culture it's very rude to stay silent when someone is trying very hard to resolve a misunderstanding."

The next day Janet went to see her friend Qian, who had lived in Canada for over a year. Qian listened to Janet's story and said, "She is angry!" This was a surprise to Janet.

"What is she angry about? Why won't she talk to me?"

Janet never found out. Deng moved out soon after.(Linell Davis, 2001)

Analysis:

In this case, the Canadian woman Janet relies on direct talk to make an agreement or to resolve a conflict, while her Chinese partner Deng uses indirection and silence. Obviously Janet does not know that direct criticism would result in Deng's losing face in Chinese culture while Deng does not realize that the normal way of solving problems in Canadian culture is face-to-face talk which might sound very aggressive to her. Both of them should not apply their home culture rules in the new situation and should learn to know what is really behind their own actions.

Part Five   Knowledge Practice

Translation

I. Translate the following passage into Chinese.

The prevailing trend in some Western countries is toward informality. Formality has become equated with lack of substance. The author recently attended an inauguration ceremony of the university's 12th president in a certain Western country. The master of ceremony，who was the graduate of the same institution and currently served as a member of the Board of Visitors，consistently referred the person being inaugurated as "Bob," rather than "Dr. Smith" or"President." By doing so，he was expressing his familiarity and even his personal friendship with the president as well as his fondness for informality even during one of the most important formal occasions at the university. Using the person's first name in such a formal occasion is unthinkable in East Asia countries and would be perceived as extremely inappropriate and rude behavior. The master of ceremony was also expressing extreme individualism since he was in a sense boasting of his personal friendship at the expense of the appropriate rituals for that ceremony.

II. Translate the following passage into English.

有位语言心理学家说过交流是双行道,没有回应的谈话是无效谈话,说话艺术最重要的应用就是与人交谈。交谈的过程实质上是交谈双方交互发出信息与交互接收信息的过程。双方必然自始至终扮演既是听者又是说者的双重角色,双方都要自觉地围绕某一共同的话题,各抒己见,互相反馈。因此,交谈者不仅要会说还要会听,听说兼顾,互相配合,才能达到真正的交流。如果各说各的,互不相干,或只有一方说,另一方被动地听,都不利于交谈的顺利进行。

Case Study

I. Case 1

Getting Angry at the Way of Giving Message

Miss Liu，a college English teacher from China，went to a university in Britain for an exchange program. When she arrived at the university in Britain，the university arranged home-stay for her. According to the arrangement，she should pay the host $300 per month. She moved in on September 30, and it was November 2 when she joined a group of Chinese visiting scholars for a seven-day trip to London. When she came back, Miss Liu was shocked to find a note in her room which said: "You moved into our home on September 30, you've only paid &300. And this month's rent was due on November 1, but today is November 9." When she read this note, Miss Liu got very angry. She regarded it as an insult to her. So she gave the host the money that is asked from her and moved out to other place immediately.

Questions for discussion:

1. Why did Miss Liu feel irritated when she read the note on her room given by the host?
2. What do you think the differences between language style culture between Chinese and English?

II. Case 2

Understanding the Cultural Background

A woman from China who sells insurance in central Illinois has developed the Asian community as her major clientele. She has been extremely successful with that group and attributes her success to the cultural and linguistic adaptation of American insurance practices to the values of the Asian clientele. She has business cards and brochures printed in Japanese, Chinese, and Korean, the languages of her major client groups and she works very hard at pleasing her clientele. This saleswoman has adapted to the culture of the United States in many ways; she is assertive and outgoing, and she has a good grasp of the concept of profit. She also knows, given her own background, that she must be more indirect and willing to enter into long-term relationships with her clients that in many cases go beyond a typical American business relationship. A number of her clients ask her to give marital advice to their children, act as a go-between in marriage arrangements, and help with other personal matters. (Gao Yongchen, 2010)

Questions for discussion:

1. What makes the insurance saleswoman so successful?
2. What do you think is the most important factor influencing intercultural communication?

Unit 4
Daily Verbal Communication

Learning Objectives

By the end of this unit, you should be able to
1. Understand cultural differences in addressing;
2. Understand cultural differences in greeting;
3. Understand cultural differences in conversation topics;
4. Understand cultural differences in visiting and parting;
5. Understand cultural differences in compliments and compliment response;
6. Understand cultural differences in expressing gratitude and thanks.

Part One Warming Up

Watch the following movie clip from *Swing Vote* and then answer the questions below the script.

Questions for discussion:
1. Why does the daughter address her father as "Bud" instead of "Father"? Can it be acceptable in Chinese culture? Why?
2. What culture is shown in the way that the daughter and father make the conversation between each other? And can this way be accepted in Chinese culture? Why?

3. Suppose the daughter and the father are both Chinese, how would the daughter address her father, and how would they make the conversation?

Part Two Basic Knowledge of Daily Verbal Communication

As people's social behavior must be in line with social rules, speech behavior must be in accordance to rules of speaking. When the rules are broken, errors may be made. If you use address forms based on Chinese rules by saying "Where are you going?" as a greeting to a Westerner, you make an error, because you break the rules of English greeting.

Cultural influence in speech acts is shown in many aspects of social interaction. Chinese and English speakers differ when conducting daily verbal communication, such as addressing, greeting, visiting, etc..

1. Addressing

In daily verbal communication, there are some differences in the ways of addressing people. If people are unaware of those differences between different cultures, intercultural communication break-down may occur when people from different cultures communicate with each other. Therefore, in order to survive in other cultures, it is very necessary to learn some knowledge of the basic cultural differences in this field.

How to address others is one of the first problems closely related to interpersonal relationship. People from both English-speaking countries and China have two kinds of personal names — a surname and a given name. But there are some differences in the order and use of those names between English and Chinese. In Chinese the surname comes first and the given name follows the surname, while in English this order is reversed, as shown in the following examples:

Table 4.1 Order of Chinese name

	Surname	Given name
Chinese	Zhao	Xianhe

Table 4.2 Order of English name

	Given name	Surname
English	Christian	Lewes

In Chinese, for a man called Zhao Xianhe, he is mostly addressed by the following addresses: Zhao Xiansheng; Zhao Laoshi; Zhao Shifu or (Zhao + other professional titles); Zhao Xianhe; Xianhe; Xiao Zhao; Lao Zhao. While in English, for a man called Christian Lewes, he is mostly addressed by the following addresses: Mr. Lewes; Christian; Chris.

When addressing foreigners, Chinese speakers frequently make such mistakes as follows: Lewes; Mr. Christian; Teacher Lewes; Teacher. One reason why people use Lewes or Mr. Christian to address the man called Christian Lewes may be attributed to the Chinese concepts of the degree of relationship between people and the ways of showing respect. If a Chinese person uses Xianhu to address the Chinese man called Zhao Xianhu, it indicates that the Chinese person has intimate relationship with the man called Zhao Xianhu. However, in English, a man named Christian Lewes may be called Christian or Chris, which does not indicate intimate relationship between the addresser and the Christian Lewes.

Nowadays, many people from English-speaking countries, especially from America, tend to address others by their given names even when meeting for the first time. This applies to people of the same age, different ages and of different social statuses. And it is common for a child to call a much older person Peter, Mary, John, etc., and children even call their parents or grandparents by their given names. It is very common for college students call their professors by their given names. The professors regard this as an indication of their being friendly and being easy to approach instead of being disrespected. This is opposite to Chinese custom. In Chinese, if a child call his/her grandparents by their given names, or a student call his/her teachers by their given names. A quick scold would be surely given to the child or the student, because, in Chinese, addressing others who have higher social status than the addressers by given names is regarded as disrespectful.

Therefore, Chinese should keep it in mind that the Chinese custom of addressing members of one's family, relatives or close neighbors as "大姐", "大伯", "三婶"and the like should not be used to address people from English-speaking countries. In English, it would be enough that the given name alone, whether for man or woman, is used to address others such as addressing one's parents by their given names and addresses like Dad, Mom, Mum, or mother, one's grandparents by their given names and addresses like Grandpa, Grandma, and sometimes older relatives by their given names and Aunt Mary or Uncle Peter. It should be mentioned that it is the given name, not the surname is used. And sometimes Americans may just use the given name to address their relatives without considering the degree of relationship. Another thing should be kept in mind is that in English "Brother" or "Sister" would commonly be used to address persons who belong to a Catholic group, some religious or professional societies.

The usage of the surname and given name in English and Chinese can be summarized as follows:

Table 4.3

	English	Chinese
Formal relationship/situation	Title ＋ surname	Surname ＋ Title
Neutral relationship/situation	Title ＋ surname，Given name	Surname ＋ Title
Close relationship/situation	Given name	Given name

Due to the differences mentioned above，Chinese often feel uncomfortable when using a westerner's given name to address him/her，feeling that it indicates there is a close relationship between them. Westerners，on the other hand，may feel that if a Chinese insists on using their surnames to address them，it indicates that the Chinese is unwilling to be friendly to them，and they feel that the Chinese way of addressing them maintains a gap between them. So the above mentioned address form like Mr. Christian or Lewes may be a Chinese form. With Mr. Christian，the use of the given name indicates friendly relationship，but the adding of the title indicates the respect they should show. With Lewes，the lack of a title indicates friendly relationship，but the use of the surname prevents it sounding intimate.

Apart from the above mentioned ways of addressing others by Chinese speakers，another common way of addressing others is to use a person's title，office，or profession，such as "王老板""张经理""刘院长". While in English，only a few occupations or titles like Doctor，Judge，Governor，Mayor，Professor，Nurse and ranks like Captain are used to address people with such a title，office，or profession. These can be used either singly or with the person's surname. (Deng Yanchang，et al.，1989)

2. Greetings

Like addressing，in daily verbal communication，there are also some differences in the ways of greeting people. Being unaware of those differences between different cultures may lead to intercultural communication break-down when people from different cultures communicate with each other. So in order to survive in other cultures，it is very necessary to learn some knowledge of the basic cultural differences in this field.

Greetings are common phenomena in both English and Chinese. When people meet，they usually greet each other. The purpose of greeting is to establish or maintain social contact instead of transferring information. Therefore，formulaic expressions are often used in both English and Chinese. In English，the following greetings are often used in their daily life.

— Hi!

— Hey!

— Hello!

— How's life?

— How's everything?

— Good morning/afternoon/evening.

— How are things?

— How are things with you?

— How are things going?

In Chinese，the following greetings are often used in their daily life，which are very similar to those English greetings.

— 吃了吗？（Have you had your meal?）

— 上哪儿去？（Where are you going?）

— 去过哪啦？（Where have you been?）

Most English-speaking people would react to these greetings by using such words as "It's none of your business!" or "Are you going to invite me to dinner?"

3. Conversation Topics

In daily verbal communication，there are some differences in the ways of initiating conversation and selecting conversation topics between Westerners and Chinese. Being unaware of those differences may lead to intercultural communication break-down. Therefore，in order to survive in other cultures，it is very necessary to learn some knowledge of the basic cultural difference in this field.

Studies show that Western ideas of privacy are somewhat different from those of the Chinese. And due to that reason，Chinese often irritate Westerners by the way they try to start conversations. For example，Chinese frequently start conversations by asking Westerners questions like：How old are you? Are you married? How much do you earn? They don't know they have invaded Westerners' privacy by asking these questions which Westerners regard as private matters. Therefore，when communicating with Westerners，Chinese should be careful about topics that are regarded as privacy in English-speaking countries，but not in China. The following are such topics.

3.1 Age

Generally speaking，in Western countries，it is unacceptable to ask people a direct question like "How old are you?" in conversation，because it is regarded as impolite in Western culture to ask people their ages，especially women who are over thirty. They would feel their privacy is intruded. The most acceptable topic of conversation in an English society is the weather，which suits people well because that is an impersonal topic.

3.2 Money

In the West, one's salary is regarded as personal and private affair. A person's salary is not usually known by other people, not even by their family members. This does not mean that the relationship between family members is not close. So it is wise to avoid asking Westerners questions like "How much do you earn?"

In China, it is very common to ask people how much they paid for a particular item. But in the West, although people may discuss prices in general, it is unacceptable to ask people directly how much they paid for something. If one wants to know the price of an item, he or she can get it indirectly. The following example can well illustrate a possible approach:

Xiao Zhang: That's a beautiful book shelf! Where did you buy it?

Peter: At the furniture shop on Huashan Road.

Xiao Zhang: Oh, I'd like to buy one myself. Was it very expensive?

Peter: Not really. In fact, I thought it was quite reasonable. I paid fifty yuan for it.

3.3 Health

In China, when someone is sick like having a cold, he or she usually hears expressions like "Drink plenty of water", "Put on more clothes" or "Take medicines". In fact, these expressions just function as advice used to show concern. But Westerners often feel offended at being told such things. Phrases like "Put on more clothes" have protective, parental cares, and hence sound inappropriate to the Westerners who want to be thought as independent. In the West, if one wants to show concern in such circumstances, normally phrases as follows are used.

A. I do hope you'll get better soon.

B. Look after yourself.

C. Have you been to the doctor?

D. Try and get some rest.

3.4 Family

In China, it is natural to assume that everyone over 25 or 30 is married with children. But in the West, it is unwise to assume people in that way because some Westerners marry late, some marry but don't ever have children, and some even never marry at all. Therefore, in order to prevent an embarrassing situation from occurring, the following questions should be avoided:

A. Is your husband/wife with you?

B. How many children do you have?

C. I'm so sorry that you are not married at such an age.

In the West, if one doesn't know whether the person is married or not when communicating, the following general questions can be used.

A. Do you have a large family?

B. Are there many members in your family?

These kinds of questions allow the option of talking about parents, brothers and sisters, spouse or children.

4. Visiting and Parting

4.1 Visiting

If someone pays a business visit, the Westerners prefer to arrange the time in advance, and they expect him or her to go straight to the point, rather than make a long preparation chatting before going to the point. If someone pays a social visit, the situation is more flexible, and depends on individual preferences. However, when planning a visit in advance, one should pay more attention to the use of language. It is common that Chinese often make statement or command when they want to make a request. For example, if Chinese want to express the request like "Can I come and see you this afternoon?" They often say words like "I'm coming to see you this afternoon." Since this wording carries the implication "You must stay at home this afternoon because I'm coming to see you." Westerners may feel unhappy. Therefore, it is necessary for Chinese to learn the suitable expressions in English of making requests. The following are some suitable expressions:

A. I haven't seen you for a long time. I was wondering whether I could come round to visit you sometime.

B. I'd like to come and see you sometime. Would you be free one afternoon next week?

C. I would like to come and visit you. Would it be convenient for me to come Wednesday evening?

Westerners are used to organizing their time, so if Chinese want to invite them to take part in some important activities, it is helpful to give them notice in advance, usually at least a week in advance. Otherwise, they may feel offended, and refuse to attend.

In the West, if people go to visit someone, they are almost immediately asked if they would like to take off their coats. If they do not take off their out-door clothing, it means that they are only want to stay for a few minutes. If they take off their coats, they will be asked to sit down, and then they will be offered something to drink like tea or coffee. And the offer is normally given by a phrase like "Would you like a cup of tea?" The guests are expected to give the answer honestly. If they say no, the hosts will not give them any. If they accept, they will be given a cup and expected to drink it all. After finishing it, they will be offered a second one.

Unlike the Westerners, when Chinese go to visit someone, and when the host offers a cup of tea, they may refuse out of politeness for at least one time before accepting. If the host does not make more offers, they may think the host is not so hospitable. And after they accept the cup of tea, they usually don't drink it all to show their respect for the host. Therefore, if Chinese don't act as Westerners do when visiting them, misunderstanding may occur. For example, one of my students told me when he visited his friend Kathy in UK, he declined the offer of some drink. Later he grew very thirsty but was too shy to ask for a drink.

When Chinese have visitors, they are often very hospitable in offering food. If guests are invited for a meal, Chinese prepare more dishes than can be eaten at the time. Conversely, Westerners prepare the meal size based on the guests' appetites, both the quantity and variety of the meal are much less than those in China.

During dinner, the Chinese host often constantly puts the best pieces of food on the visitor's plate, which is an expression of hospitality. The visitor's refusals are usually ignored, because in Chinese culture, "no" can often be a polite form of "yes". Unlike Chinese, Westerners usually let the guests to help themselves and do not keep asking them to eat more. In China it is acceptable to leave food on the plate, while it is impolite to do so according to Western custom.

As a result, misunderstandings may occur. If the Chinese are invited to dinner by a Westerner, they may feel the Westerner is ungenerous because he/she prepares the small amount of food and does not constantly encourages them to eat more. They may feel hungry even after dinner since the food is not offered a second time after their polite initial decline. The Western visitors in a Chinese home, on the other hand, often have a pile of food on their plate including what they do not particularly want, which they should finish eating according to their culture. As a result, the more they eat, the more they are given. The cultural differences of offering food to visitors between Chinese and English hosts often lead to misunderstanding.

4.2　Parting

Parting can be a difficult task in any culture. And in different cultures, the ways of parting are quite different. So it will be particularly difficult for a person in another culture. The guest has to decide how long it is proper to stay, when to leave and needs to know what to say.

In Western culture, it is common for the guest to initiate the phase by noting that he/she should depart soon, but no immediate move to depart is made. He or She may make a couple of minutes' small talk while preparing for leaving. For example, "Well, it's been interesting to see you, but I must go soon. I hope we can get together again soon ..." or "Thank you for a lovely evening. I must go soon." The host will see the guest to the door, and then say something like "Thank you for coming."

In contrast to that, Chinese visitors often stand up suddenly and say, "I'm leaving now". This seems quite abrupt to the Westerners. Unless the host strongly insists that he or she stay longer, the guest will walk towards the door and say "不要送了", "回去吧", "再见". For important guests, the Chinese hosts will see the guests to the building gate, sometimes even to the bus stop and say "请走好", "不远送了", "有空再来".

5. Compliments and Compliment Responses

Compliments and praises, part of daily verbal communication, are of important social functions which including greeting people, expressing thanks or congratulations, encouraging people, softening criticism, starting a conversation, or even overcoming embarrassment. In almost all cultures compliments occur. But cultural differences exist. The following are some differences between Chinese and English compliments.

In America, although many women do not compliment men, it is common for a man to informally compliment a woman on her look or clothing:

Man: You look terrific tonight, Jessica.

Woman: Flattery will get you nowhere, Mr. Green. (laughing)

While this conversation can indicate subtle relationship between the man and the woman, it is common and does not make people feel unpleasant. However, if a Chinese man gave the same compliment to a Chinese woman, such compliment would most likely be taken as a kind of flirtation.

On the whole, Chinese people give fewer compliments to each other than Americans do. Chinese people are cautious about the line drawn between compliment and flattery. They often do comment on things and people favorably. In such circumstances they will make it clear that they do not intend to flatter:

A: Your skirt is beautiful. How much did it cost?

B: Only 80 yuan.

A: That's reasonable. I think I'm going to buy one tomorrow.

Positively commenting on something can indicate that the speaker likes to possess it. So the Chinese will quickly add that she intends to buy it, to avoid the possibility of expressing a request.

When it comes to responses to compliments, in different situations, the responses to compliments may vary greatly. At an informal level among close friends, reactions tend to be formulaic or even uniform in both English and Chinese. However, these conventional formulas between cultures are different.

The following are examples.

American English:

A: You did a good job.

B：Thank you/Thanks.

Chinese：

A：你干得不错。

（You did the job very well）.

B：大家共同努力的结果。/还差得远哩。

（That's the result of joint efforts./There's still much room for improvement.）

These most commonly used responses show that native English speakers tend to accept the compliments，at least in form，while native Chinese speakers tend to expressing with words about their not being worthy of the praise，although they do feel comfortable about the compliments.

6. Gratitude and Thanks

Expressing thanks is universally held as being civilized. But there exist differences of expressing gratitude between Chinese and Western cultures. "Thank you" is used far more frequently in English than "谢谢" in Chinese. Saying "thank you" is very common in Western cultures，even between parents and children，husband and wife，even for very small and most ordinary things. So they give thanks to people all day long. For instance，a customer will thank the saleswoman for her service. A teacher will say "Thank you "to a student for his answering the question. A husband will thank his wife for bring him a glass of water. A wife will thank her husband if he helps her with her chair.

In contrast，in traditional Chinese culture，people often neglect expressing "谢谢" for minor favors that others have done for them，like lending a pencil，pointing directions，passing a message，etc.，especially among close friends and members of the family. Many Chinese often regard Westerners' frequent use of "Thank you" as unnecessary. Westerners，on the other hand，sometimes think the Chinese attitude of not explicitly giving thanks as a sign of rudeness or lack of sincerity.

All cultures require their members to respond to gratitude，but they have different expressions. For example，some English expressions like "It doesn't matter" or "Never mind" can be confusing to Chinese. They are considered the responses only to apology，not to thanks in Chinese. On the other hand，some Chinese expressions like："This is what I should do" or "It is my duty to do so" are confusing to native English speakers. They are responses to thanks in Chinese，but not so in English.

Glossary

1. **reverse** *vi*. move backwards 倒,倒退
2. **Catholic** *adj*. of the Roman Catholic faith 罗马天主教的

3. **verbal**　*adj.* of or in words　词语的，言语的，字句的

4. **break-down**　*n.* failure to function or continue　故障；中断

5. **formulaic**　*adj.* constituting or containing a verbal formula or set form of words　公式的，俗套的，刻板的

6. **intrude**　*vi.* put oneself deliberately into a place or situation where one is unwelcome or uninvited　侵入，闯入

7. **inappropriate**　*adj.* not suitable or proper in the circumstances　不恰当的，不相宜的

8. **spouse**　*n.* a husband or wife，considered in relation to their partner　配偶（指丈夫或妻子）

9. **hospitable**　*adj.* friendly and welcoming to strangers or guests　好客的，殷勤的

10. **initial**　*adj.* existing or occurring at the beginning　最初的，开始的

11. **abrupt**　*adj.* sudden and unexpected　突然的，意外的

12. **compliment**　*n.* a polite expression of praise or admiration　恭维，赞美

13. **flattery**　*n.* excessive and insincere praise，especially given to further one's own interests　（尤指为获更多私利而说的）溢美之词，奉承话，谄媚

14. **conventional**　*adj.* based on or in accordance with what is generally done or believed　传统的，习惯的

15. **joint**　*adj.* shared，held，or made by two or more people together　共有的，共享的，联合的

16. **sincerity**　*adj.* free from pretence or deceit；proceeding from genuine feelings　诚挚的，真心真意的，真诚的

17. **accordance**　*n.* in agreement or conformity with　一致，和谐，符合

18. **surname**　*n.* a hereditary name common to all members of a family，as distinct from a Christian or other given name　姓

● Comprehension Check

I. Decide whether the following statements are true (T) or false (F).

1. （　） All cultures require and value politeness, but the ways in which politeness is achieved may vary significantly.

2. （　） Addressing forms like "Miss White", "Green" by Chinese may be a form of cultural compromise.

3. （　） Chinese hospitality toward the Westerners is always greatly appreciated.

4. （　） The Chinese way of showing concern is usually appreciated by the Westerners.

5. （　） "Thank you for coming!" is a typical expression used by Western hosts when the guests just arrived.

6. (　) In informal situations, a large number of compliments are used to make people feel comfortable.

7. (　) Chinese people give more compliments in daily life than Americans.

8. (　) If a guest compliments something in another person's home, the Chinese host or hostess will probably give that thing to the guest.

9. (　) "Thank you" is used far more frequently in English than "谢谢" in Chinese.

10. (　) The social functions of Chinese and English compliments are roughly the same.

II. Answer the following questions.

1. What are the differences of addressing between Chinese and English-speaking countries?

2. What are the differences of conversation topics between Chinese and English-speaking countries?

3. What are the differences of visiting and parting between Chinese and English-speaking countries?

4. What are the differences of compliments and compliment responses between Chinese and English-speaking countries?

III. Fill in each of the blanks in the following passage with an appropriate word from those listed below.

A. interaction　　B. span　　　　C. affected　　　D. dilemma

E. especially　　 F. overlook　　　G. representing　 H. influence

I. evolved　　　 J. communication

Language is important to human ___1___ so much so that we take speaking and writing for granted; that is, we frequently ___2___ the significant influence language has on human behavior. Over millions of years, we have ___3___ the organ necessary to produce and receive sounds; in a much shorter ___4___ of time, we have created cultural systems in which those sounds have taken on meaning by ___5___ things, feelings, and ideas. Culture and language are intertwined, and they certainly make an attractive couple, as in the chicken and egg ___6___ — which came first, the language or the culture? Culture is ___7___, and culture has such a pervasive ___8___ on communication. In intercultural context, communication gets complicated like everything else. What people say, how they say it, what they don't say — and ___9___ what they mean by what they say — are all deeply ___10___ by culture.

(L.A. Samovar., R.E. Porter & L.A. Stefani, 2007)

Part Three Knowledge Expansion

Communication Styles: Direct and Indirect Ways

Most cultures have numerous forms of ways to express politeness. However, they are sometimes misleading. For instance, Americans give orders or requests often by asking questions (Would you like to ...?). There are certain words or types of conversation, which are considered appropriate for certain situations in a culture, e.g. introducing people to one another or asking someone for a favour. The amount of directness or indirectness one chooses is different, and so are the structures of conversations.

Most cultures exhibit both direct and indirect communication. However, the degree to which one is preferred differs from culture to culture. In direct communication style, speakers say what they mean, mean what they say, tell it like it is; they are less likely to imply and more likely to say what they really think. Direct styles are tend to be used in low-context, individualistic cultures such as the United States, England, Australia, and Germany. In the United States, people often use the expression "for sure", "no question", "without doubt" and value verbal precision and self-expression. For example, in intercultural business negotiation settings, American negotiators are mission-oriented, and they express their offers directly. If they come across a conflict with any party concerned, they like to be challenged openly for the negotiation, and they think it is quite normal because of their direct communication preference.

However, in an indirect communication style, speakers don't always say what they mean or mean exactly what they say; listeners have to read between the lines; speakers are more likely to suggest or imply than to directly say what they think; yes may mean maybe or even no. Indirect communication style is often seen in high-context and collectivistic cultures with the characteristic of using ambiguous and vague words. In high-context cultures, true understanding is implicit, coming not from words but from actions in a certain context. Many Asian countries, such as China and Japan, tend to use indirect style to save face and maintain harmony in social relationships. Direct expressions of one's need are avoided to reduce the possibility of losing face or causing conflict. Compared to American negotiators of the direct style, Chinese negotiators who follow the indirect style usually expect long-term cooperation. Thus, there is generally a slow "warm up" of the negotiation, followed by tentative suggestions. Chinese negotiators try to avoid negotiations anticipating conflict, and they are always trying to "save face" for both parties.

Both direct and indirect features are present in any culture with a different degree of preferences. Generally, Americans tend to use the direct style while the Asian countries are favor of the indirect one. The following dialogue takes place between a young couple who have been dating for a short time. The man is a student from the U.S., and the woman from an Asian country. The misunderstanding that results from the use of direct and indirect modes of communication needs to be noted.

Jim: You know, Michiko. I really enjoy the time we spend together. I really like you. I've been so happy since we met.

Michiko: Hmmm, thank you.

Jim: I mean, I feel like I've learned so much about you and your culture.

Michiko: Yeah, it's very interesting.

Jim: I'm so glad you came to the United States. Do you like it here?

Michiko: Well, it's pretty big. It's very nice here.

Jim: What do you think about Americans?

Michiko: I don't know. Maybe I haven't been here long enough to know.

Jim: You must think something.

Michiko: Well, I'd probably have to think about it.

Jim: I mean, do you like us?

Michiko: Well, I don't really know that many Americans yet.

Jim is probably not going to get a specific answer from Michiko. Throughout the dialogue, she used rather general answers all the time to Jim's very specific and direct questions. Michiko might assume that Jim is being far too direct and aggressive. Besides, she may think it is indicative of her desire to be in the United States of America because of her experience of traveling halfway around the world. Moreover, Michiko cannot possibly say something critical about the United States because she would lose face as a non-native. So she relies on imprecise and indefinite answers, which frustrates Jim.

To sum up, when people from different cultural backgrounds communicate with each other through language, verbal intercultural communication happens. It is generally admitted that language helps in communicating with people from different backgrounds, while people may be less aware that cultural literacy is necessary to understand the language being used.

In case of using a word or phrase without being aware of its cultural implications, one may at best communicate ineffectively and at worst send entirely incorrect information. Therefore, words in themselves do not always carry the meaning. The meaning comes out of the context, the cultural usage, not mere the words. Generally, people use a dictionary to explain one's words in another language, but literal translation often doesn't mean the same thing because the certain context and culture's influence on the words' meaning. Cultures not only influence the vocabulary but also its usage. Intercultural communication can be greatly improved if one knows the different ways of addressing, greeting, giving compliments, etc.. (Craig Storti: 1999)

Comprehension Check

I. Answer the following questions.

1. What is direct communication style and indirect communication style?
2. Why do people in China prefer to communicate in an indirect way?
3. What role does culture play in the communication style?
4. What is the significance of Chinese knowing the different styles in communication?

II. Translate into Chinese the following passage in the essay.

In case of using a word or phrase without being aware of its cultural implications, one may at best communicate ineffectively and at worst send entirely incorrect information. Therefore, words in themselves do not always carry the meaning. The meaning comes out of the context, the cultural usage, not mere the words. Generally, people use a dictionary to explain one's words in another language, but literal translation often doesn't mean the same thing because the certain context and culture's influence on the words' meaning. Cultures not only influence the vocabulary but also its usage. Intercultural communication can be greatly improved if one knows the different ways of addressing, greeting, giving compliments, etc..

Reading 2

The Culture Grip Influences Cross Cultural Communication

Most of us probably think of ourselves as persons who operate through our own free will. Much of the time, however, this is not true. A Mexican visitor and a Peruvian guard participated in a communication exchange that was deeply embedded in the hierarchy and formality inherent in Mediterranean-based cultures. With the interrogation, the guard had addressed the visitor with the familiar verb form in Spanish. The familiar form of address in most Spanish-speaking countries is used only with family members, close friends, former classmates, or children. The Mexican visitor was indignant, even though the circumstances were dangerous. He responded "Do we know each other?" It was a powerful cultural rebuke. The automatic response of the guard was to amend his discourtesy and reply in the formal style of address for the visitor to please go about his business. Fortunately for the Mexican visitor, this incident turned out well. He would not have responded in such a manner if he had stopped to think about the logic of challenging a gun with indignation and three Spanish words, but the point is that he did not think. Cultural conditioning controlled the behavior of both men, including the one who held the gun and the apparent power. Neither man went through a conscious thought process.

Our behavior is taught to us from birth, and it is taught to us so that we will conform to the culture in which we live. We learn when to speak up and when to keep quiet. We learn that certain facial expressions meet with approval and others provoke a reprimand. We are taught which gestures are acceptable and which are not, and whether we can publicly unwrap a gift; we learn where to put our hands when at the table, whether or not we can make noise with our mouths when we eat, which utensils to use or not to use, whether toothpicks are acceptable and, if so, in what fashion we may use them. We learn how to address people in a manner approved by our culture, what tone of voice to use, what posture is censored and what is praised, when and how to make eye contact and for how long, and countless other things that would be impossible to consciously remember and use all at the same time when interacting socially.

This behavior is learned so well, so that we can pass social scrutiny by the ever-alert antennae of our peers and be admitted to their group that the behavior becomes internalized below the level of our conscious thought. We operate in great part on this elaborately written subconscious program, leaving only a small percentage of our actions to be governed by conscious choice and thought. We most often become aware of the subconscious behavior that we expect from ourselves and therefore from others when someone violates the pattern that we have come to expect. Such a violation raises our internalized rules to a conscious level of awareness. (Novinger, Tracy, 2011)

● Comprehension Check

I. Answer the following questions.

1. How does culture gap influence cross cultural communication?
2. Why does the Mexican visitor feel uncomfortable after hearing the Peruvian guard' addressing him or her?
3. What is considered polite to address a stranger in most Spanish-speaking countries?

II. Translate into Chinese the following passage in the essay.

Our behavior is taught to us from birth, and it is taught to us so that we will conform to the culture in which we live. We learn when to speak up and when to keep quiet. We learn that certain facial expressions meet with approval and others provoke a reprimand.

We are taught which gestures are acceptable and which are not, and whether we can publicly unwrap a gift; we learn where to put our hands when at the table, whether or not we can make noise with our mouths when we eat, which utensils to use or not to use, whether toothpicks are acceptable and, if so, in what fashion we may use them. We learn how to address people in a manner approved by our culture, what tone of voice to use, what posture is censored and what is praised, when and how to make eye contact and for how long, and countless other things that would be impossible to consciously remember and use all at the same time when interacting socially.

Part Four Knowledge Application

Case Analysis

I. Case 1

A Misunderstanding at the Dinner Table

Roger was a student majoring in East Asia Studies in an American university. He started an e-mail correspondence with Li Zhang, a sociology major in China, who was introduced to him through a mutual friend.

Upon graduation, Roger received a generous gift from his grandfather — Grandpa would pay for a round-trip ticket to China. He told Li Zhang the good news, and the two decided to meet.

Li Zhang decided to give Roger a very special welcome: she and the three students from her dormitory would cook him an authentic Chinese meal, as Roger had told her that he loved Chinese food.

However, when Roger was presented with the dinner, he was almost terrified by some of the food: pork stomach soup, pig liver with ginger and spring onion, and chicken with mushrooms in which the chicken had been cut to pieces with bones still attached.

Fortunately, there were courses like tofu (bean curd), stirred fried beef, steamed fish and vegetables that Roger loved. He tried to stick to them, but Li Zhang kept putting food he did not like on his plate. When she asked how he liked the liver, Roger said, "It's very unusual ... and interesting." This seemed to make Li Zhang happy, and she gave him more liver. Roger tried to stop her, but she would not be stopped. Roger was so frustrated that he told her that he did not really like it that much.

"But you said it was unusual and interesting!" Li Zhang said.

"Well, they both mean something less than positive," Roger said carefully, trying not to hurt their feelings.

Li Zhang and her friends became concerned at this, "So you don't like the food?"

"I'm not used to eating liver, that's all. But I do like the chicken, the beef, the tofu, and the vegetables. I have had more than enough to eat. I never make this much food at home," Roger was eager to let them know how much he appreciated their effort. "Trust me, I'm enjoying the food. I know what I like."

Having said that, he found a piece of chicken that was less bony, held it in his hands to eat it, and then licked his fingers.

Li Zhang and her friends looked at each other in shock.

It was not an ideal first meeting for either Li Zhang or Roger.

Analysis:

If the case is analyzed from the Chinese perspective, it can be explained as follows. Li Zhang wanted to be a good hostess. She had deliberately made pig stomach soup, pig liver, and other dishes to give Roger a taste of authentic Chinese food. In China, internal organs and intestines are considered more culinary and more expensive than lean pork. At the dinner table, an attentive hostess would serve helpings to the guest. Typically, the guest would say "no" to what is offered the second time out of politeness (and sometimes being truthful to his/her taste). Most of the time, the hostess simply ignores what the guest says and serves anyway. That was why Li Zhang kept putting food onto Roger's plate.

The words "unusual" and "interesting" sounded positive to Li Zhang, or at least they were translated that way in Chinese. It was disturbing for her that it was not what Roger meant.

Moreover, Roger's table manner was not acceptable to Li Zhang: licking one's finger is one of the worst things to do over dinner table in China.

If the case is analyzed from the American perspective, it can be explained as follows. This case raises several cultural differences. A few words are needed about "interesting" and "unusual". Americans use these terms as a tactful response to something they don't understand or don't like. By describing something they dislike as "interesting", they feel they are not lying as they would if they said they liked it and they hope to avoid hurting the other person's feelings.

Americans generally have limited experience with foreign foods. The range of foods, especially offal, in grocery stores and restaurants is generally limited. Organ meats, especially, are no longer very common. This may be because their taste is often strong, or because they look "gruesome". With a plentiful supply of familiar foods, Americans usually don't feel the need or have the interest in being adventurous with their diet.

II. Case 2

The Cancellation of the Dinner Party

Stan Brown from New Zealand was called to a staff meeting by his principal. Stan had been teaching in the Philippines for two years and was enjoying his life at the international school in Manila. Jose, who had developed a close relationship with Stan, was also invited to the meeting. The principal asked Stan to discuss his proposal about a mathematics curriculum development project that Jose provided, the content of which was known to the others at the meeting. Only slight changes were necessary. It was agreed to take the next step toward possible implementation. Since this had taken less time than expected, the principal asked Jose to say a few words about his curriculum development project he was working on. While Jose gave his project outline, Stan asked some difficult questions that forced Jose to think with efforts to defend some of his earlier assumptions. After the meeting, Jose told Stan that he could not meet him for dinner as earlier planned. Stan was puzzled by Jose's cancellation. (adapted from ibid.)

Analysis:

In New Zealand, a friend can openly provide constructive criticism. Stan took this for granted, as it is a common practice among Westerners. In fact, if Stan did not make such suggestions to a friend in his country (these suggestions are helpful in the long term), the friend would be angry that Stan did not help him when he had the chance. In the Philippines, however, a person cannot be a friend and a critic at the same time, or at least not in public. If Stan had made those suggestions to Jose privately, most likely, Jose would not have harbored such a hostile feeling toward him. Therefore, Stan should find some other way to voice his comments, that is, a way acceptable to the Filipinos (including the southeastern Asians).

Part Five Knowledge Practice

Translation

I. Translate the following passage into Chinese.

In many societies with a high-context communication style, such as Japan or Mexico, it is considered impolite to respond with "No" to a request. The courteous response of "maybe" or "I will try" is clearly understood as "No" to a person familiar with that culture and contextual ritual. A person from a low-context culture will typically ignore the ritual (context) because he is accustomed to focusing on the words. He takes the words spoken literally and treats them as being information specific. This low-context person is then incensed or offended when he does not get what he expects. If he protests, the high-context person cannot understand why the low-context person wants to force a rude response, or why the low-context person is being rude by insisting.

II. Translate the following passage into English.

交谈通常不须做书面准备,多半是边想边说。语言信息传递得非常快,说话人没有过多的时间对语言加工润色,一般使用通俗平易、浅白清晰、好说易懂的语言说话,不太讲究词语的华美,所以口语色彩相当鲜明。主要表现在三个方面:一是句式短,话语简洁明快,容易上口入耳,方便信息快速传递;二是带有丰富的口语词汇,如方言、俚语、行话、流行语等;三是话语连贯性不强,甚至省略了某些内容。由于双方同在一个语境中,交谈的目的、内容明确,所以说话即使不连贯,有较多的省略语,双方都能听得懂,即便是说错了或对方听不明白,也可以纠正、重复、解释和补充。

Case Study

I. Case 1

Drinking Twelve Cups of Tea

When Helen, a British lady, who had no idea about Chinese tea-drinking, went to visit a Chinese family in Hong Kong, she was immediately given a cup of tea. Although she was not thirsty and did not particularly like that type of tea, she finished the cup out of politeness. But the more she drank, the more she was given. Although she kept insisting that she did not want any more, but the host took no notice. As a result, she drank about twelve cups of tea that afternoon! She felt she was in a very awkward situation, but she did not know how to avoid getting more tea poured. (Adapted from Helen Oatey: The Customs and Language of Social Interaction, 1987.)

Questions for discussion:

1. How could you help Helen in this case out of the awkward situation?

2. What do you think are the differences of drinking culture between China and Britain?

II. Case 2

Misunderstanding Implied Meaning

Christian was a British student studying Chinese in a university in Britain. He had been to China for one year. During his stay in China, he ate much Chinese food and liked Chinese food very much. One day two Chinese exchange students, who were studying

English literature in the university where Christian was studying Chinese in Britain, invited Christian and other three British students to have dinner together at their apartment. Apparently, Christian enjoyed the food prepared by the two Chinese exchange students very much, and he also liked chatting and watching TV programs with them. When the other three British students left, he was still in the Chinese exchange students' apartment. The Chinese exchange students felt very sleepy and wanted to go to bed, but they didn't tell Christian about it. Christian didn't leave until 1 a.m. The two Chinese students felt very uncomfortable. About five weeks later, Christian told the Chinese exchange students that he hoped they could make a time and have dinner together just like what they had last time again. Although the Chinese exchange students didn't want to invite him to have dinner anymore, they said OK. But unlike last time, this time the Chinese exchange students also invited a Chinese girl student Miss Sheng who was studying in a different British university. They told Miss Sheng about their problem, and they hoped she could help them to let Christian leave early from their apartment after dinner without making him feel Chinese people are impolite to him. After dinner, all of them sat down in the sitting hall chatting and watching movie. When it was eleven, Miss Sheng stood up and asked Christian: "I want to leave, are you going with me, it's already eleven and it's very dark outside." She expected Christian to accompany her. But Christian said he didn't go to bed until 2 a.m. and he would prefer to stay there and watch movie. The two Chinese exchange students went mad.

Questions for discussion:

1. Why didn't the Chinese exchange students tell Christian that they hope Christian to leave so that they can go to bed as they wanted?
2. Why did Christian stay in the Chinese exchange students' apartment until 1 a.m.?
3. What's the implied meaning of Miss Sheng's words: "Are you leaving with me, it's already ten thirty and it's very dark outside."?
4. Why did Christian misunderstand Miss Sheng's meaning?
5. Why did the Chinese exchange students go mad?

Unit 5

Nonverbal Communication and Culture

Learning Objectives

By the end of this unit, you should be able to:

1. Understand the significance of nonverbal communication;
2. Explain the relationship between nonverbal communication and culture;
3. Understand the definition of nonverbal communication;
4. Understand the functions of nonverbal communication;
5. Understand the classification of nonverbal communication;
6. Understand the differences of nonverbal communication among cultures.

Part One Warming Up

Watch the following movie clip from *The Parent Trap* and then answer the questions below the script.

Questions for discussion:

1. What does the hug between Martin and Anne mean in English culture?
2. What does the body language of shaking hands between Martin and Anne mean before they say goodbye to each other? When is the body language of shaking hands usually used in Chinese culture?

3. What does Martin's kiss mean in the selected movie clip?

Part Two Basic Knowledge of Nonverbal Communication and Culture

1. Significance of Nonverbal Communication

People often communicate whether consciously or unconsciously, by using their hands, their eyes or by giving a nod, a smile, etc.. People wave their hands when saying goodbye to each other. Students let the teachers know that they are listening carefully by having eye contact with their teachers. People may have wondered why they sometimes take an immediate liking to a person they have just met. People may have worried about why someone they were talking to suddenly became cold and distant. The reasons may be that it wasn't anything that was said, but something that happened: an eye contact, a gesture, a movement or a frown. In fact, people convey a whole variety of information and emotions to others with their bodies, which is non-verbal communication. But most people are not aware of the importance of nonverbal means of communication, and therefore do not realize their full potential. Communication theorists assert that, in face-to-face communication, less than 30% of the information is communicated through speaking, and over 70% of the information is sent by nonverbal means.

One study done in the United States demonstrated that in the communication of attitude, 93% of the message was conveyed by voice and facial expressions, whereas only 7% was transmitted by words. (Mehrabian A., Wiener M., 1967)

From the above mentioned, it can be concluded that nonverbal communication is so important that it deserves much of people's attention.

Nonverbal communication is important because people use the actions of others to learn about others' affective or emotional states to form impressions of them. And as the statement "Your body doesn't know how to lie" indicates, the message sent by body movement tend to be more believable when they contradict the verbal message, because many of people's nonverbal actions like blushing are not easily controlled. As Greek philosopher Heraclitus stated, "Eyes are more accurate witness than ears."

Nonverbal communication is particularly important to the study of intercultural communication. Though some nonverbal behaviors speak a universal language, differences are found in nonverbal expressions of different people from different cultural backgrounds. Often what can be perfectly accepted in one culture may be considered rude or even obscene in other cultures.

2. The Relationship between Nonverbal Communication and Culture

As with verbal communication, nonverbal communication is also closely associated with culture. People from different cultures have diverse means of sending messages without using words. Like culture, nonverbal communication is also invisible, and much of our nonverbal behavior tends to be elusive and frequently beyond our awareness.

Nonverbal communication expresses meaning or feeling without words. Universal emotions, such as happiness and fear, are expressed in a similar nonverbal way across the world. However, there are differences in nonverbal expression of the same meaning or feeling across culture that may become the source of confusion for foreigners. For example, friendship exists everywhere, but its expression varies. Embracing each other between men is acceptable in some countries, but in other countries, such way of display affection may be shocking. So understanding the culture differences in nonverbal communication can help people to communicate successfully with members from other cultures. To do so, we should watch carefully how people in another culture act and how they react to us. In doing so, we may learn as much about our own cultures as about the others.

2.1 Nonverbal Communication Is Culturally Bound

Although some nonverbal messages like the V sign and the laugh can be used as intercultural and interracial communication means, nonverbal cues are not universal. Same nonverbal signals may be attached to different meanings by people from different cultural backgrounds. For example, in Western cultures, eye contact can symbolize honesty, whereas in other cultures, it may signify rudeness. Smiling is another good example of expressions of nonverbal behaviors. Even if smiling is a kind of expressions of nonverbal behaviors who are universal and governed by biological necessity, its meaning varies across cultures.

Likewise, there are different rules that govern nonverbal behaviors in different cultures and different contexts in which nonverbal communications take place. For instance, people kiss in most cultures, but there are different rules that determine who kisses whom, and in what contexts who is kissed by whom. When French friends meet and greet each other, they often kiss on both cheeks, but they never kiss on the mouth. In the United States only after long absence, friends can kiss when they greet each other, and the kiss usually is accompanied by a warm hug. The rules that govern kissing also vary among different genders.

The understanding of nonverbal signals is more complicated by the fact that even people in the same cultural background use different signals when they conduct similar communication behavior. For example, men and women usually use different nonverbal language in conversation. Compared with men, when women chat with each other, they take up less space, keep closer distance from each other, use more contact, use more facial expressions, smile more, and are more expressive. Take People from different social class or positions for another example. People from the upper social classes or people with high positions may be more assertive and outspoken in many cultures when they communicate with people from lower social classes and lower positions.

According to Varner and Beamer (2006), about seven factors influence nonverbal communication. They are cultural background, socioeconomic background, education, age, gender, personal preference and idiosyncrasy. When people understand the meaning that nonverbal behaviors signify or nonverbal language communicates, all these factors should be considered.

2.2   The Culture Implication Nonverbal Behavior Communicates

Nonverbal communication reveals cultural differences and conveys relation messages. For instance, smile and nod indicates that we are satisfied with what we see or agree with what we heard from other people. Nonverbal behavior also communicates social status and power. For example, a leader may be able to touch his employees, but it is usually unacceptable for an employee to touch his or her boss. People often associate broad and expansive gestures with high status and associate, converse, small, tight gestures with low status.

2.3   Main Cultural Patterns the Nonverbal Behavior Reflects

Main cultural patterns in the nonverbal behavior are worth searching for because noting cultural differences in nonverbal patterns is not sufficient. Like the researches about values, studies on nonverbal communication patterns vary with different cultural patterns. For instance, different ways of arranging office space in the United States and France can reflect different cultural values of power distance in the two countries. If a large room is given to Americans, they will distribute themselves around the walls, and leave the center of the room open for group activities. To be more specific, the center belongs to the group of people, and is often marked off by a table or something like that placed there. In the contrast, the French do not make way for each other in the way that the Americans do. In a French office, the seat in the middle of the room is arranged for the man in charge. He can govern everything so that all things run smoothly. And if a new colleague comes, Frenchmen do not divide up the space with him or her, but give him/her a small desk in a dark corner in the room. The way of arrangement of space in a French office reflects that the French pattern emphasizes hierarchy that reflects high power distance values in which there is a centralized control in the office, and the new comer is not treated equally with former ones. However, in an American office, when a new person comes to an office, almost everyone in the office will move their desk to leave space to the newcomer to share with them. The American pattern emphasizes equality that reflects lower power distance values for the USA. (Cheng Wenjuan, Yan Xiaofeng, 2012: 222 - 226)

3. Definition of Nonverbal Communication

Scholars give different definitions of nonverbal communication from different perspectives. According to Martin and Nakayama (2005), nonverbal communication is communication through means other than language. For example, facial expression, personal space, eye contact, use of time, and conversational silence. Dodd states that nonverbal communication involves not only the actions but also the cultural interpretation of those actions in relation to the verbal communication uttered simultaneously. (Dodd, 1998: 135) Samovar et al (2007) claim that nonverbal communication involves all those nonverbal stimuli in a communication setting that are generated by both the source (speaker) and his or her use of the environment and that have potential message value for the source of receiver or listener. (Samovar et al, 2007: 197)

Based on the above mentioned, nonverbal communication can also be viewed as communication without the use of words contrary to verbal communication.

4. Functions of Nonverbal Communication

Nonverbal communication has its unique functions in interpersonal or intercultural communication. The following are some basic functions of nonverbal communication.

4.1 Emphasizing/Accenting

When people communicate with others, they can use nonverbal signals to emphasize their words. If people use forceful gestures to accompany their words, change their vocal volume or speech rate and make pause, etc. properly, they can achieve good effect in their communication behavior. For instance, when people express their anger verbally, and shake their fist to emphasize their verbal message of being anger, their anger can be expressed effectively.

4.2 Repeating

People often use nonverbal messages to repeat a point they are trying to make. For example, when people say "the new school is north of that building", they usually point in a certain direction. In such a situation, the gesture and words have a similar meaning and reinforce one another.

4.3 Complementing

When people tells someone that they are pleased with his or her performance, and at the same time they pat the person on the shoulder. In such a situation, nonverbal communication adds more information to messages. That is to say, physical contact places another layer of meaning on what is being said.

4.4 Substituting

If people in a group are boisterous, one who wants to say something might place his or her index finger to his or her lips as an alternative to saying, "Please calm down so that I can speak." In such a situation, nonverbal behavior is a substitution for all the words that it would take to convey the same meaning.

4.5 Regulation

In conversation, people often regulate and manage communication by using some forms of nonverbal behavior. People nodding their head means that they agree with what their partners want to convey in communication and that their partners should continue talking. People's motioning someone to come closer indicates that they want to talk to him or her. Having direct eye contact with someone is to let him or her know the channels of talking are open. Such examples can be listed out.

4.6 Contradicting

On some occasions, people's nonverbal actions send signals that are opposite to the literal meanings contained in their verbal messages. For example, just before an important examination, although a person tells others that he or she is relaxed and at ease, yet his or her voice quavers and hands shake.

4.7 Complementing

When people use nonverbal communication to complement verbal communications or vise verse, they can express their message or make accurate interpretation of messages from others easier. People can use nonverbal cues to elaborate on verbal messages to reinforce the information they sent out when trying to achieve communicative goals. For example, if you are a teacher, when you are pleased with a student's performance, you can tell the student your satisfaction by speaking out, at the same time you pat the student on the shoulder, and an extra meaning like encourage will be added with the message of the satisfaction. Previous studies have shown that messages can be remembered better by people when nonverbal signals affirm the verbal message exchange.

5. Classification of Nonverbal Communication

In a broad term, nonverbal communication covers four areas: kinesics (body language), proxemics (space language), paralanguage (voice modulation), chronemics (time language). And each of these broad areas includes over twenty topics. The following are some of the common topics that most communication theorists address:

(1) Kinesics (body language): facial expressions, eye contact, hand gestures, and touch, etc.

(2) Proxemics (space language): body distance and body touch.

(3) Paralanguage (voice modulation): speed, volume, pause, silence, etc.

(4) Chronemics (time language): punctuality, time orientation, what is early or late, long or short, etc.

5.1　Kinesics

Kinesics is the term used for communicating through various types of body movements, including facial expressions, gestures, postures and stance, and other mannerisms that may accompany or replace oral messages. The term *kinesics* itself comes from the Greek word *kinein* (to move). It was first used (in 1952) by Ray Birdwhistell, an anthropologist who wished to study how people communicate through posture, gesture, stance, and movement. Part of Birdwhistell's work involved making film of people in social situations and analyzing them to show different levels of communication not clearly seen otherwise. The study was joined by several other anthropologists, including Margaret Mead and Gregory Bateson. In 1970, Julius Fast published a best-selling book called *Body Language*, which did much to advance public interest in how people communicate through movement. Social scientists collectively categorize all communicative body movements under the general term of kinesics. It covers a broad range of nonverbal activity, including facial expressions, pacing and other leg movement, body posture and gestures of hands, arms, head, and torso. Kinesics cues can send messages as follows: (1) one's attitude toward the other person (standing face to face with a friend, called direct body orientation, or leaning forward may show that he or she is relaxed). (2) one's emotional state (tapping on the table or playing with coins can mean that he or she is nervous). (3) one's desire to control his or her environment (motioning some person to come closer means wanting to talk to the person).

While all people use movement to communicate, culture teaches people how to use and interpret these movements specifically. In the following sections, a few cultural differences in facial expressions, posture and gestures will be discussed.

5.1.1　Facial Expressions

Facial expressions, as a kind of kinesics, are the most obvious and important source of nonverbal communication. For example, in China, there is a saying that "a person's character is clearly written on his or her face". In Mexican, people consider one's face as the mirror of one's soul. And in Yiddi, there is a proverb which says that the face tells the secret. It can be concluded that people everywhere in the world have been attracted by the face. And facial expressions are frequently used in people's communication across the world.

Although facial expressions play an important part in the study of intercultural communication, the specific implications of facial expressions are not easy to understand.

According to Samovar, et al., people have three faces: the first face which is called the assigned face that you were born with can be changed with the influence of the state of your age, health, and even cosmetics and surgery; the second face you can manipulate at your will, you can smile, frown, and so on; the third face be changed by surroundings and messages that you receive, and can show fear, happiness, sadness, and something like that.

Study shows that in most societies, at least six basic emotions, which include happiness, sadness, disgust, fear, anger, and surprise, are communicated by similar facial expressions. And these six facial expressions are universal, carrying the meaning throughout the world.

However, there exist variations of facial expressions from one culture to another. The power of the face is recognized by different cultures, and many rules are produced to regulate the accepted facial behavior in social interaction, and the way it may be to attend to faces of other people during social interaction. For example, in the Middle East, the facial behavior of grief or sadness is exaggerated by people there. It is common to see men crying in public in countries in the Middle East. However, in America, most people hide the facial behavior of grief or sorrow.

1) Smiling

Smiling is one of the facial expressions that people in every culture conduct at times, but there are variations in the meaning of smile from culture to culture. Smile can indicate quite different meanings in specific situations in different cultures. For example, in one culture it can indicate joy and amusement, and in another culture, it can indicate embarrassment.

In the United States, people smile a lot in their life. A smile can signify the meaning of happiness or friendly affirmation. And smile is used with much regularity. People in the U.S. even smile to strangers. But in most Asian countries, since culture in this aspect is different from that of the U.S., people don't smile the way Americans do. They will smile or laugh softly when they feel embarrassed or want to hide any discomfort. In Japan, people may smile when they want to express their emotion of happiness and affection or to avoid embarrassment and unpleasantness. In Korea, it is considered inappropriate for adults to smile on public occasions. And in China, people rarely show emotions because of the concept of saving face. In Thailand, people smile even much more than Americans. That is the reason why Thailand has the name of the "Land of Smile". In Germany, people smile much less than Americans. There is such a saying in Germany: "Life is severe and there is very little to smile about." So smile is used with far more discretion. People only smile when they meet persons they know well and really like.

2) Showing Anger

The expression of anger is shown in different ways in different cultures. In Western cultures, frowning is used to show one of the milder forms of anger. But in cultures where people do not like to show their feelings with open expressions, they may use much subdued frowning. Take Japanese culture for example, people think it is inappropriate that open frowning is used to show anger.

In some cultures, the way of shouting and gesturing are used to show anger. For example, in Germany, Canada, and Arab countries, people often raise their voices when they are angry.

In many Mediterranean cultures, intense and expressive gesturing is used to show anger. People in that region often use big gestures to accompany their verbal tirades. When they are in anger, their whole body is in movement to show anger and outrage, and it seems that they are affected entirely.

In many Asian cultures, people seldom raise their voices when they are in anger. People from Asian cultures can read the subdued message of anger. However, people from Western cultures tend to understand the more subtle code of facial expression in terms of anger. And it is harder for an outsider to judge how angry a person from the Middle East really is since their maximum facial expression comes easily.

There are also different ways of using facial expressions between different groups of people even within a culture. For example, compared with men, women tend to use more facial expressions, smile more, and are more attracted to others who smile. As far as showing anger is concerned, cultural values determine who can do it and how to do it. Older people, men, and people in authority may show anger more readily than younger people, women, and people in lower positions.

5.1.2   Gestures

As an important aspect of body language, gestures include movements of the hands, arms, head, face, eyes and the body, such as waving hands, nodding head.

Researchers have identified gestures as the following broad categories: ① emblems or symbols: 'V' for victory. ② illustrators: police officer's hand held up to stop traffic. ③ regulators: glancing at your watch to signal that you are in a hurry. ④ affect display: someone's face turns red with embarrassment.

Gestures are frequently used in people's daily lives. People express themselves with gestures often without thinking. They wave their hands when they express Goodbye to someone, they point when they give directions to someone, and they use their hands when arguing or speaking animatedly. However, in some cultures and regions, meaning of the same gesture may be quite different. In some cultures, a certain gesture signifies positive, humorous implication, while in other cultures and regions, the gesture may have the opposite meaning. For example, in the U. S., the gesture of pointing usually does not carry negative connotations. However, in China, pointing at someone can be viewed as a sign of rudeness. Therefore, it's important for people to be careful to avoid misinterpretation.

The following are some main gestures, including head movement, hand gestures and arm movement, which will be presented to show how culture influences the meaning of gestures.

1) Head Movement

Nodding or shaking one's head are universal head gesture. In most cultures, nodding one's head is considered as agreement and shaking one's head is seen as rejecting. But there are still some cultures where nodding one's head is interpreted as disagreeing, while shaking heads means agreeing, in Bulgaria, people just do in this way. Similarly, in southern India, moving one's head from side to side is not considered a negation.

In the United States, nodding has more meanings, and it also means understanding. In regions like Asia, the Middle East, and the Pacific Islands, people often see nodding as, "I hear you speaking.", but not consider nodding as understanding the message or agreeing. In Greece, when people express "yes", they nod similar to people in most countries like the United States, but when they express "no," they jerk their heads back and raise their faces, and lifting one or both hands up to the shoulders strongly emphasizes the "no', which is quite different from other countries like the United States.

2) Hand Gestures

Hand gestures are widely used by people to communicate in the world. Hand gestures have a large range, including crossing of fingers, the nose-tap, the eye-lid pull, the ring sign, the vertical horn sign, the horizontal horn-sign, the thumb-up sign, the ear touch, and the V sign.

Culture, to a large extent, determines the use of hand gestures. For example, people in different cultures use different fingers to point. In American culture, people use index finger; in German culture, people use little finger; in Japanese culture, people use the entire hand (in fact most Asians consider pointing with index finger to be rude). Similarly, same hand gestures have different meanings in different cultures. Using hand to count is a good example. In German culture, thumb means 1; in Japanese culture, thumb means 5; in Indonesia, middle finger stands for 1.

Since the connotations of hand gestures are determined by cultures, it is necessary to know some guidelines for gesturing in various cultures. The following are such guidelines (Axtell. 1991).

(1) The hand gesture of "V", which is made by holding two fingers upright, with palm and fingers faced outward, means victory in many countries, including the United States, Britain, and so on. However, it should be noted that in England this hand gesture has a rude connotation when the palm of the hand is used to face in.

(2) The hand gesture of the vertical horn gesture, which is made by raising fist,

index finger and little finger extended, has an insulting connotation in Italy, but it means good luck in Brazil and Venezuela. And in Italy and Malta, the horns symbolize the meaning of driving away evil spirits. This hand gesture has various meanings in U.S. subcultures, such as positive meaning associated with the University of Texas Longhorn football team, but Satani cults (cult recognition sign signifying the devil's horns).

(3) The hand gesture of thumbs-up has a positive connotation means "everything is O.K." or "good going" in many cultures, especially in North America and most of Europe. However, in Australia and West Africa, it has been considered as a rude gesture.

(4) The hand gesture of "O.K." sign, which is made by jointing the thumb and forefinger together to form a circle, is seen as a positive gesture in American culture, but it is considered obscene in Brazilian culture. And this hand gesture means money in Japanese culture.

(5) The beckoning gesture, which is made by upturning fingers, with palm facing the body, is used to summon a waiter by Americans. However, it is used to beckon animals and prostitutes by Filipinos. And in Vietnam and Mexico, it is seen as a negative gesture, meaning offensive.

It is worth knowing that people should learn the meanings of hand gestures before they use them when they communicate in international settings to avoid being misunderstood by people in another culture.

3) Arm Movements

Arm movements are usually used to accompany speakers' words to have a better communication effect. If a speaker uses big arm movements, he or she can make the listener feel feared and make himself or herself appear more powerful. In different cultures, the degree of arm movements is used differently. Generally speaking, people in South America, Africa, Italy, and the Middle East usually have big and intense gestures of arm movements when they speak. For example, the Arabs would use vigorous gestures when they are speaking to make their emotions appear stronger. They wave arms to accompany every spoken word. The Brazilians use hand gestures and broad arm gestures when they talk. The Chileans also use hand gestures when speaking. Unlike the above mentioned countries, people in Asian countries, Germany and the United States use moderate or small hand gestures when speaking. For instance, people in the United States use moderate gestures, in which elbows rarely go above shoulder level because that is seen as being too emotional or even angry; waving hello or goodbye is an exception. Chinese and Japanese people rarely use hand gestures and arm movement when speaking because they regard such outward activity as a lack of manners and restraint. Germans also see big gestures accompanying spoken words as uncomfortable behaviors.

In addition, there are differences of gestures between different genders. In most cultures, men tend to use larger gestures, while women tend to use fewer and smaller gestures when speaking. Even in the same culture, there exists difference of gestures. For example, in the United States, the whites use moderate movements when communicating, while African Americans think a greater variety of movements can make communication lively and expressive, and they tend to use various hand movements when speaking to others. (Samovar, et al. 2007: 208)

5.1.3 Posture and Stance

Posture is an important kind of body behaviors which includes how people stand, sit or walk. Posture can convey messages like social status, self-confidence and interest. Posture mainly includes direction of body orientation, arm position, and body openness through which messages of certain posture is understood. The posture of standing erect and walking with strength indicates that people who do that have confidence. While people lacking confidence usually walk with stooped shoulders and are slow and hesitate. People with higher status usually stand relaxed, while subordinates stand with tense. Leaning forward demonstrates being interested in what is said, while sitting back communicates a lack of interest in a conversation.

Culture largely determines posture, and posture can reflect culture. In the United States, it is accepted that people sit in a relaxed manner and slouch when standing, while in Germany people see this behavior rude, a person's slouching is considered as a sign of his or her poor upbringing. In Germany, sitting and standing straight is considered as good character.

In Asian countries, bowing can reflect status in communication. For instance, in Japan, giving bowing first and with a deeper bow indicates the giver has lower status than the other person. And the superior in the communication can determine when to end the bow. When the communicators have equal rank, they give the bow in the same way. In Thailand and India, people have a similar bow manner. It reflects larger power distance in culture structure because status and rank are considered important in communication.

The way people position their legs while sitting can also reveal their cultural background. For example, if a man makes an act of ankle-to-knee leg crossing, it indicates that he comes from America because most American males tend to have an act of ankle-to-knee leg crossing. In contrast, if a person comes from Saudi Arabia, Egypt, Singapore, or Thailand, he would not do such a posture because the act of ankle-to-knee leg crossing is considered as an insult. In Arab countries, the gesture of showing the sole of the foot or pointing one's foot at others should be avoided when seated because in Arab culture, the lowest part of the body is seen as unclean.

Culture differences can be revealed by different gender postures. Sitting with legs and ankles together and arms close to their bodies indicates that the sitter is a female, and she has a middle-class or upper-class family background. While sitting by crossing the ankle on the knee demonstrates that the sitter is a male, and he seems to own space and take up more space when communicating with other persons.

5.2　Haptics

Haptics is a kind of nonverbal communication, and it means the way in which people communicate through touching behaviors. These behaviors include kissing, hugging, hand shaking, high five, hand holding, and so on.

The manner of touch is determined by culture. And the meaning conveyed by people through a certain touch behavior can be different in different cultures. In some cultures, people feel comfortable when they have body contact with others, while in other cultures, people try to avoid body contact since touching may be understood as a form of sexual harassment. In countries like Italy, Spain, and Portugal, it is acceptable that both males and females walk along the street holding hands or arm-in-arm. Similarly, in the Latin American countries and the Middle East, men can be seen touching each other, and it is considered quite acceptable. In Mexican culture, males can have close touch with each other, such as standing closely to each other, or even holding other one by the lapel or shoulder. It should be mentioned that, in the Middle East region, people should avoid touching a person with his or her left hand because the left hand is considered unclean. However, in some cultures like American culture, touching between men should be avoided because it may be considered as an indication of homosexuality.

Hand shaking is one of the most common touch behaviors across the world. However, the way of handshake varies from culture to culture. In Germany and the United States, people prefer to shake hands firmly because they regard firm handshakes as strength. Unlike Germans and Americans, French people generally shake hands softly. So when a German shakes hands with a Frenchman, the German may feel uncomfortable with the limp handshake of the French, and the French may wonder why the German gives a grip in the handshake. In the Middle East countries, people may put the free hand on the forearm of a person when they are shaking hands with the person. In Japan, if people shake hands with foreign partners, they may keep their arms firmly extended to keep a greater distance and their handshakes are relatively weak and short since they are used to greeting guests by a bowing gesture. In Canada, people tend to give a midrange grip, with number of pumps accompanying common handshaking behavior. Most Canadian business people would shake firmly and for several pumps of the hand. When a Canadian businessman shakes hands with his Japanese partner, both the Canadian businessman and the Japanese businessman feel uncomfortable. And even misunderstanding may occur between them. For example, the Canadian businessman may think the Japanese partner is not serious considering his weak and short handshake while the Japanese partner may assume the Canadian businessman is showing off his power given his firm and long handshake. Therefore, it is important to learn cultural difference in touch since tactile behavior is highly cultural.

Similarly, kissing is also a very common touch behavior around the world, and it differs from culture to culture. In many countries in the region of Eastern Europe and countries in Arab world, people will kiss when they meet their friends. In Mexico and Spain, even same sex persons touch each other. For instance, men will embrace when they greet each other. In Costa Rica, when two women greet each other, they will kiss on one cheek and put a hand on the shoulder. In Asian countries, people seldom touch in public. In many countries in the region of Southeast Asia, people avoid touching when meeting and have very little physical contact in their conversation. In China, men and women seldom show physical affection in public. In Japan, people even borrowed the word of kiss from the English language, and made Japanese word *kisu* for kiss.

Cultural differences of touch also exist between males and females. Females generally have more touch behavior than males. For example, in China, girls can be seen walking hand in hand or arm in arm with each other, but not males. And for females, they use the touch behaviors of hugs and embraces more frequently than males do. And they use these touch behaviors to enhance their relationship with other people. Men use touch to strengthen their power.

5.3 Oculesics

Oculesics is a kind of nonverbal communication, and it means the way that people use their eye behavior when communicating with other people. The main forms of such behavior are eye contact and gaze. Eye contact is a common form of nonverbal communication, which means that two people look at each other's eyes at the same time when they are involved in the process of social communication. Eye contact can reveal a person's interest, attention, and so on. Gaze contains the behaviors of looking while talking or listening, the amount of gaze, and the frequency of glances, and so on.

People use eye contact in different ways to communicate different messages and meanings. For example, study shows that when people recall something, they often move their eyes up and to the left, and when people imagine something that they have never seen, they often move their eyes up and to the right. If people want to send the message of inviting someone for communication, they may stare at a person at a distance, and if the person wants to send back the message of accepting the invitation, he or she may return the gaze. Besides, there are more mutual eye contacts among friends than others.

Eye contact is also determined by culture, so the frequency and interpretation of eye contact vary from culture to culture. In the United States, Canada, Britain, and Eastern European countries, direct eye contact is accepted, and such direct eye contact is not steady and lasts for a second or two. And if someone avoids eye contact when communicating with others, he or she may be seen as disrespectful or inattentive because in these countries, eye contact signifies respect and attentiveness.

In other countries, there is little direct eye contact. For instance, in Japan, people feel uncomfortable at the direct eye contact throughout the conversation, and if people look someone in the eye in Japan, they may be considered as invading someone's space. In China and Indonesia, people consider the prolonged eye contact as bad manners, and lowering the eyes signifies respect during a conversation.

In some cultures, the eye contact is very intense. For example, In the Middle East countries, people will concentrate on the eye movement of others to be able to read their real intentions. And they may move closer to other people in order to see their eye more clearly, such eye contact behavior makes non-Arabs feel uncomfortable.

Previous researches conclude the degree of eye contact as follows (Thiederman, 1991.)

Degree of Eye Contact	Group of People
Very direct eye contact	Middle Easterners Some Latin American groups The French
Moderate eye contact	Mainstream Americans Northern Europeans The British
Minimal eye contact	East Asians Southeast Asians East Indians Native Americans

Since there are different meanings of the way of eye contact behaviors among different cultures, the meaning of eye contact behaviors may be misunderstood. For example, very direct eye contact can be misinterpreted as hostility or aggressiveness when such behavior is used actually to convey the message of showing interest. Minimal eye contact may be misunderstood as lack of interest, dishonesty, fear, or shyness, when such behavior is used actually to show respect or being friendly. A prolonged gaze or stare may be misunderstood in the United States, Japan, Korea, and Thailand as rude.

(Chen Wenjuan, Yan Xiaofeng, 2012.)

5.4 Proxemics

Proxemics refers to the study of how human beings and animals use space in the communication process. The space between the sender and the receiver of a message influences the way the message is interpreted. Like other aspects of nonverbal communication, the perception and use of space varies significantly across cultures and different settings within cultures. Previous researches show that the study of proxemics is concerned with ① personal space ② public space ③ seating ④ furniture arrangement.

5.4.1　Personal Space

All people maintain a sphere of space around them for comfort — personal bubble.

If someone invades that personal bubble, he or she feels violated.

In the United States that bubble is about the length of an arm, and people talk about keeping relationship at arm's-length to mean that they want to keep someone at a distance and not allow that person into their personal sphere, and that bubble is a little bit smaller in France, but larger in the Netherlands and Germany. It is even larger in Japan but much smaller in Latin American countries and the Middle East. The size of the personal space also is influenced by social status, gender, age and level of authority, further complicating the interpretation of space in communication.

People's attitudes toward space reflect their attitudes toward privacy. Northern Europeans cherish their privacy and arrange their dwellings accordingly. Property boundaries are marked carefully, and everyone ensures that they are not violated. Fences and hedges separate gardens. Traditionally, a German house had a fence around the front yard with a gate that was closed and in many cases locked.

In contrast to Germany, houses in the United States may have fences and hedges surrounding the backyard, but the front yards are wide open and inviting. Doors tend to be open, an invitation to come in. If someone tends to be alone, the door may be closed.

In Japan privacy is defined altogether differently than it is in the United States and Germany. Japan is a crowded country, and space is costly; therefore, houses and apartments are smaller. Walls and doors are thin, traditionally made of wood and parchment paper. Sound carries easily. Yet within this crowd the Japanese are able to create a private sphere. The private bubble and the personal space are more a creation of the mind than an actual space. Americans connect privacy with physical space, whereas Japanese people connect privacy with mental space.

5.4.2　Public Space

The way people arrange and use public space also reflects cultural attitudes towards space and privacy. Business people from the United Sates who go to Japan or China often comment on how crowded the cities are and state that there just is not enough breathing space. That may be true by U.S. standards, but the Japanese and Chinese may interpret the conditions differently. Two people from different cultures may look at the same space yet come to entirely different conclusions.

People from the United States carry their idea of individuality over into public spaces.

They consider it their right to walk and play on the grass in the park. After all, it is their park; their taxes paid for it. Government buildings in the United States are open to the public. Anyone can go into the Capitol in Washington or the various state capitols. In no other country is the residence of the president open to the public.

The Germans organize their public spaces in the same way they organize their private lives. Order is an overriding concern, and detailed provisions are made to guarantee that order. Germans tend to not have problems with this control because they grew up with an emphasis on order. As a result, parks tend to be clean and neat; the grass is not trampled upon. This order is achieved through the use of numerous signs; "It is forbidden to step on the grass" is typical and is enforced. However, during the last decade the universal acceptance of the tight regulation of public spaces began breaking down. One of the side effects has been more littering in parks and plazas. This change in behavior indicates that the nonverbal language of space can change over time. The study of nonverbal communication therefore is an ongoing activity.

Germans tend to be very aggressive in crowds. The British queue at the bus stop, in stores, and at the theaters. Theatergoers in London, for example, follow strict unwritten rules on queuing to get tickets; it is expected that everyone will follow the unwritten honor system. Germans, in contrast, form throngs and push and shove without any order at all, and they are surprised at the voluntary order of the British.

Generally, people from Northern Europe prefer a larger physical space and therefore stand farther apart in waiting lines. People from Latin American countries, in contrast, have a smaller physical space and stand closer. Seeing space in lines at Euro Disney, Latin American visitors frequently try to fill in the space left by people from Northern Europe. This annoys the Northern Europeans.

5.4.3   Seating

Seating arrangements are also used as a form of nonverbal communication. For example, in America, people tend to talk with those opposite them rather than those sitting or standing beside them. In China, people often feel uneasy when they face someone directly or sit on opposite sides of a desk. Besides, the seating arrangements reflect status and role distinctions when people take seats at a meeting or at a dinner table. In Korea and Japan, seating arrangements are also based on hierarchy. For Koreans, the seat at the right is considered to be one of honor. For the Japanese, the most senior person is arranged to sit in the middle, and those who sit to the left and right of this senior person have lower ranks but nearest to the senior position. And people with extreme low rank will be seated away from the table.

5.5   Furniture Arrangement

The relationship between human beings and the furniture arrangement, as an aspect of nonverbal communication, can reflect values of cultures. In China, the traditional philosophy of *fengshui*, an art of manipulating the physical environment, determines how furniture should be arranged so as to establish a harmonious natural environment. Arranging furniture based on *fengshui* reflects Chinese traditional value of pursuing happiness, prosperity, and health. In the United States, furniture is arranged in such a way that space, measured and divided according to the American traditional value, meets the idea of protecting the privacy of people, who are working in the same office, and avoiding the interactions among them. This way of furniture arrangement reflects American cultural value of equality and standardization of the segments. In French offices, furniture is arranged in such a way that the cultural value of centralization is reflected. The seat of the manager is arranged in the center, and others are arranged to sit around the manager, which signifies the meaning that the manager is the controller and observer of everything that goes on in the office. In Japan, cultural value of group orientation weights over personal privacy, so desks or tables are arranged hierarchically in the center of a large, common room absent of walls or partitions. And in business building, people seldom tend to have private offices. In Germany, since privacy is stressed, office furniture is spread throughout the office. Similar to private houses, German office doors are closed. So when people go to an office to do something, they often first knock at the doors and wait for "Herein (Come in)". This is quite different from that of Japan.

As far as space use of different genders is concerned, in most cultures, there exist differences of space use between men and women. Women normally establish closer proximity to others than men. According to Leather, women claim less personal space than men since they want to keep closer relations with others, while men tend to defend violations of their territories more actively, so men claim more personal space than women. And men often walk in front of their female partners. (Leather, 1986: 236)

5.5.1 Voice Quality

The voice quality is composed of the recognizable characteristics of people's voice, including pitch range, quality of articulation, rhythm, resonance, and pace. Each person has his or her distinctive voice quality. The distinctive features of the voice some people have may be muffled, childish, or nasal, and that of the voice other people have can be breathy, resonant, or melodious. And certain types of voice quality carry cultural stereotypes. For instance, in America, if a woman has a high-pitched, strident voice, she may be judged as discontent, while if a woman has a low-pitched, breathy voice, she may be seen as sexy. In Japan, if a man has low-pitched voice with great volume, he is judged to be more masculine or authoritarian. The association between voice quality and its implication has been learned by communicators. And some aspects of voice quality can be interpreted fairly universal, so voice quality can be used by listeners to interpret honesty, emotional state, rank, and general attitudes when communicating with others.

5.5.2　Vocalization

Vocalization consists of vocal segregates, which include "um", "uh", "eh", sniffs, harrumph, and similar noises, and vocal characteristics, which include giggling, moaning, yelling, snicker, whining, crying, and groaning.

Vocal segregates are fairly universal across the world. When it comes to punctuating their speech, people in the U.S. may use un's to punctuate their speech, people in France may use eh's, and the upper-class British use er's, and all three of the vocal duration, placement, and use are similar, so they can be easily interpreted across cultures.

The messages sent by vocal characteristics vary from culture to culture. The meaning of a certain vocal characteristics is learned by communicators. For instance, in Islam, the seeming natural act of sneezing is seen as a blessing from God. In addition, the messages of some vocal characteristics are determined by culture. laughing and giggling convey different messages in different cultures. In America, people use laughing and giggling to express their enjoyment, while in southern Asian countries, if people feel extremely embarrassed or discomfort, they laugh and giggle.

5.5.3　Vocal Qualifiers

Vocal qualifiers, as important characteristics of voice, can convey people's emotions and personality. Vocal qualifiers refer to the volume ranging from soft to loud, low to high pitch, and word elongation that people produce. There are differences of vocal qualifiers in different cultures. For example, loudness of speech appears differently in different cultures. In Arabic countries, people tend to speak loudly since loudness means strength and sincerity. In Britain, people generally speak in a quieter, less intrusive volume. In Japan, people prefer a gentle and soft voice which reflects Japanese cultural values of good manners and social harmony. As for the rate of people's speaking, people in the north of America usually speak faster than people in the south. People in Italy and Arabic countries speak faster than Americans.

There are also differences between different genders. For instance, men usually speak louder than women. And men also speak in a pitch than women.

Misunderstanding may occur if people have no knowledge of vocalization. So it is important to learn how to infer the content and character made from the paralinguistic sounds that people produce and to learn the nuances in speech affecting verbal messages people make, and these knowledge can help people have smooth communication with persons from other cultures.

(Cheng Wenjuan, Yan Xiaofeng, 2012)

5.6　Chronemics

Chronemics is about the concepts of time and the rules that determine the use of time. What people consider time, how people structure their time, how people react to time can be an effective communication means to help construct a platform for their communication. When it comes to the way people see time and use time, there exist culture differences among different cultural backgrounds. As Hall advanced, as a form of communication, *monochronic* time and *polychronic* time are the most important time systems.

5.6.1 Monochronic Time

A monochromic time system means that people do one thing at a time, and time is separated into concise and small units. Based on this system, time is planned and managed. Cultures, including Germany, Canada, Switzerland, the United States, and Scandinavia, are monochromic cultures.

From the perspective of monochromic concept of time, time is seen as a commodity which can be got, lost, spent, or saved. And time is considered as a linear, which means that at a time one event happens. Generally speaking, in monochromic cultures, people consider it valuable to be punctual, complete tasks in time, and keep to schedules. American culture is a typical monochromic culture, where time is considered such a precious treasure that it can't be wasted. For example, common Americans plan their daily lives and events by arranging a precise time table, and they force themselves to follow the schedules. In American universities, most staff and teachers hold the monochromic concept of time. All the things like classes, meetings, and office appointments are carried out according to schedule. Teachers see one student at a time, hold one meeting at a time, and keep appointments with the exception of emergency. For both teachers and students, family problems are not considered good reasons for not fulfilling academic obligations.

As a result of this perspective of time, people in America and other countries with monochromic cultures attach great importance to schedules and tasks. People in countries with monochromic cultures are committed to planned schedules, and may consider those who do not have the same perception of time as being disrespectful. As Hall stated, promptness is considered valuable in American life. Those who are not prompt are often regarded as an insult or as being unreasonable (Hall, 1990a: 144).

Apart from segmenting and scheduling time, Americans pay much attention to looking ahead and orienting almost entirely toward the future, they think that people should look forward to the future and not pay too much attention to the past. Their future is not far. People must try to obtain results in the foreseeable future which can be one or two years or at the most five or ten years (Hall, 1990a: 7 - 8).

5.6.2 Polychronic Time

A polychromic time system means that people can do several things at once. In countries, including Egypt, Africa, Greek, Mexico, India, the Philippines, and Spain, polychromic system of time is used. In polychronic cultures, scheduling time is considered a more important thing in people's life. For example, in Latin America, it is very common for one person to have a number of simultaneous jobs in the period of time at which one can either carries on from desk or moves between desks, with a small amount of time spent on each. People in polychromic cultures normally deal with life in a holistic manner.

From the perspective of polychromic culture, people focus more on relationship instead of watching the clock. Therefore, if family members or friends are late for a event like gathering, being "late" is not a problem because the relationship is what really counts. As a result of polychromic concept and use of time, people in polychromic cultures consider that precise calendars and schedules can not rule people, and they think it impossible to keep on schedule. For example, in Iran and Afghan istan, people don't treat appointments much seriously. It's very usual for one person to make dozen appointments in order to meet a friend. And because of differences in the concept and use of time, many international business negotiations and technical assistance projects are carried on with difficulties and have even failed. For instance, U.S. business people often complain that business people in the Middle East countries do not start meeting "on time", and that during meetings, people do things unrelated to their business theme, and people may cancel meetings due to their personal obligations. In addition, people often can not accomplish tasks due to their personal relationships. In contrast, international students and business personnel found that Americans seem too tied to their schedules, and they found that Americans care little about personal relationships, and often sacrifice time with their friends and family to accomplish tasks and keep appointments.

Unlike monochromic cultures which are steeped in task, polychromic cultures are deeply rooted in tradition. As Hall stated, in Arabic countries, people look back two to six thousand years for their own origin, and carry out almost every modern action based on related history. As a result, Arabs often first develop the historical aspects of their subject before they start a talk or a speech, or analyze a problem (Hall, 1990a: 144)

Victor (1992) summarized the characteristics of polychronic time orientation culture as follows: ① interpersonal relations supercede preset schedules; ② appointment time is flexible; ③ people handle many tasks simultaneously; ④ personal ties dominate breaks and personal time; ⑤ time is flexible and fluid; ⑥ personal time and work time are not clearly separated; and ⑦ organizational tasks are measured as part of the overall organizational goal.

5.7　Silence

Silence, as a form of nonverbal communication, can be interpreted in various ways, according to the specific situation, the duration of silence, and the specific culture. Silence can be interpreted as the meaning of agreement, lack of interest, or contempt, one giving the topic some thought. And silence can be used to suggest displeasure in America and other cultures. In a word, silence is seen as an important communication tool, and in different cultures, silence is interpreted as different meanings. And the differences in the use of silence can best be testified by looking at high-context and low-context cultures. (Vaner and Meamer 2006)

5.7.1 Silence in Low-Context Cultures

In low-context cultures, people convey messages by explicitly encoding their meaning into words, and often interpret silence as the absence of communication. To them silence is seen as a break that has occurred in the process of communication. In low-context cultures silence is considered ambiguous, which makes it more difficult to interpret silence than words when silence occurs in communication. Therefore, silence does not fit with the low-context cultural emphasis on explanation and clarity, and people in low-context cultures (mainly Westerners) generally are not used to silence. Studies show that reducing uncertainty is the main task for people to fulfill in initial interactions when communicating verbally. In American communication contexts, people adopt active uncertainty reduction strategies namely asking questions. They often consider it as a responsibility to start a conversation or keep it going, regardless of being with friends or strangers.

5.7.2 Silence in High-Context Cultures

Unlike low-context cultures, people in high-context cultural countries have a different attitude to the use of silence. Sometimes people use silence as a kind of strategy to reduce uncertainty. People in Eastern countries feel comfortable with the silence in talk or noise, and are not trying to filling every pause when communicating with other people. In many Eastern traditions, people believe that words can affect the rich meaning in an experience, and only silence can help to gain the inner peace and wisdom. According to Buddhism, what is real may become unreal when it is spoken out. Similarly, the Chinese philosopher Confucius held that silence could be seen as a friend who never betray. Many Asian people use silence as a means to avoid quarrel or conflict.

Concerning high-context attitude toward the use of silence, perhaps Japan is the most typical country, where silence is very complex and can be used to pursue a variety of purposes, though other Asian countries share the similar attitude towards silence. First, in Japan, silence is used as a way of talking among family members. Between parents and their children, they can understand each other enough through a glance at the face and a glance back even under the condition that parents and children do not speak out to each other when communicating. Second, people often relate silence to credibility. The saying that "It is the duck that squawks that get shot." can reflect that Japanese see the value of silence in communication. While the American saying "The squeaky wheel gets the grease." reflects that Americans see silence as a negative means in communication.

Therefore, when people representing these two divergent styles communicate with each other, the use of silence might create communication problems between them. For example, when business people from Japan and the U.S. come together and negotiate with each other, their different attitudes toward the use of silence can stand in their way. The Japanese use the silence as a bargaining tool to consider the Americans' offer, while the Americans interpret the silence as a rejection and will offer a lower price to get the discussion going again. Similar to Japanese culture, in Indian culture, silence plays a dominant role in communication because people think self-realization, salvation, and peace can be achieved in a state of meditation and introspection. In addition, in many Scandinavian cultures such as Finland, Sweden, Denmark, and Norway, silence can be used to convey interest and consideration. Similarly, when many American Indians communicate with persons of authority, age, and wisdom, they use silence to show their respect to those persons.

So it is very important for anyone to know the use of silence with culture differences from their own when interacting with people from different cultures.

(Cheng Wenjuan, Yan Xiaofeng, 2012)

○ **Glossary**

1. **contradict** *vt*. be in conflict with   与……矛盾,与……抵触,相悖
2. **blushing** *adj*. becoming red (in the face) from shame or confusion   脸红的
3. **obscene** *adj*. offensive or disgusting by accepted standards of morality and decency   淫秽的,下流的
4. **elusive** *adj*. difficult to find, catch, or achieve   难以分辨(或捉摸、得到)的
5. **embrace** *vt*. hold (someone) closely in one's arms, especially as a sign of affection   拥抱,怀抱
6. **boisterous** *adj*. (of a person, event, or behaviour) noisy, energetic, and cheerful   (人、事件、行为)喧闹的,吵吵嚷嚷的,兴高采烈的
7. **index** *n*. an indicator, sign, or measure of something   指示,标志,测量
8. **quaver** *vi*. (of a person's voice) shake or tremble in speaking, typically through nervousness or emotion   (人的嗓音)颤抖(尤指因紧张或激动而引起的)
9. **kinesics** *n*. the study of the way in which certain body movements and gestures serve as a form of non-verbal communication   人体动作学,举止神态学
10. **proxemics** *n*. the branch of knowledge that deals with the amount of space that people feel it necessary to set between themselves and others   空间关系学(研究人与人之间所需间距的学科)
11. **paralanguage** *n*. the non-lexical component of communication by speech, for

example, intonation, pitch and speed of speaking, hesitation noises, gesture, and facial expression 副语言(如语音、语调、语速、停顿、手势和表情)

12. **chroneme** *n*. 时位

13. **modulate** *vt*. exert a modifying or controlling influence on 调节,调整

14. **punctual** *adj*. happening or doing something at the agreed or proper time 守时的,准时的

15. **disgust** *n*. a feeling of revulsion or profound disapproval aroused by something unpleasant or offensive 反感,憎恶

16. **affirmation** *n*. the action or process of affirming something 肯定

17. **taboo** *n*. a social or religious custom prohibiting or restricting a particular practice or forbidding association with a particular person, place, or thing 禁忌

18. **insult** *vt*. speak to or treat with disrespect or scornful abuse 辱骂,侮辱,凌辱

19. **bow** *vi*. bend the head or upper part of the body as a sign of respect, greeting, or shame 鞠躬,欠身;屈膝

20. **haptics** *n*. the study concerned with the perception and manipulation of objects using the senses of touch and proprioception 触觉学

21. **bubble** *n*. ① a thin sphere of liquid enclosing air or another gas 泡,水泡,泡沫 ② (figurative)used to refer to a state or feeling that is unstable and unlikely to last. (喻)泡沫,幻想,泡影;空想

22. **parchment** *n*. a stiff, flat, thin material made from the prepared skin of an animal, usually a sheep or goat, and used as a durable writing surface in ancient and medieval times 羊皮纸

23. **provision** *n*. a condition or requirement in a legal document 条文,条款;规定

24. **paralinguistic** *n*. 副语言学,辅助语言学,派生语言学,超语言学

25. **segregate** *vt*. set apart from the rest or from each other; isolate or divide 隔离,使分开

26. **resonant** *adj*. (of sound) deep, clear, and continuing to sound or ring (声音)响亮的,洪亮的;回响的

27. **melodious** *adj*. of, producing, or having a pleasant tune; tuneful 产生优美旋律的,悦耳的

28. **strident** *adj*. loud and harsh; grating 大声的,刺耳的

29. **high-pitched** *adj*. (of a sound) high (声音)高的

30. **low-pitched** *adj*. (of a sound or voice) deep or relatively quiet (声音、嗓音)低沉的,柔和的

31. **masculine** *adj*. ① having qualities or appearance traditionally associated with men 具有男子气质的 ② of or relating to men; male. 男人的,男性的,雄性的

32. **authoritarian** *adj*. favouring or enforcing strict obedience to authority, especially

that of the state，at the expense of personal freedom （国家）专制的；独裁主义的

33. **belch** *v.* to send out large amounts of smoke，flames，etc. （大量）喷出，吐出

34. **groan** *v.* make a deep inarticulate sound in response to pain or despair （因痛苦或失望而）呻吟，发哼哼声

35. **hiccup** *n.* an involuntary spasm of the diaphragm and respiratory organs，with a sudden closure of the glottis and a characteristic sound like that of a cough 打嗝

36. **moan** *n.* a long，low sound made by a person expressing physical or mental suffering or sexual pleasure 呻吟声，呜咽声

37. **sigh** *v.* emit a long，deep，audible breath expressing sadness，relief，tiredness，or similar 叹气，叹息

38. **sneeze** *v.* make a sudden involuntary expulsion of air from the nose and mouth due to irritation of one's nostrils 打喷嚏

39. **snore** *v.* make such a sound while asleep 打鼾

40. **variation** *n.* a change or slight difference in condition，amount，or level，typically with certain limits 变化，变更，变动

41. **rhetorical** *adj.* of，relating to，or concerned with the art of rhetoric （与）修辞（有关）的

42. **monochronic** *adj.* 出现一次的

43. **polychronic** *adj.* 出现多次的

44. **foreseeable** *adj.* able to be foreseen or predicted 可预见的，可预测的

45. **discrete** *adj.* individually separate and distinct 分离的

46. **segment** *n.* each of the parts into which something is or may be divided 部分，片段

47. **tangible** *adj.* perceptible by touch 可触摸的，可触知的

48. **supercede** *v.* 代替，取代；接替；紧接着……而到来；延期；推迟行动

⊙ Comprehension Check

I. Decide whether the following statements are true (T) or false (F).

1. (　) Speaking is just one mode of communication. There are many others.

2. (　) Some researchers assert that in face-to-face communication，about 70% of information is communicated by speaking，and over 30% is sent by nonverbal means.

3. (　) Much of our nonverbal behavior，like culture，tends to be elusive and frequently goes beyond our awareness.

4. (　) In some cultures，eye contact should be avoided in order to show respect.

5. (　) Western women usually like Chinese to touch their babies or small children.

6. ( ) Latin American, African, Arab and most Asian cultures are polychronic time cultures.

7. ( ) Arabs belong to touch cultures.

8. ( ) The inappropriate physical contact should be avoided in order to show respect or obedience.

9. ( ) A smile eye gesture might be interpreted in a diversity of meanings across cultures.

10. ( ) How closely people position themselves to one another during a discussion or talk cannot communicate what type of relationship exists between them.

II. Answer the following questions.

1. What's the relationship between nonverbal communication and culture?

2. What are the major differences between verbal and nonverbal communication?

3. What cultural patterns are reflected in the nonverbal behavior?

4. What are the functions of nonverbal communication?

5. What is the classification of nonverbal communication?

6. What the content of the kinesics, proxemics, paralanguage and chronemics?

7. What happens if a firm fails to take notice of the cultural differences in nonverbal communication?

III. Fill in each of the blanks in the following passage with an appropriate word from those listed below.

A. turn	B. recognizes	C. cultures,	D. meaning
E. message	F. actions	G. expresses	H. behavior
I. frown	J. gesture		

Just as we noted with verbal communication, non-verbal forms are organized. In fact, we can identify trends among people by carefully observing their non-verbal __1__. Let's look at a specific example of this. When it comes to turn taking, some non-verbal elements can constitute a person's turn. So, for example, in the following dialogue, Mary __2__ her turn with a frown:

Who's doing the presenting?

Mary: Are you ready to present this at the meeting?

Jack: Actually, I thought that you were going to be presenting.

Mary: (frowns)

Jack: But I suppose I could, if you don't want to.

This slight facial __3__ clearly communicates to Jack that something is not right here. In fact, Mary is not in agreement with his first statement. He interprets her __4__ to mean that she does not want to present the given material; after her silent frown he reworks the task assignment and takes the presentation on himself. In this sense, a small element of non-verbal behavior, in this case a simple frown, has taken the place of talk in a __5__ . Notice that the behavior is organized in the sense that Mary __6__ that this will constitute her turn, and she places it exactly where talk would otherwise be. What this means is that elements of non-verbal __7__ can be used by speakers in the same ways that talk is used, structured, and organized. In fact, sequentially, Mary could have used either talk or the frown to express her position. Jack, from his side, recognizes both the turn and its __8__ , and adjusts accordingly.

Not all forms of non-verbal behavior correlate so precisely to the turn-taking schema. Non-verbal communication can also be used to produce single statements, which can be seen throughout advertising and marketing campaigns. Pictures of smiling children might signify the superiority of some new breakfast cereal; a thumbs-up can, in certain __9__ represent the quality of a product or service; even a joyous leap into the air has been used as an advertising tool by banks to represent financial freedom through their services. Such elements of behavior communicate to the recipient the intended __10__ : namely, that this product or service is worth buying! Some auto manufacturers depend on non-verbal messages to present the spotlessness, speed, and quality of their products.

(Melanie Moll, 2012: 83 – 84)

Part Three Knowledge Expansion

Reading 1

Appearance: A Special Way of Communication

The way we dress also communicates. Dressing according to custom and expectations shows respect for form and establishes a foundation for future dealings. Subtle aspects of dress can let people know where one is from.

When one is examining appearance in intercultural communication, one must ask a number of question, such as:

(1) What is appropriate business dress for men and women in a particular culture?

(2) What is the difference in attire when doing business in one's own culture and doing business with another culture?

(3) What degree of importance is attached to one's attire?

(4) What are the penalties for inappropriate attire?

In some ways business dress for men is universal around the world, yet there are differences. The suit, the dress shirt, and the tie are generally acceptable, but the styles may vary widely. Europeans tend to wear suits that are more tailored and youthful than businessmen in the United States do. The severe business suit, sometimes described as the IBM look, is disappearing in Europe. The Japanese, in contrast, remain conservative. They tend to wear either gray or dark blue suits with white shirts. Arabs may wear Western suits, but when doing business in Arab countries, they usually wear traditional dress, the white flowing robe and the headdress.

In Southeast Asia the European business suit, with its origin in cool and cloudy England, is giving way to a new uniform: slacks and a short-sleeve shirt worn outside the pants with a collar and an attached belt. However, when a businessman from that part of the world travels to the United States or Japan for business, he will wear a conservative business suit.

For women dress is more complicated. Businesswomen from the United States tend to wear suits. Even though the suits have softer lines and are less masculine and even though dresses have become more acceptable, business dress for American women in managerial position is still more severe than it is in Western Europe.

A German student, after finishing her MBA in the United States and looking for a job in her native country, discovered very quickly that her American business suit was totally inappropriate for interviews. It was too severe and too conservative. No young businesswomen were wearing that kind of suit. A short skirt with a stylish blouse was the norm.

French female students who go back to France from the United States make the same comment. They also find that French businesswomen dress more femininely than their American counterparts dress. These returning students feel uncomfortable in the typical American business dress; however, they also point out that although women in French or German business tend to dress more fashionably, very few are in managerial positions. That, of course, is another question, a matter of tactics, perhaps. If women want to succeed in business, they have to dress and look the part.

In Japan women often work as office ladies who serve tea and greet customers. They do not have to worry about what to wear; the company provides them with a uniform, usually a conservative suit with a blouse, white gloves, and a hat. However, as more women enter management training programs at Japanese firms, they may change their appearance to indicate the different status.

In most cultures dress also identifies a person as belonging to a specific group and having a certain status. Dress can offend, but it also can protect. With the growing number of assaults on foreigners in Germany, the Japanese issued a dress code for after-business hours for all Japanese employees in that country. Immediately, all Japanese had to wear dark conservative suits with white shirts, ties, and dress shoes at all times to establish them as business people. The business dress, it was assumed, would identify a person as doing business.

With the growing emphasis on comfort and leisure time activities, attitudes toward appearance and dress are changing in many cultures. In many cases young people around the world have more in common with young people from other cultures than with the older generation of their own culture when it comes to dress. Jeans, tennis shoes, and sweatshirts are taking the place of formal business attire.

A few years ago Germans were very conservative in their dress both in business and in their private lives. It was expected that one would dress up for the office and on Sundays. Every German man from age 14 on owned a black suit to be worn at weddings, funerals, and other important occasions. During final examinations in the Gymnasium (high school) and the university, both men and women were expected to wear black suits to acknowledge the importance of the occasion. Much of that has changed. The young people are very informal, and many go to interviews in casual dress. Although older Germans may bemoan casual dress as a sign of lack of respect and the general decline and downfall of behavioral norms, young people are enjoying the more relaxed attire.

If a person from a more casual culture with an emphasis on comfort does business with someone older from a conservative and formal culture, dress can become a serious issue.

(Iris Varner Linda Beamer, 2006)

Comprehension Check

I. Answer the following questions.

1. What happens if a company fails to take notice of the cultural differences in nonverbal communication?
2. Could you give out examples to show that attitudes towards punctuality vary from one culture to another?
3. Do the same gestures always have the same meaning in different cultures? Give examples to explain why or why not.
4. What is the custom of gift-giving in China? Please give your comment on it.

II. Translate into Chinese the following passage in the essay.

In most cultures dress also identifies a person as belonging to a specific group and having a certain status. Dress can offend, but it also can protect. With the growing number of assaults on foreigners in Germany, the Japanese issued a dress code for after-business hours for all Japanese employees in that country. Immediately, all Japanese had to wear dark conservative suits with white shirts, ties, and dress shoes at all times to establish them as businesspeople and distinguish them from other Asians who might be in the country illegally and involved in illegal dealings. The business dress, it was assumed, would identify a person as doing business in Germany rather than wanting to immigrate illegally.

Reading 2

A Picture Conveys Various Meanings

Advertising and marketing campaigns can tell us a great deal about how a culture understands values such as health, wealth, and beauty. While the metaculture has admittedly had an enormous influence on advertising norms, it is still a prime area indicating how people communicate their values non-verbally. Business dress standards will often be a direct reflection of how local cultures have been influenced by global advertising.

The television tells us that beauty is external. Commercials of all sorts proclaim the superiority of their product, and leave the viewer with the impression that buyers of that product will be as attractive as the model advertising it. Many Maybelline cosmetic products, for example, flout gorgeous movie stars who tell us that they buy Maybelline products "... because I'm worth it!" As study shows, some cultures are rather obsessed with cosmetic products and their ability to mask the natural body odors and features. One French woman described it this way: "I don't leave my apartment unless I have makeup on!"

The enormous cosmetic market is a good indication of how many cultures globally value personal appearance standards which are often set by the various media. While this is the case, we do find some interesting differences in certain geographical regions. One modern cosmetic market research organization offered hundreds of cutting-edge statistical reports for Europe, North America, and Asia, while market information and availability for Africa, the Middle East, Central and South America, and various island cultures numbered far less — in the twenties and thirties. Only three reports were available to detail the statistics of the Caribbean. What this indicates is that these cultures do not extensively promote the value of the same processes of beautification that are normal in some others.

What counts as healthy often displays the basic cultural division of wealth. In developed nations, where food is plentiful, being healthy often is associated with a strong, lean body. Being able to practice sports of various kinds, not being overweight, and physical mobility are benchmarks for health. For example, the Swiss culture promotes this view of health throughout both the educational arena as well as the general public. Schools place an enormous importance on sports, both in and outside the classroom, and most Swiss students are expected to learn to ski or snowboard. In fact, schools have mandatory ski trips where the entire class is bussed to a ski resort to learn this important cultural sport. The Swiss combine their active lifestyles with walking; again, school children are expected to walk to school in rain, snow, or sunshine. Biking is regularly organized from early on, and walking, biking and traffic laws are taught to the children as early as kindergarten.

Such attention to fitness is carried into the business arena. Many companies will offer multiple sports events throughout the year to their employees, and employees are expected to participate. One job-seeker was actually told on the phone not to bother to come to an interview unless he was physically fit, since the company wished to stress a healthy image through its products and employees.

Other cultures, such as that in Vietnam, depend upon this sort of lifestyle as crucial to transportation determination, and less as a predetermined means of fitness. Economic considerations prohibit many people from owning cars, so an active physical lifestyle is imperative to get to work. Here the values have less to do with health, and more to do with absolute necessity.

There are times when a collision of values occurs. When this happens, we are able to clearly identify how social values are communicated or violated. For example, the well-known social issues photographer Olivero Toscani created quite a stir when he launched a campaign against deadly eating disorders, specifically anorexia. Using painfully thin model images, Toscani publically portrayed a naked human body and the results of such a disorder. He argued that this was an attempt at slowing the growing reaction to fashion advertising in the West which portrays only thin women and men as beautiful. His photography was shocking to some. Critics argued that such images not only exploited the women suffering from eating disorders, but they also encouraged such women to continue these patterns of behavior in order to achieve publicity and visibility. Toscani countered that the risk this campaign takes is worth it to counter pervasive stereotypes of attractive women globally.

When it comes to images, it is also important to note that scenery, especially regionally valued views, is an indication of the importance of the physical earth, its features, and its preservation. Whereas in some areas artwork focuses on survival issues, such as hunting, other areas place the focus on the earth itself in relation to human existence and development. Such attention to the environment is growing, usually in direct connection with the spread of globalization and industry. In fact, recently even the Vatican published a list of "new sins" that are apparently brought about by modern times.

One of these sins included pollution that causes permanent environmental damage.
(Melanie Moll，2012：99 – 102)

Comprehension Check

I. Answer the following questions.

1. Can you give examples to explain the power of nonverbal communication?
2. What's the function of touch in communication?
3. What is the appropriate distance between persons that American can accept?

II. Translate into Chinese the following passage in the essay.

The enormous cosmetic market is a good indication of how many cultures globally value personal appearance standards which are often set by the various media. While this is the case, we do find some interesting differences in certain geographical regions. One modern cosmetic market research organization offered hundreds of cutting-edge statistical reports for Europe, North America, and Asia, while market information and availability for Africa, the Middle East, Central and South America, and various island cultures numbered far less. Only three reports were available to detail the statistics of the Caribbean. What this indicates is that these cultures do not extensively promote the value of the same processes of beautification that are normal in some others.

Part Four Knowledge Application

Case Analysis

I. Case 1

Body Distance

Mark had recently moved from Denmark to Sydney, working as a salesperson for a large Australian company. Three weeks later, he was invited to take part in a local club, and Mark was thrilled by his admission to the club. During the first few weeks of the club's activities, Mark was either standing in a corner talking with someone or sitting in a sofa listening to other people chatting. With the passage of time, he was familiar with most of the club members and seemed to enjoy talking with them. One day at an evening party, one of the ladies came up and showed some interest in chatting with him. As a matter of fact, he paid attention to that lady the first time he was attending the club's activities, and her willingness to talk with him now was sort of cliff hanger. He immediately showed his aspiration to strike up a conversation with her and they began talking about the atmosphere of the party before the lady began to ask him questions about his motherland. At first, the talk between them seemed to be quite favoring, but as the talk went on, the lady seemed to step back again and again while Mark went forward, looking at her in an indeterminate way. The lady obviously seemed uneasy. Just when Mark was about to ask her questions about Australian social customs, another man standing by shoot a glance at the lady and then, she excused herself and went to talk with that man, leaving Mark standing there alone and wondering why their talk came to such a sudden end.

(Wang Fuxiang & Ma Dengge, 1999)

Analysis:

This is a typical case of misunderstanding caused by different perceptions about body distance. There is a lot of evidence to show that body distance varies with different people, different circumstances, and different cultures. In Denmark, at a formal event, the intimate space is usually between 20 to 30 centimeters; while in Australia, such an occasion requires a body distance of 40 to 50 centimeters. Therefore, when a Dane talks with an Australia, the problem arises: the Dane is accustomed to a close distance while the Australian is comfortable with a great distance. In this case, Mark, by trying to establish his normal intimate space, infringed on the Australian lady's space. Because of this, she felt somewhat threatened and lost her sense of comfort. At that moment, the nearby man offered her the opportunity to excuse herself from Mark. If Mark had had some knowledge about the expected personal space for Australians, the encounter might have been totally different.

II. Case 2

Monochronic Americans and Polychronic Mexicans

A large American telecommunication company introduced a technically superior product on the world market. It planned to focus specifically on increasing sales in Latin America, where it had not been very successful previously. The only serious competitor was a French company which had an inferior product, but whose after-sale support was reputedly superior.

The Americans went to great pains to prepare their first presentation in Mexico. "Judgment Day" would begin with a video presentation of the company and its growth potential in the medium-long term. After this, vice-president of the group would personally give a presentation to the Mexican minister of communications. Also meticulously planned was the two-hour lunch. Knowing Mexican culture, they believed this was where the battle would be fought. The afternoon session was reserved for questions and answers. The company jet would then be ready to leave Mexico City in the last departure "slot". It was tight, efficient and appreciated, right?

Wrong, the Mexican team threw off the schedule right away by arriving one hour late. Then, just as the Americans were introducing the agenda for the day, the minister was called out of the room for an urgent phone call. He returned a while later to find that the meeting had gone on without him. The Mexicans were upset that the presentation had proceeded, that the after-sales service contract was separate from the sales contract and that the presentation focused only on the first two years after installation rather than the long-term future together.

The French, on the other hand, prepared a loosely structured agenda. They determined some of the main goals to be attained by the end of the two-week visit. The timing, the where and the how were dependent on factors beyond their control, so they left them open. A long presentation on the historical background of the French state-owned company was prepared for the minister and his team. It had done business with Mexico's telephone system as early as 1930 and wanted to re-establish a historic partnership. As far as the French were concerned, the after-sale service, which extended indefinitely, was part of the contract. It was the French who received the order for a product known in the industry to be technologically less sophisticated.

Analysis:

The American telecommunication company, technically superior and working with high efficiency, fails to get the order. It is a fine example to show how an international company should take every detailed nonverbal cultural information into consideration when making decisions. America and Latin America have different orientation towards time, and as a result, what are highly rewarded in one culture may not work well in another culture.

Contrary to the American telecom company who provided a seemingly efficient and tight one-day agenda, the French delegation, just prepared a loose and open two-week agenda without any definite and detailed plan. Despite the fact that the American company may introduce to them a technologically superior product, the Mexican chose to extend their welcome to the French company who emphasized a long term relationship.

From this case, we know that different cultures have different notions of punctuality and promptness. As we've described before, Hall in 1976 elaborated on two time systems: Monochronic Time (M-Time) and Polychronic Time (P-Time). M-Time culture applies to American, Western and Northern European cultures, while Latin American, African, Arab and most Asian cultures are typical P-Time cultures. In M-Time cultures, time is perceived as a linear structure just like a ribbon stretching from the past into the future, and schedules are particularly observed. On the other hand, a P-Time culture is less clock-bound, more flexible and more easily influenced by human factors. They lay less emphasis on punctuality and promptness which are greatly valued by M-Time cultures.

The difference in time culture may account for why the highly-efficient timetable of the American telecompany makes the Mexican company feel pressed, suffocating and less friendly.

Part Five   Knowledge Practice

Translation

I. Translate the following passage into Chinese.

Although we may not realize it, when we converse with others we communicate by much more than words. By our expressions, gestures and other body movements we send messages to those around us. A smile and an outstretched hand show welcome. A frown is a sign of displeasure. Nodding one's head means agreement — "Yes". Waving an outstretched hand with open palm is the gesture for "goodbye". Leaning back in one's seat and yawing at a talk or lecture shows lack of interest and boredom. These gestures have come to be accepted in general as having the meanings mentioned, at least to Chinese and Americans. They are part of the way in which we communicate. This "body language", like our verbal language, is also a part of our culture.

II. Translate the following passage into English.

在英语国家,盯着对方看或看得过久都是不合适的。即使用欣赏的目光看人——如对方长得漂亮——也会使人发窘。许多外国人到其他国家去旅行,因当地人盯着他们看而恼火,感到很别扭,认为那里的人"无礼",因而感到气愤,殊不知在该国是常事,看的人不过是好奇而已。

Case Study

I. Case 1

The Ways of Handling Time

Ms. Sheng Lu was sent to a University in Britain as an exchange scholar. The program director, Professor Huang, arranged Ms. Sheng to tutor eight students in Chinese. Of the eight students, five were British, and three were Arabs. She made the schedule plan as the following: Ms. Sheng and the students were to meet at the Library in the University she was conducting exchange scholar research program every Tuesday afternoon and Friday afternoon from 1: 30 p.m. to 5: 30 p.m., and she would teach four students a day, with fifty minutes for each student.

After teaching for four times, Ms. Sheng found that the attitudes towards studying between the British students and the Arab students are quite different. The British students were always punctual while the Arab students were either late or absent without any notice or apology. Ms. Sheng was satisfied with the British students very much. But she was angry with the Arab students because every time Ms. Sheng had to wait for the Arab students, and when they didn't arrived she had to call them. And what made she feel surprised was that the Arabs never answered with an apologetic tone. Sometime they didn't arrive on time even after she had called them, and Ms. Sheng had to wait for one or two hours for the three Arabs to come. She was really irritated by the Arab students' "impoliteness".

Questions for discussion:

1. Why were the three Arab students late or absent for their study frequently?
2. Why didn't the three Arab students feel ashamed for their being late or absent for study?
3. What are the differences of the way of handling time between British persons and Arabs?

II. Case 2

Being Puzzling About My Co-workers' Thoughts and Emotions

Janaser Zabi from Lebanon has been working for a Swedish company for several months. When she arrived in January, she did not think she would last very long; the short days and the cold winter made her wonder how anyone could live in such an environment. But now that summer has arrived, she is getting used to the climate and her surroundings. She likes her work, and her colleagues are friendly, but she doesn't have a real feel for them. What do they think? How do they live? What do they do in their free time? What are their hobbies? In her previous job in Beirut, for example, she would socialize with her co-workers after hours. She knew about their families, and in the office there was an easygoing relationship. Janaser misses the enthusiastic greetings with co-workers and the hugs with the other female employees.

In Stockholm her co-workers are friendly but more distant. Janaser is used to speaking with her whole body, using her arms to emphasize her points, and showing her. Increasingly she is wondering how she is doing. Her boss, Arby Gustaf, seems to appreciate her work, but sometimes she has doubts. He never just comes out and says, "Great job!" Yesterday he called her into his office to set the agenda of an upcoming negotiation session with managers from Malaysia. Janaser knows that the company faces severe competition and a joint venture with the Malaysian firm would help open the Asian market. Arby discussed the negotiation strategy and gave her several assignments for the negotiation. He was all business, objective but without emotion. Janaser is wondering: Is he confident that this Malaysian negotiation will go well? Does he have any doubts? What does he think is going to happen? Is she doing her part? His words sound confident, but during her time in Sweden she has found that she has not been very successful at reading the thoughts and emotions of her co-workers.

(Iris Varner & L. Beamer, 2006.)

Questions for discussion:

1. What do you think are the differences between Janaser's communication style and that of her boss?
2. Why couldn't Janaser feel certain about what her colleagues and boss are thinking about?

Unit 6
Contrasting Cultural Values

● Learning Objectives

By the end of this Unit, you should be able to:

1. Know what value is;
2. Understand the differences between Chinese values and Western values;
3. Know cultural dimensions;
4. Understand the core of Chinese culture.

Part One   Warming Up

Watch the movie clip from *The Gua Sha Treatment* and answer the questions below the script.

Questions for discussion:

1. Why did Datong and John misunderstand each other?
2. What are the differences between Chinese thought pattern and American thought pattern?

| Part Two | # Basic Knowledge of Contrasting Cultural Values |

1. Value

Values fundamentally influence our behaviors in society. They do not describe how we act in a culture but dictate what we ought or ought not to do. Values tend to be the basis of all the decisions we make and provide standards for us to evaluate our own and other's actions. Thus a value can be defined as a conception, explicit or implicit, distinctive of an individual or characteristic of a group, of the desirable which influences the selection from available modes, means, and ends of action.

Values are a learned organization of rules for making choices and for resolving conflicts. These rules and guideposts are normative and teach us what is useful, good, right, wrong, what to strive for, how to live our life, and even what to die for. A value system represents what is expected or hoped for, required or forbidden. It is not a report of actual conduct but is the system of criteria by which conduct is judged and sanctions applied.

Values are useful in explaining and understanding cultural similarities and differences in behaviors; thus, understanding values and their cultural basis is helpful for people who are working in the global workplace. If they understand how values vary from culture to culture, they are more likely to accept and interpret correctly behavioral differences. This acceptance and correct interpretation, in turn, enables people to interact effectively with others whose values and behaviors are different.

2. Cultural Values

Every culture has its ways of doing things in daily life, such as ways of eating, drinking, dressing, finding shelters, making friends, marrying, and dealing with death. People have to learn the cultural ways of their community to satisfy their basic human needs. These ways are not something that the people in the group are born with. Instinctive behavior, on the other hand, is a pattern of behavior than an animal is born with. Spiders spinning their webs is an example. The mother spider does not teach her babies how to spin webs. In fact, she is not even there when they are born. We have to remember that, most of the time, the different customs of different cultures are neither right nor wrong. It is simply that different people do things in different manners.

Although each of us has a unique set of values, there are also values that tend to permeate a culture. These are called cultural values.

3. Comparison Between Chinese Values and Western Values

Many scholars have made studies about cultural differences between the West and the East. Among these differences, three are highlighted as: cognition, relationship with nature, and concept of truth. Western people are said to incline to think in a linear fashion. A cause leads to an effect. In Eastern culture, a cause can lead to an effect and it can be an effect as well. Past, present and future are interconnected and affect one another. Western culture tends to be toward mastery over nature while Eastern culture seeks harmony with nature. Regarding the concept of truth, the view of Western culture on ultimate truth or reality is based more on scientific and empirical explanation while that of Eastern culture is based more on existing truth. Cultural differences between the East and the West have a significant impact on the communication behavior and pattern. As a result of the differences in cognition, relationship with nature and the concept of truth, people from the West and the East are further different in the following aspects.

3.1 Differences in Symbolization

Symbolization is how people imagine or regard something. It actually reflects the way people think. The Chinese and Westerners are different in symbolizing. In the *APEC Summit* held in Shanghai in 2001, with the closing day coming, Presidents from all over the world were invited to wear the traditional Chinese Tang suits for a photo together. The Tang suits were ready and then the Presidents were asked to choose the colors of the suits by themselves. However, it was quite interesting to find that most of the Easterners chose red while most of the Westerners preferred blue. Red means fortune in most Eastern cultures but stands for blood, revolution in the West. Blue means something noble or significant in the Western culture.

3.2 Differences in Time Consciousness

The Chinese relatively pay more attention to the past. They cherish old classmates and friends. If they happen to visit a city, they will squeeze their time to have a get-together with friends there. Westerners, particularly Americans, usually are less interested in the past. Instead, they focus on what is going on for the time being. They believe that life is like a fast moving train. If you miss it, you are out of date.

3.3 Differences in Conception of the Self

The Chinese are collectivist, placing high value on group cooperation and individual modesty. So many Chinese are used to beginning their English conversation with "My English is poor." The Westerners, particularly Americans, are individualists, placing high value on self-reliance and freedom from externally imposed constraints. At the beginning of a presentation, the American will say: "I believe that my presentation will be of great value to anybody present."

3.4   Differences in Approaches to Tasks

The Chinese are relationship-oriented. They often maintain a harmonious relationship with some people, which has priority over accomplishing tasks. They don't care as much about schedules or timelines. Meetings may run long. The Westerners, particularly Americans, are task-oriented. They focus on a scheduled timeline and would like to put all their efforts on the tasks. In their opinion, relationships are less important than getting the work done.

3.5   Differences in Social Relationship

The Chinese have formal and hierarchical social relationships. They feel uncomfortable while they are chatting with someone who holds a higher position. The Westerners, particularly Americans, have informal and egalitarian social relationships. People tend to minimize the importance of social rankings.

4. Cultural Dimensions (文化维度)

For those who work in international companies, it is sometimes amazing to see how different people in other cultures behave. We tend to have a human instinct that all people are the same — but they are not. Therefore, if we go to another country and make decisions based on how we operate in our own country, the chances are we will make some poor decisions. Geert Hofstede's research gives us insights into other cultures so that we can be more effective when interacting with people in other countries.

After making profound studies about the social behaviors of people who come from different cultures, Hofstede developed a model that identifies four primary dimensions for differentiating cultures: power distance, individualism and collectivism, masculinity and Femininity and uncertainty avoidance.

4.1   Power Distance (权力距离)

Power distance means the extent to which the less powerful members of institutions and organizations within a country, expect and accept that power is distributed unequally. It just shows how much subordinates can consent or dissent with their superiors. It is the distance between the superior and the subordinate. Among most oriental corporate cultures, there is hierarchism, greater centralization, sometimes called "poser-oriented culture," due to historical reasons. The superiors make the decision and are entitled more privileges. Their decision and supervision are always positively evaluated by subordinates. In this situation, it does not matter if subordinates have a disagreement with their managers, especially in some Asian countries.

In some Asian countries, power distance is also associated with "the family culture".

"The family culture at its least effective drains the energies and loyalties of subordinates to *buoy up* the leader." In this kind of culture, the manager is like the "caring father" who knows better than his subordinates what should be done and what is suitable for them. The subordinates always esteem the managers because of their position and experience. There are both positive and negative aspects in the family cultures. It is just an easy managing system. But sometimes it is hard to get young creative employees work well because of the hierarchy.

4.1.1　Small Power Distance Culture

Small power distance culture values horizontal relationships where everyone is on a level playing field. Status symbols and privilege invite ridicule, and those who would set themselves above others are cut down to size. While a boss has power and authority, he must be careful to respect workers and share the benefits of that power whenever possible. Everyone is expected to have a voice in decision-making and each person or group has rights and feels free to complain when those rights are violated. There is a strong sense of what is fair, and when workers sense they are being treated unfairly, they feel free to complain and negotiate to improve their situation.

Hosfstede found countries, like Australia, New Zealand, the United Sates, Denmark, and Finland enjoy small power distance culture. In these cultures, superior and subordinates feel relatively comfortable with shared decision-making and decentralization. Employees are not expected to rigidly conform to authority, and people have a certain latitude for disagreement.

Small power distance countries hold that inequality in society should be minimized. People in these cultures believe that they should have access to power. To them, a hierarchy is an inequality of roles established for convenience. Subordinates consider superiors to be the same kind of people as they are, and superiors perceive their subordinates the same way. People in power, such as supervisors or government officials, often interact with their constituents and try to look less powerful than they really are. In small power distance societies the emphasis is on impersonal "truth" that can be obtained by any competent person.

4.1.2　Large Power Distance Culture

Large power distance culture emphasizes the unequal distribution of power in institutions and organizations in a hierarchy of privilege. A few people have a lot of power; the vast majority has little. Power is experienced as a personal attribute, something to be felt rather than enforced. Members of large power distance culture will usually be quiet, soft-spoken, and polite, whether they are powerful individuals or not. And if they feel that you are being unfriendly or uncaring, they will be silent. People of large power distance culture will show their trust in you by asking for help and direction and will show their respect by remaining formal and lowering their eyes.

Hofstede found that some Asian countries enjoy large power distance culture. In these societies, people respect formal hierarchical authority, and employees seldom violate chains of command or openly question decisions by their superiors.

In large power distance societies, communication is traditionally superior-centered. The superiors initiate all communication, outline the path of progress, and the subordinates should follow. The superiors are never publicly criticized or contradicted. The emphasis is on the personal "wisdom".

4.2　Individualism Versus Collectivism (个体主义和集体主义)

Hofstede defined the second dimension of individualism and collectivism as: "individualism pertains to society in which the ties between individuals are loose. Everyone is expected to look after himself or herself and his or her immediate family. Collectivism as its opposite pertains to societies in which people from birth onwards are integrated into strong, cohesive groups, which throughout people's lifetime continue to protect them in exchange for unquestioning loyalty." (Hofstede, 1994)

Individualists prefer self-sufficiency while collectivists give more recognition to their interdependent roles and obligations to the group, Studies of social categorization and intergroup relations show that people use salient characteristics as the basis to "group" others. The group that the categorizer feels similar to and identifies with is called the "ingroup" and other groups are called "outgroups." People from all types of culture categorize others in this way, but the importance of the distinction is much greater for people from collectivist cultures.

4.2.1　Individualistic Culture

Individualistic culture believes that people are supposed to take care of themselves and remain emotionally independent of groups, organizations, or other collectives. Self-emphasis is important, even in budding friendships. Individuals can do whatever they want, and their "freedom" and their "rights" are of necessary values. They build contracts to protect their right from others and to protect their dignity. Their high level of self-respect does not keep them from enjoying a good time and occasional adventure, even if they might feel guilty later. When they are with friends, they are very open, but they can be very critical toward enemies. Individuals like to debate but will withdraw and become defensive with somebody they don't trust. When they are interested, they can be loud with lots of questions but they are likely to look away when they get bored. They judge others by how much they need them. Individuals are major units of social perception.

The United States, Australia, and Great Britain are societies high in individualism, where individual achievement is highly valued and clearly a mark of success. The characteristics of individual-oriented societies can be clearly shown as follows:

A. Other's behavior is explained by personal traits.

B. One's success is attributed to his own ability.

C. Self is defined as individual entity.

D. One knows more about self than others.

E. Achievement is made for one's own sake.

F. Personal goals are over group goals.

G. Self-assuredness is valued.

H. Autonomy and independence are valued.

I. Dependence on others is avoided.

J. One bears casual connections to many groups.

K. Task completion is important.

L. One has few obligations to others.

M. Confrontation is acceptable.

Individualism, as described above, is the attitude of valuing ourselves as separate individuals with responsibility for our own destinies and our own actions. Proponents of individualism believe that self-interest is an appropriate goal. Take American culture for example, the individual-collective dimension displays in the following aspects:

(1) The ideal of the individual is deeply rooted in the social, political, and economic institutions. The individual is the source of moral power, totally competent to assess the effects of his own actions, and is expected to be responsible for those actions.

(2) Family ties tend to be relatively unimportant. Family remains the primary group to which most Americans have their strongest loyalties. Nevertheless, when compared with other cultures, Americans divide their time and emotional energy between family and a wider variety of social groups, including church, school, labor union, workplace, and a host of voluntary organizations.

(3) The physical layout of the typical American house, designed to maximize individual space, clearly reflects the emphasis placed on individualism and personal privacy. Parents are expected to acknowledge the private space and possessions of their children's rooms, and children are usually restricted in their use of the space that is considered the domain of the parents.

(4) The concept of individualism is instilled from an early age in the United States by constant encouragement of children to become self-sufficient. Children are taught to make their own decisions, clarify their own values, form their own opinions, and solve their own problems. Children are encouraged to search out answers for themselves, rather than rely on teachers or adults.

As a Swiss saying goes, "Everybody takes care of his own business and the cows will be well guarded." People in individual-oriented culture do not like to get involved in others' affairs; problems and things are usually kept within the family. A common saying is:"One washes his dirty laundry in the family." People will assume that if you are in trouble, it must be because you have done something wrong and until you prove the contrary, they will not interfere. Not that their hearts are made of stone, but remember that this is a people who had nothing but mountains and poverty 100 years ago, so they just do not blindly expect everything to come from the state or from others. Heaven helps those who help themselves.

4.2.2 Collectivist Culture

Collectivist Culture emphasizes the ingroup, such as the organization or the extended family. Collectivists value harmony and avoid direct confrontation. They emphasize building relationships with others through *rituals* and politeness, and task accomplishment becomes an indirect or secondary goal. Each individual represents the group to which he belongs, so if an individual is hurt, the group is hurt; if an individual is helped, the group is helped; if an individual is ashamed, the group is ashamed. The communication style is typically indirect.

Asian, Latin American, and West African nations are societies low in individualism but high in collectivism. In these societies, people would likely *endorse* group harmony, social order, conformity in group relationships, deference to group norms, family relationships, loyalty, and *consensus of* viewpoint. The characteristics of collective-oriented societies can be illustrated as follows:

A. Groups are major units of social perception.

B. Others' behavior is explained by group norms.

C. Success is attributed to the help of group.

D. Self is defined in terms of group.

E. One knows more about others than self.

F. Achievement is for the benefit of group.

G. Ingroup goal is over personal goal.

H. Modesty is valued.

I. Interdependence is valued.

J. Ostracism is feared.

K. One has strong connections to a few groups.

L. One has many obligations to others.

M. Harmony is expected.

N. Relationships are important.

Collectivism emphasizes common interests, conformity, cooperation, and interdependence. It regards a group of individuals as having a single identity similar to a person. It has purposes, and it acts to achieve goals. The individual-collective dimension is displayed in the collective-oriented societies in the following aspects:

(1) People tend to identify or define themselves primarily as members of a group rather than as individuals. When asked "Who are you?", most Americans would give their names, professions, and where they live, probably in that order. When asked the same question in China, for example, one is likely to give his name only, including his given name and surname, no more.

(2) Property, such as land, is controlled by the large group rather than being individually owned. Whereas Americans own property (to the extent that they have total control over it), people in collectivist societies have only limited rights to property that is ultimately controlled by the large group.

(3) Collectivist societies have a strong sense of responsibility to the group (e.g., like country, family, company). If an individual does not make his best effort, it is seen as letting down the entire group. In other words, both success and failure are kind of "team affair".

(4) There is considerably less privacy. Children, even in homes with ample rooms, frequently share the same sleeping areas with their parents and *siblings* until well into *adolescence*. Clearly, they do share a room with other siblings.

4.3 Masculinity Versus Femininity

Masculinity focuses on the degree the society reinforces, or does not reinforce, the traditional masculine work role model of male achievement, control, and power. In high masculinity cultures, males dominate a significant portion of the society and power structure, with females being controlled by male domination. A country of low masculinity culture has a low level of differentiation and discrimination between genders. In these cultures, females are treated equally as males in all aspects of the society.

4.3.1 Masculine Culture

In high masculinity societies, people tend to believe that matters of material comfort, social privilege, access to power and influence, status and prestige, and ability to consume are related to ability and that with enough opportunity any individual who wants these benefits of society can have them. High masculinity societies tend to reward financial and material achievements with preferential social prestige and status, and to attribute strong character and spiritual values to such high achievers.

In societies labeled masculine, such as Japan, Austria, Mexico, and Argentina, men are expected to hold the primary jobs and women are expected to remain at home and raise families. Male offspring are groomed for work roles and higher education, while female children are relegated to supporting roles. More detailed characteristics are given as follows:

A. There is a high occupational segregation by gender.

B. Gender inequality is common.

C. Careers for males are mandatory.

D. Few women are in powerful jobs.

E. Accomplishments are highly valued.

F. High level of job-related stress.

G. People are highly competitive.

H. People are task-oriented.

I. The art of combat is valued.

J. The bigger, the better.

K. Family and work life are separated.

L. One lives to work.

In masculine culture, power means the right to make others do what you want them to do. Masculine people like to show off by being the biggest, best, and fastest. They like to be noticed when they come into the room. They like to dominate discussions and to compete, especially when there is a chance of winning. The males in particular like sports, often roughhouse with other males, and love to use sports metaphors. People in masculine culture tend to argue and criticize others, even when they do not intend to be antagonistic. They look up to heroes and look down on losers.

The following are some illustrations of masculine culture.

(1) There is a great deal of gender-role segregation; women are expected to do certain jobs and men do others.

(2) Fewer women will be in high government positions. To illustrate, in Morocco less than one percent of national legislators are women compared with 43 percent in Sweden.

(3) Adult women in certain African and Middle Eastern countries cannot receive a driver's license, bank account, passport, or contraceptives without the explicit permission of either their fathers or their husbands.

(4) People (particularly men) tend to be defined in terms of what they do for a living. Consequently, when people retire, they have great problems of adjustment because "who they are" has been taken from them.

(5) A strong emphasis is placed on achievement, with the greatest respect given to those who are the high achievers.

4.3.2   Feminine Culture

In feminine societies, men and women are considered socially equal. Homosexuality is not a threat. Love and tenderness are for men and women alike. Intimate relationships without sex are allowed. Children need love, and parents spend much time with them.

The so-called feminine societies include all the Scandinavian countries, Portugal, Spain, and several Pan-American nations. In these cultures, women are in more prominent and professional fields. Organizations accommodate women's needs for maternity leave and childcare, and working environments tend to be less assertive and stressful. We can see more information about the feminine culture as follows:

A. There is little occupational segregation by gender.

B. There is relative gender equality.

C. Careers for males are optional.

D. More women are in powerful jobs.

E. Nurturing is highly valued.

F. The level of job-related stress is low.

G. People are highly cooperative.

H. People are relationship-oriented.

I. The art of comprise is valued.

J. The smaller, the more beautiful.

K. Concern for family issues is present in workplace.

L. One works to live.

Feminine culture expects both males and females to be cooperative and nurturing in their relationships. They are supposed to be sensitive to the needs of the disadvantaged and are quick to offer help to those who need it. Modestly, they downplay their accomplishment or power in society and depend on soft negotiation and compromise rather than forcing a conclusion by confrontation. To say how good you are is considered bragging and very unacceptable. Small talks are a favorite pastime. Femininity considers the feelings of others important to a relationship.

Some illustrations of feminine culture are listed below.

(1) Employers are likely to provide parental-leave programs for both mothers and fathers.

(2) People prefer shorter working hours to higher salaries. (Hofstede, 2001)

(3) Men and women are more likely to study the same subjects in college than are men and women in tough societies. (Hofstede, 1998)

(4) Family issues are taken into consideration as part of the corporate decision-making process. Thus, the sanctity of family vacations is preserved at all costs, maternity and paternity leaves are generous, and persons who work abroad are selected, at least in part, with an eye toward family responsibilities. In short, the role of the employee as a family member is more clearly recognized and respected.

(5) Dominant religions stress complementarities of the sexes, not male dominance.

4.4 Uncertainty Avoidance

According to Hofstede (1998), uncertainty avoidance refers to the lack of tolerance for ambiguity and uncertainty and the need for formal rules and high-level organizational structure. The unpredictability of the future, and the resultant anxiety that this produces, is part of the human experience. Nevertheless, cultures differ in the degree to which they can tolerate ambiguity, cope with uncertainties, and adapt to the future. Hofstede's uncertainty-avoidance measure indicates the extent to which a culture conditions its members to feel either comfortable or uncomfortable in unstructured, ambiguous, and unpredictable situations.

In cultures with high uncertainty avoidance, emotions are displayed in the way that everything different is dangerous. They resist changes and worry about future. They are open for new things and changes. They don't have feelings of uncertainty about future.

4.4.1 Low Uncertainty Avoidance

Cultures of low uncertainty avoidance have less concern about ambiguity and uncertainty and have more tolerance for a variety of opinions. This is reflected in a society that is less rule-oriented, more readily accepts change, and takes more and greater risks.

Societies with dualistic social philosophies or multidimensional religions place little value on any absolute truth. Instead, these "uncertainty-accepting" cultures practice religions and social relativism, and they tolerate ambiguity relatively easily within their organizations. The United States, Canada, Great Britain, and several African nations are examples of such societies. People in these societies make their behaviors informal compared with societies with highly structured environments, and they associate comparatively little particular ceremonies with social rituals. The critical components of low uncertainty avoidance dimension can be depicted in the following way:

A. There is a strong willingness to live day by day.

B. There is less emotional resistance to change.

C. People are more risk-taking.

D. There is a willingness to change the employer.

E. One hopes for success.

F. One shows little loyalty to one's employer.

G. Sometimes rules can be broken.

H. Conflict is natural and to be expected.

I. Initiative of subordinates is encouraged.

J. Differences are tolerated.

K. People have low level of stress.

L. There are few emotional expressions.

M. Superordinates may say "I don't know".

N. Less formal organizational structures are desired.

People of low uncertainty avoidance take life easy. They tolerate and even celebrate ambiguous situations; the more unfamiliar the challenge, the greater the adventure.

There is a tendency to avoid setting rigid rules and laws but to resolve any conflict that might arise. There is an easygoing attitude toward structure and schedules along with a tendency to "win it", to work out solutions to problems on the spur of the moment. They tolerate very different behaviors and avoid conformity whenever possible. Characteristics of the culture of low uncertain avoidance can be further interpreted as follows:

(1) People are more willing to make experiment with new techniques and procedures.

(2) People are not as threatened by workers from other countries as are those from high-uncertainty avoidance cultures.

(3) People have a preference for a broad set of guidelines rather than a formal set of rules and regulations.

(4) People are more likely to accomplish tasks effectively in groups or teams.

(5) Leaders are more likely to be innovative, creative, and approachable.

4.4.2 High Uncertainty Avoidance (高度不确定性规避)

Cultures of high uncertainty avoidance have a low tolerance for uncertainty and ambiguity. This creates a rule-oriented society that institutes laws, rules, regulations, and controls in order to reduce the amount of uncertainty.

To prevent uncertainty, societies set up laws and rules. Take companies for example, in companies, duties and rights (internal and external) are controlled by authorities. Some cultures tend to have strong uncertainty avoidance like France. In France many strict regulations are used and tasks are heavily centralized in companies. There will be a much higher demand for details when creating a contract. This is to avoid any circumstances which could cause any kind of uncertainty. Organizing is therefore rather inflexible concerning changes which occur in business life. The critical components of high uncertainty avoidance dimension can be depicted as follows:

A. There is greater anxiety about the future.

B. There is more emotional resistance to change.

C. People are less risk-taking.

D. There is a tendency to stay with the same employer.

E. Failure is feared.

F. One shows considerable loyalty to employers.

G. Rules should not be broken.

H. Conflict is undesirable.

I. Initiative of subordinates is discouraged.

J. Differences are considered dangerous.

K. People have high level of stress.

L. Emotional expression is acceptable.

M. Superordinates have all the answers.

N. Formal organizational structures are desired.

People of high uncertainty avoidance have no tolerance for ambiguity. They like a safe and predictable world. When they are friendly, they will respond in details, being formal and unambiguous. When they are unfriendly, they become vague in `their responses and seek to end the interaction. They trust you; they will debate and argue heatedly from either side of a polarized right/wrong, good/bad position, seeking to find the truth through argument. If they distrust you, they will be openly critical and challenge your credentials directly. They show interest by being task-oriented and by asking many questions. The following will help you understand high uncertainty avoidance culture more.

(1) People are not likely to try anything new because its results are highly unpredictable.

(2) People are likely to resist the hiring of immigrants or others seen to be "outsiders."

(3) People feel much more secure with a highly structured set of policies, rules, and regulations. Moreover, they have little tolerance for bending the rules under any circumstances.

(4) People are considerably less comfortable working in problem-solving teams.

(5) Leaders are not likely to be innovative or approachable. (Wang Weibo, Chen Lijuan, 2008)

5. High-context and Low-context Culture Orientations

Another tool for examining cultural differences is the approach described by the anthropologist Edward Hall. He maintained that, although all cultures contain some characteristics of both high and low variables, most can be placed along a scale showing their ranking on this particular dimension, that is, context really is a cultural dimension that ranges from high to low.

In high-context cultures most of the information is in the typical physical context or is internalized in the people who are a part of the interaction. Very little information is actually coded in the verbal message. In low-context cultures, such as American, German and Swiss cultures, most of the information is contained in the verbal message, and very little is embedded in the context or within the participants. In high-context cultures, such as those of Japan, China, and Korea, people tend to be more aware of their surroundings and their environment and do not rely on verbal communication as their main information source. The context of the message is well understood by both the sender and the receiver. Take the following case for example. A very distinguished 73-year-old Chinese scholar and statesman was being honored by a university in the eastern United States. He and his wife had just made the 24-hour flight from Beijing, and they were met at the airport by some friends who exclaimed, "You must be very tired!" His response was *keyi*, meaning "it is possible" or "it is OK". Of course he was tired! He was an old man who had sat on airplanes or in airport for 24 hours straight. But the context communicated the obvious. Here the context refers to such things as the meeting in an airport at night, the fact of his long journey, his age, his slightly glazed eyes, etc..

Yet it is not hard for a Western imagination to suppose the situation in reverse. A traveler to Beijing gets off the plane after 24 hours of continuous travel. In response to the same comment, "You must be tired!" he replies, "Tired! I've never been so tired in my life ! I've been sitting on planes or in waiting rooms for 24 hours and wondered if my legs would work again! My eyes are so gritty with sleep that they feel like the Gobi desert was in that plane!" and so forth. (Beamer & Varner, 2006)

From this example, we can see members of low-context cultures, like the Western traveler, put their thoughts into words. They tend to think if thoughts are not in words, then the thoughts will not be understood correctly or completely. When messages are in explicit words, the other side can act upon them. But members of high context cultures, like the Chinese old man, have less tendency to trust words to communicate. They rely on context to help clarify and complete the message. The following table summarizes the major differences in how high-context and low-context cultures affect the settings.

Comparison between low context and high context

Low context	High context
Tends to prefer direct verbal interaction.	Tends to prefer indirect verbal interaction.
Tends to understand meaning at one level only.	Tends to understand meaning embedded at many socio-cultural levels.
Is generally less proficient in reading nonverbal cues.	Is generally more proficient in reading nonverbal cues.
Values individualism.	Values group membership.
Relies more on logic.	Relies more on context and feeling.
Employ linear logic.	Employ spiral logic.
Says "no" directly.	Talks around a point, avoids saying "no".
Communicates in highly structured messages, provides details, stresses literal meanings, gives authority to written information.	Communicates in simple, ambiguous, non-contexted messages; understand visual messages readily.

(Dou Weiling, 2011)

6. The Core Value of Chinese Culture

In China, Confucian thought has dominated the Chinese way of life for almost 2,000 years. So the widely accepted traditional values derive largely from the influence of Confucian philosophy on Chinese culture and they are at the very core of Chinese identity. According to Li Yunchuan（2008）, the core values of traditional Chinese culture can be summarized as follows:

6.1   Society and Hierarchy in China

First, in Chinese tradition, the community always stands before the individual. The integration of individuals in a social context comes from the high influence of the family. Moreover, age and position are seen as signs of wisdom and rich experience. It is always proper to show respect for the suggestion or opinions of others.

6.2   Role of Family

The traditional view of family life in China is one of a strong family unit led by the father and husband, who largely has absolute rule and control of the family. The Chinese still emphasize the values of family and to maintain family links. However, much of the old structure and many old values of the traditional Chinese family have been replaced by new structure and new values of modern family.

6.3   Politeness

Politeness has an ethical dimension in China. The reason for that is Confucian concept of mannered behavior. The foundation of Chinese Politeness is modesty, which means humbling oneself. Showing respect to others, which means appreciating other people, is equally important for both men and women.

6.4   Face

Face is one of the most valuable things in China. Face can be saved, lost, given and taken very easily. "Save someone's face" means not embarrassing people in front of others. Face also refers to somebody's status. When challenging authority and another person's standing within a community, Chinese will often attempt to cause a loss of face.

6.5   Reciprocity（互惠）

In China, the long process of development in the agricultural society formed a unique pattern of relationship between man and nature, that is, Heaven and Man, man and nature coexist. The Confucian theory of "Doctrine of the Mean"（中庸之道）urges individuals to avoid competition and conflict, and to maintain a harmonious relationship with each other. If there is no harmonious relationships, trust can't be established, face can't be maintained, reciprocity will not continue, and further *Guanxi*（关系）also can not be established.

We may add collectivism to the core Chinese value, according to which, we should give more consideration for others and individuals should put self-existence and development in the second position for the sake of the country.

（Dou Weiling, 2011）

● Glossary

1. **criterion**   *n*.(*pl*. criteria-rɪə) a principle or standard by which something may be judged or decided   原则,标准

2. **sanction**   *n*. a threatened penalty for disobeying a law or rule   处罚,制裁

3. **instinctive**   *adj*. relating to or prompted by instinct; apparently unconscious or automatic   (出于)本能的,无意识的,自发的

4. **ultimate**   *adj*. being or happening at the end of a process; final   最后的,最终的

5. **empirical**   *adj*. based on, concerned with, or verifiable by observation or experience rather than theory or pure logic   以观察(或经验)为依据的,单凭经验的,经验主义的

6. **cognition**   *n*. ① the mental action or process of acquiring knowledge and understanding through thought, experience, and the senses   认识,认知   ② a result of this; a perception, sensation, notion, or intuition   认识(或认知)的结果;感觉;知觉,观念;直觉

7. **squeeze**   *vt*. extract (liquid or a soft substance) from something by compressing or twisting it firmly   榨取,榨;挤出

8. **conception**   *n*. the forming or devising of a plan, idea, or work   (计划、想法、作品或产品的)构思,构想,形成,设计

9. **collectivism**   *n*. the practice or principle of giving a group priority over each individual in it   集体主义(做法或原则)

10. **modesty**   *n*. the quality or state of being unassuming or moderate in the estimation of one's abilities   谦虚,谦逊,谦恭

11. **individualism**   *n*. the habit or principle of being independent and self-reliant   个人主义

12. **constraint**   *n*. a limitation or restriction   限制,约束,束缚,局限

13. **hierarchical**   *adj*. of the nature of a hierarchy; arranged in order of rank   等级制度的,分等级的

14. **egalitarian**   *adj*. of, relating to, or believing in the principle that all people are equal and deserve equal rights and opportunities   (与)平等主义(有关)的,主张人人平等的

15. **masculine**   *adj*. having qualities or appearance traditionally associated with men   具有男子气质的

16. **feminine**   *adj*. having qualities or an appearance traditionally associated with women, especially delicacy and prettiness   女人味儿的,女性的(尤指娇美的)

17. **institution**   *n*. a society or organization founded for a religious, educational, social, or similar purpose   (以宗教、教育、社交等为目的的)协会,机构

18. **subordinate** *adj.* lower in rank or position   下级的，级别低的

19. **consent** *n.* permission for something to happen or agreement to do something   同意，赞成，准许

20. **orient** *v.* align or position (something) relative to the points of a compass or other specified positions   使朝向，以……为方向

21. **horizontal** *adj.* parallel to the plane of the horizon；at right angles to the vertical   水平的，横向的

22. **decentralization** *vt.* ［often as *adj.* decentralized］ transfer (authority) from central to local government   分（权）

23. **latitude** *n.* the angular distance of a place north or south of the earth's equator, or of the equator of a celestial object, usually expressed in degrees and minutes   纬度

24. **perceive** *vt.* become aware or conscious of (something); come to realize or understand   认识到，意识到；理解

25. **superior** *adj.* higher in rank, status, or quality   （官衔、地位、质量）较高的；上级的，高质的

26. **contradict** *vt.* deny the truth of (a statement), especially by asserting the opposite   否定……的真实性

27. **integrated** *adj.* having been integrated, in particular   结合的

28. **salient** *adj.* most noticeable or important   值得注意的，重要的

29. **assured** *adj.* confident   有信心的

30. **confrontation** *n.* a hostile or argumentative situation or meeting between two or more opposing parties   对峙，敌对，对抗，冲突

31. **endorse** *vt.* declare one's public approval or support of   公开赞同（或支持），认可

32. **conformity** *n.* compliance with standards, rules, or laws   （对标准、规则、法律的）遵守，遵奉；顺从

33. **consensus** *n.* ［usu. in sing.］ a general agreement   一致

34. **illustrate** *v.* explain or make (something) clear by using examples, charts, pictures, etc.   举例说明，以图表说明

35. **ostracism** *vt.* exclude (someone) from a society or group   放逐，流放

36. **dimension** *n.* an aspect or feature of a situation, problem, or thing   （局势、问题、事物的）方面，特征

37. **surname** *n.* a hereditary name common to all members of a family, as distinct from a Christian or other given name   姓

38. **sibling** *n.* each of two or more children or offspring having one or both parents in common; a brother or sister   兄弟，姊妹，同胞

39. **discrimination** *n.* the unjust or prejudicial treatment of different categories of people or things, especially on the grounds of race, age, or sex   区别对待；歧视

40. **prestige** *n.* widespread respect and admiration felt for someone or something on the basis of a perception of their achievements or quality 声望；威望，威信

41. **label** *v.* (labelled，labelling，美 labeled，labeling) attach a label to (something) 给……贴标签

42. **relegate** *vt.* consign or dismiss to an inferior rank or position 把……降级，把……置于次要地位

43. **segregation** *n.* the action or state of setting someone or something apart from other people or things or being set apart 隔离，分隔

44. **mandatory** *adj.* required by law or rules；compulsory 法律（或规则）规定的；强制的，必须遵守的

45. **antagonistic** *adj.* showing or feeling active opposition or hostility towards someone or something 有对立情绪的，对抗的，敌对的

46. **legislator** *n.* a person who makes laws；a member of a legislative body 立法者，立法机关成员

47. **contraceptive** *n.* device or drug intended to prevent pregnancy 避孕器，避孕药

48. **explicit** *adj.* stated clearly and in detail，leaving no room for confusion or doubt 详述的；明晰的，明确的

49. **homosexual** *adj.* (of a person) sexually attracted to people of one's own sex （人）同性恋的

50. **prominent** *adj.* important；famous 重要的；卓越的，著名的

51. **accommodate** *vt.* (of physical space，especially a building) provide lodging or sufficient space for （空间，尤指建筑物）容纳；为……提供膳宿（或足够空间）

52. **assertive** *adj.* having or showing a confident and forceful personality （性格）果敢的，有冲劲的

53. **nurture** *vt.* care for and encourage the growth or development of 养育，培养

54. **brag** *v.* say something in a boastful manner 吹牛，吹嘘，夸耀

55. **sanctity** *n.* the state or quality of being holy，sacred，or saintly 圣洁，神圣

56. **maternity** *n.* motherhood 母性，母亲身份

57. **paternity** *n.* (especially in legal contexts) the state of being someone's father （尤用于法律）父亲身份

58. **complementarity** *n.* a relationship or situation in which two or more different things enhance or emphasize each other's qualities or form a balanced whole 互为补充，相辅相成

59. **ambiguity** *n.* uncertainty or inexactness of meaning in language （语言）意义不明确，含糊

60. **unpredictable** *adj.* not able to be predicted 无法预测的；不确定的

61. **duality** *n.* the division of something conceptually into two opposed or contrasted

aspects, or the state of being so divided 二元性

62. **philosophy**   *n*. the study of the fundamental nature of knowledge, reality, and existence, especially when considered as an academic discipline 哲学

63. **multidimensional** *adj*. of or involving several dimensions 多维的

64. **ritual**   *n*. a religious or solemn ceremony consisting of a series of actions performed according to a prescribed order （宗教等）庄严仪式

65. **component**   *n*. a part or element of a larger whole, especially a part of a machine or vehicle （尤指机械或车辆的）部件,零件；（构成整体的）组成部分,成分

66. **initiative**   *n*. the ability to assess and initiate things independently 首创精神,创造力

67. **procedure**   *n*. an established or official way of doing something 程序

68. **superordinate**   *n*. a thing that represents a superior order or category within a system of classification （分类中）上一级的事物

69. **credential**   *n*. (*usu. pl*.) a qualification, achievement, personal quality, or aspect of a person's background, typically when used to indicate that they are suitable for something 证书,文凭

70. **immigrant**   *n*. a person who comes to live permanently in a foreign country 移民,侨民

71. **anthropology**   *n*. [mass noun] the study of humankind 人类学

72. **distinguished**   *adj*. very successful, authoritative, and commanding great respect 非常成功的；权威的；受尊重的

73. **derive**   *v*. (derive something from) base a concept on a logical extension or modification of (another concept) 从……得出,源自

74. **Confucianism**   *n*. a system of philosophical and ethical teachings founded by Confucius and developed by Mencius 孔子学说,儒学,儒教

75. **humble**   *v*. lower (someone) in dignity or importance 卑躬屈膝,低声下气

76. **prevail**   *vi*. prove more powerful than opposing forces; be victorious 占优势,占上风；获胜

77. **possession**   *n*. the state of having, owning, or controlling something 拥有,所有

78. **sustain**   *vt*. strengthen or support physically or mentally （在体力、精神方面）支持,支撑

79. **reciprocity**   *n*. the practice of exchanging things with others for mutual benefit, especially privileges granted by one country or organization to another （尤指国家、组织之间在利益上、特权上的）互给,互换,互惠；对等

80. **internalize**   *v*. (psychology) make (attitudes or behaviour) part of one's nature by learning or unconscious assimilation （心理）（通过学习或无意识吸收）使（态度、行为）成为本性的一部分

81. **mutual**   *adj*. experienced or done by each of two or more parties towards the other or others （感情、行动）相互的,彼此的

82. **doctrine** *n.* a belief or set of beliefs held and taught by a church, political party, or other group 教义,信条

Comprehension Check

I. Decide whether the following statements are true (T) or false (F).

1. (　) A high-context message is one that is mostly in the explicit code rather than in the underlined context.

2. (　) Chinese culture holds that human nature is good.

3. (　) In collectivistic cultures, people emphasize "I" than "we".

4. (　) Native Americans regard that the relationship between human being and nature should be harmonious.

5. (　) Low power distance countries expect and accept power relations that are more consultative or democratic.

6. (　) One's speech acts are totally independent of his or her culture.

7. (　) In high-context cultures, that of North America, for example, a large portion of the message is left unspecified and accessed through the context.

8. (　) In low-context cultures, people judge what someone is talking about not only by what he is saying but also by the context in which the message occurs.

9. (　) In high-context communication the listener is already "contexted" and so does not need to be given much background information.

10. (　) Chinese culture is a high-context culture; American culture is a low-context one.

II. Answer the following questions.

1. What are the differences between Chinese values and Western values?

2. What are the differences between individualism and collectivism from the value perspective?

3. What are the differences between high-context and low-context culture orientation from the value perspective?

III. Fill in each of the blanks in the following passage with an appropriate word from those listed below.

A. weapons	B. Philosophy	C. relationship	D. control
E. nature	F. encounter	G. independent	H. realized
I. origins	J. imbalance		

On the problem of "conflict between man and nature," in 1992, 1575 scientists, including half the Nobel laureates, signed the "World Scientists' Warning to Humanity," which stated that human beings and the natural world are on a collision course. In my opinion, the warning signaled that human kind will ___1___ a serious crisis if the world continues as it is now. Advanced science and technology can benefit people, but as a part of nature, people not only __2__ a lot of instruments to destroy nature but also control __3__ which can be used to destroy human beings in the process of conquering nature. The never-ending exploitation and destruction of nature results in consequences such as the waste of natural resources, the depletion of the ozone layer, the evaporation of the ocean, environmental pollution, the sudden and sharp growth in the human population, and ecological __4__ . The result is the destruction of "a harmonious nature" and "the harmonious relationship between man and nature," threatening conditions for human existence. These situations have a relationship with the subject-object dichotomy in Western philosophy. For instance, in A History of Western __5__ , Russell said: "The philosophy of Descartes ... it brought to completion, or very nearly to completion, the dualism of mind and matter which began with Plato and was developed, largely for religious reasons, by Christian philosophy ... the Cartesian system presents two parallel but independent worlds, that of mind and that of matter, each of which can be studied without reference to the other." It means that for a long time, spirit and matter have been regarded as __6__ and isolated in Western philosophy. Therefore, this kind of philosophy is established on an "external relationship" ("man" and "nature" are two unrelated factors), or it can be said that they regard "mind" and "matter" as two independent dual factors, and when Western philosophers study one, they do not involve the other (but Western philosophy has changed, for instance, Whitehead criticizes the dualism in the traditional way of thinking in his Process Philosophy). It means that Western thought involves the dualism of "subject-object" ("mind" and "matter," or "nature" and "man") from Plato in the Axial Age. But Chinese philosophy is different because it is based on "the unity of Heaven and man".

One of the __7__ of Chinese philosophy is Zhou Yi 周易 (The Book of Changes). There is an important passage on the Chu Bamboo Slips unearthed in Jing Men, Hubei province, in 1993. Those bamboo slips were written around 300 B.C. They say that "Change communicates with the Dao of __8__ and the Dao of man." It means that the Book of Changes studies the Dao of Heaven (law of Heaven or nature) and the Dao of man (order in society) and why they are connected through a comprehensive study of the subjects. That is, people in ancient times had already __9__ that they had to include "man" when studying "nature" and when studying "man," they had to involve "Heaven" too. This is "the unity of nature and man". In fact, this had already been revealed in Confucius' Analects. Zi Gong said: "I cannot hear Master Confucius' saying about nature and the Dao of nature." Although Zi Gong had never heard Confucius speak about "nature and the Dao of nature", he brought forward this issue, which indicates that there was great interest in the __10__ between "human nature" (man) and "the Dao of Heaven (nature)." When looking at the development of human society, people originally came across the relationship between "man" and "nature (Heaven)" because humans cannot live without "nature." Therefore, the ancient Chinese always paid attention to "the relationship between man and nature." (Yijie Tang, 2015: 17 - 18)

IV. Group Discussion.

1. How do values affect communication?

2. Can you cite examples to illustrate the term "ethnocentrism"? What is the solution to ethnocentrism?

3. When members of different value systems encounter, what should they do in order to achieve mutual understanding?

4. Would you make a list of major Chinese traditional values? Have some of them changed? If so, what caused those changes?

Part Three Knowledge Expansion

Reading 1

Three Fundamental Values of the Chinese

Before briefly discussing Chinese values, we should note that what we are calling Chinese society is in actually the society of the Han, the dominant ethnic group in China. About 92% of the Chinese are Han people. The rest belong to the other 55 ethnic groups in the PRC, such as Zhuangs, Mongolians, Tibetans, Uighurs, and Miaos. These ethnic minorities tend to cluster in either southwest or northwest China. For example, Yunnan, one of the southwestern provinces, has as many as 26 ethnic groups living within its boundaries.

Collectivism is the term used by anthropologists and sociologists to designate one of the basic orientations of Chinese culture. This term could be placed at one end of a continuum; at the other end would be one of the basic orientations of U.S. culture, individualism.

Though collectivism originated in the agrarian economy of ancient China and in the ethics of Confucius, a few forms taken by contemporary Chinese collectivism are attributable to China's present social organizations. For example, the enveloping nature of the Chinese work unit is largely a product of that system. Another example is the relationship among neighbors. Though neighbors in China have traditionally been highly interdependent, the type of neighborhood committee that is an institutionalized provider of social services and mutual aid is quite new. In these and other ways, the tradition of collectivism has been enhanced since the founding of the People's Republic of China.

On the other hand, the burgeoning business economy of China's large cities, where Western influence is especially strong, is beginning to change the ethic of collectivism. Western businesspeople frequently complain about the job-hopping of their Chinese employees and question how this is compatible with China's ancient collectivist ethics. The answer: it isn't. Job-hopping demonstrates that individualistic values are gaining foothold in China. Nowadays it is common for young people to change their jobs one or two years after graduation from college. They gain experience and then seek higher positions, which accounts for high mobility in the business world. Those who work in foreign companies tend to change their jobs even more frequently, because they believe they may have better opportunities.

Throughout their history the Chinese have shown respect for age, seniority, rank, maleness, and family background. Confucianism embodied this attitude toward power and authority by stressing the benefits of ordered hierarchical relationships. Over the past few decades in China, however, the emphasis on socialist egalitarianism has noticeably changed this way of thinking. In Chinese families the kind of absolute power wielded by the patriarch is a thing of the past.

Perhaps the chief determinant of relative power in China is seniority. Who is older and who is younger among siblings, for instance, is of considerably importance. In Chinese, the age-neutral words brother and sister do not exist; instead, there are quite different words for elder brother, younger brother, elder sister, and younger sister. An elder sibling may call a younger one by his or her given name, but the younger one normally uses the more reverential age-relative title when addressing the older one — *gege* for elder brother and *jiejie* for elder sister. Similarly, age is important in local community affairs. What an older person says generally carries more weight in the meeting of the neighborhood committee than the opinions of younger people. Younger people are in general respectful to older ones, and informal social sanctions may be applied toward anyone who is disrespectful to seniors.

Finally, the third important fundamental value of the Chinese is intragroup harmony and avoidance of overt conflict in interpersonal relations. People from cultures the world over value smooth human relationships, but the importance assigned to interpersonal harmony varies from one culture to another. With respect to the Chinese, maintaining harmonious relationships with family members, close friends and colleagues, and other primary group members is a matter of supreme concern. The disapproval of overt confrontation and the high value placed on intragroup harmony are themes that will occur again throughout people's life.

(Hu Wenzhong, Cornelius N. Zhuang Enping, 2010)

Comprehension Check

I. Answer the following questions.

1. What are the three fundamental values of the Chinese?
2. How does the value of collectivism influence Chinese daily communication?
3. How does the value of the social power distance influence Chinese communication?
4. How does the value of intragroup harmony and avoidance of overt conflict in interpersonal relations influence Chinese people's social behavior and communication?

II. Translate into Chinese the following passage in the essay.

Though collectivism originated in the agrarian economy of ancient China and in the ethics of Confucius, a few forms taken by contemporary Chinese collectivism are attributable to China's present political system. For example, the enveloping nature of the Chinese work unit is largely a product of that system. Another example is the relationship among neighbors. Though neighbors in China have traditionally been highly interdependent, the type of neighborhood committee that is an institutionalized provider of social services and mutual aid is quite new. In these and other ways, the tradition of collectivism has been enhanced since the founding of the People's Republic of China.

Reading 2

Reflections on Datong and the Common Good

The philosophy of datong may be understood as a Chinese contribution to universal thinking about the common good. In Liyun, datong, refers to an ideal state of human social existence, probably in the mythical Golden Age of the remote past. In Datong Shu, the same term datong is used to describe an ideal world in the distant future, when social evolution has progressed to the Age of Complete Peace-and-Equality. In both of these datong worlds, "the world is shared by all alike". Human pursuits are directed to the common good of all rather than to the satisfaction of selfish or private desires. Property is held in common. The well-being of all in society is well taken care of. The practice of ren is not confined to one's family members but extends to all in a kind of universal brotherhood/sisterhood.

The theoretical foundation of datong includes the Confucian doctrine of ren. As ren means love for others and care and concern for others' welfare, it is necessary to develop criteria for determining what is good for others and what their well-being consists of. The utilitarian criterion adopted by Kang Youwei is that happiness or pleasure is good and pain or suffering is bad, with the qualification that human nature is such that individual happiness is closely related to and dependent upon sociality and solidarity within a community.

Thus human nature as ren seeks the realization of the common good of all, which consists of the minimization of suffering and the maximization of potential happiness. The philosophy of history of progress suggests that it is possible for ren to be realized in increasing degrees over the course of social evolution and historical development. The question then is how suffering is to be minimized and happiness maximized. Influenced by Buddhist thinking, Kang Youwei perceives suffering as a universal phenomenon inextricably linked to human existence. He then develops the original idea that suffering is a result of the existence of the "nine boundaries", the gradual dissolution of which will usher in the datong world of the Age of Complete Peace-and-Equality. The theory of the "nine boundaries" and their dissolution is thus Kang's most important contribution to the Chinese tradition of datong thinking. Kang's philosophy, built on a synthesis of Confucianism, Buddhism, utilitarianism, and the conception of social evolution and progress, points toward a utopian future with elements of socialism or communism and liberalism.

Kang's datong world is a far cry from today's world of global capitalism, with its gross social, economic, and political inequalities among states and classes and the extreme contrast between those living in wealth, prosperity, and freedom and those oppressed and/or living in poverty. Insofar as datong embodies a credible — or at least partially credible — vision of the common good in human social existence, we need to think seriously about the common good and how far away from it we are, especially when we consider how different the portrayals of the datong world in Datong Shu are from the world today. Is the form of capitalism that exists today consistent with the common good of humankind? Is socialism still a viable alternative, at least in the long run? The Chinese tradition of datong thinking is clearly relevant to our reflections today on these fundamental questions of social and political philosophy.

To what extent, if any, does the ancient Chinese concept of datong and Kang's adaptation of it to the modern world provide a useful contribution to our thinking about the common good? I would suggest a positive answer to this question. The Chinese character for "tong" in datong literally means "common" or "in common", while the Chinese character for "da" literally means "great". The key phrase "tianxia weigong" in the celebrated datong passage in the Book of Rites may be translated as "all under Heaven is held in common" or "all under Heaven is publicly held". The concept of datong is thus a concept that was intended by the ancient Chinese to embody a society whose organization is in accordance with the common good, or a society in which all members enjoy the good life. As pointed out above, all members of society share in the enjoyment of the benefits of social cooperation in the datong society. The welfare or well-being of all, including those who are weak, vulnerable, or unable to care for themselves, is well taken care of.

Everyone is devoted to serving the common good instead of seeking primarily to benefit oneself or one's family members. "They did not regard as parents only their own parents, or as sons only their own sons." Thus ren, benevolence, compassion, care, or love for fellow human beings is extended to all. But this datong concept was developed more than two and a half millennia ago, and in the datong passage of the Book of Rites it was only used to refer to a more perfect society in the distant past which was no longer realizable — for only xiaokang was realizable in the contemporary world. Is datong a credible vision of the common good in the twenty first-century world?

The modern welfare state seeks to ensure a minimum standard of living and a reasonable quality of life for the weak, vulnerable, disadvantaged, or underprivileged members of society. To this extent, it gives effect to the datong ideal. But the datong ideal goes further than guaranteeing minimum welfare to all. It envisages a kind of transformation of human motivation and human action from being self-centered to being altruistic. In the post-communist world of global capitalism, this core element of the datong vision would seem to be a utopian and an impossible dream. Instead, what has apparently prevailed is Adam Smith's idea of the invisible hand in the market system, which ensures that the self-interested actions of individuals, or actors in the market, will ultimately maximize the common good.

Kang's modernized version of datong is more optimistic regarding the possibility of human and social transformation. He introduces the idea of progress in history, drawing mainly on the theory of the Three Ages in Chunqiu Gongyang. In the West, belief in progress was a mark of the Age of Enlightenment, which gave rise to social movements that continue to thrive in the current day. In Kang's philosophy, progress is possible, worth striving for, and an inherent dimension of human history. Progress includes not only material and scientific progress, but also moral progress (increasing degrees of the realization of ren), cultural progress (increasing achievements in education and moral and intellectual cultivation), and social progress (reducing inequality, discrimination, injustice, exploitation and oppression, and advancing levels of freedom, equal rights, and democracy). The belief in and efforts to bring about progress in all these dimensions are still very much alive and well into the contemporary world. To this extent, Kang's datong philosophy still speaks to, and resonates within, our world today.

Even today, Kang's concepts of ren and progress can still provide a persuasive and coherent theoretical foundation for the practical struggles of fighting for a better world, in which the common good is better realized than it is today or has been in the history of humankind, and of fighting for the global realization of human rights, justice, democracy, and peace. Moreover, some of Kang's practical and concrete suggestions for a better world are still sound and yet to be realized today. For example, he understands that the ultimate solution to the sufferings of warfare can only be found in a rational and democratic system of governance at the global level. Additionally, his proposals regarding women's rights and animal welfare are still in the process of being fought for in many parts of the world.

What is most controversial in Kang's datong philosophy is the abolition of the family and of private property. Here it must first be pointed out that Kang was writing about datong in the distant future, and he made it clear that traditional family ethics have played a very important and positive role in traditional China and should continue to be respected now and in the foreseeable future. Indeed, he himself practiced the virtue of filial piety faithfully. Additionally, Kang's rejection of the family and private property for the purpose of datong should be understood in the context of China's circumstances at the end of the nineteenth century. During this time, the extended family and clan operated in many cases as a hierarchical, authoritarian, and oppressive institution, which discriminated against women and suppressed their rights (or what we would today think of as their rights) in the name of morality, and gross social and economic inequalities existed. With the benefit of hindsight, it might be said that Kang's prescriptions for remedying gender discrimination and social and economic inequality are too extreme, and that a fundamentally reformed family law (such as that which exists in many parts of the modernized world) and a social market economy are better solutions to the problems than the radical ones Kang envisaged.

(David Solomon, P.C. Lo, 2013: 97 – 100)

Comprehension Check

I. Answer the following questions.

1. What is Datong defined?
2. Does the ancient Chinese concept of datong and Kang's adaptation of it to the modern world provide a useful contribution to our thinking about the common good?
3. What do Kang's concepts of ren and progress mean to today's society?
4. What is most controversial in Kang's datong philosophy?

II. Translate into Chinese the following passage in the essay.

Kang's modernized version of datong is more optimistic regarding the possibility of human and social transformation. He introduces the idea of progress in history, drawing mainly on the theory of the Three Ages in Chunqiu Gongyang. In the West, belief in progress was a mark of the Age of Enlightenment, which gave rise to social movements that continue to thrive in the current day. In Kang's philosophy, progress is possible, worth striving for, and an inherent dimension of human history. Progress includes not only material and scientific progress, but also moral progress (increasing degrees of the realization of ren), cultural progress (increasing achievements in education and moral and intellectual cultivation), and social progress (reducing inequality, discrimination, injustice, exploitation and oppression, and advancing levels of freedom, equal rights, and democracy). The belief in and efforts to bring about progress in all these dimensions are still very much alive and well into the contemporary world. To this extent, Kang's datong philosophy still speaks to, and resonates within, our world today.

Part Four Knowledge Application

Case Analysis

I. Case 1

Are Family the Most Important?

Lisa (Chinese-American) and Shelley (American) shared a small dormitory room with each other at their university. They liked each other and went on very well until a problem came up.

One day, Lisa told Shelley, "My second cousin wants to visit the university. She may want to attend school here next year. Do you mind if she stays with us when she visits?"

"Of course not, it's pretty crowded with just the two of us. Where's she going to sleep?"

"Oh, that's not a problem. She can sleep in my bed, with me."

"Well, okay," said Shelley. "It's up to you."

"Great!" answered Lisa. "She's coming tomorrow."

Two weeks later, the cousin was still stay with them. Because she did not bring enough money, Lisa had to pay for all her meals. In order to help her cousin find her way around, Lisa missed many of her classes.

Although Lisa never complained about any of this to Shelley, Shelley decided to talk with her friend.

"Lisa," she said. "I know it's none of my business. But I don't want to see you being treated in this way. It's unfair for your cousin to take advantage of you, using your time and money like this. And how do you ever get any sleep, anyway? I think you are supposed to tell her you have your own life to live. After all, she is just your second cousin."

Lisa was surprised. She replied, "Oh, the bed doesn't annoy me! It reminds me of sleeping with my sister when I was a child. You are right, though, about my school work.

I know I'm absent from too many classes. But family comes first. I just couldn't leave my cousin here by herself."

Although having the conservation with Lisa, Shelley still could not understand her friend. Before her cousin arrived, Lisa had always seemed to be an independent, responsible person, who never skipped a class. Shelley just could not understand why she had changed.

Analysis:

One of the reasons that Shelley could not understand Lisa is this: in American culture, the nuclear family is much more important to the individual than the extended family. Most Americans feel little responsibility toward their second cousins, and may have never even met them. Therefore, Shelley was confused because Lisa put so much effort into helping "just" a second cousin. But in Lisa's culture there is not such a big difference between nuclear and extended family responsibilities. For many Hispanics, Asians, Africans, and Arabs, the extended family is very important in child rearing, social life, and caring for the elderly. In these societies, the extended family is the main financial and emotional support for people in times of crisis. This is not so for most Americans, who rely more on friends, institutions, and professionals.

Another reason why Shelley and Lisa could not understand each other is their different cultural values. Lisa felt that "family comes first", which means that her own needs come second. Shelley had a hard time understanding that point of view because in her culture the individual usually comes first. In the United States the person who can "make it on his own" without help from family is respected, although of course many people do get help from their families. For Americans, it is very important for the individual to be independent of others, and this value is true in the American family life too. In Hispanic and Asian cultures, family members depend on each other more, and families are built around the value of interdependence.

Because of these differences, it is sometimes difficult for people to understand and accept the way family members in other cultures seem to treat each other. It is important, however, to remember that families show their love in very different ways. These differences sometimes make it hard to see the reality of love of one's family in every culture in the word.

II. Case 2

Criticizing a Teacher in Public Place

Shortly after Raymond started teaching English in an English training centre in China, the Director of the program called him to the office. The Director told him in a round-about way that the students were unhappy about some of his methods and had made some suggestions about his teaching. Raymond was embarrassed, not just because the students had concerns about his teaching style, but because the students had complained directly to the Director.

(Adapted from Dai Fan, Stephen L. J. Smith: Cultures in Contrast: Miscommunication and Misunderstanding between Chinese and North Americans)

Analysis:

If this case is analyzed from a Chinese value perspective, it can be explained as follows: Chinese people place a lot of emphasis on harmonious relationship. This makes it difficult to tell a person that something is wrong about the way he or she does things. As a result, in a work environment, people tend to talk with the boss about their concerns regarding a colleague and then let the boss talk to the person about the issue. The idea is to avoid a face-to-face confrontation between one who raises an issue and the person who is being addressed. The boss is the best person to go to in such a case because his or her job is to supervise, and his or her words are not supposed to be coming from him or herself, and therefore, the employee would not feel personal about the issue.

That was why students turned to the Director about Raymond's teaching. They thought that they would upset him if they talked to him in person. So, they wanted the Director to play the role of a mediator.

If this case is analyzed from a North American value perspective, it can be explained as follows: North Americans like to maintain a harmonious working environment, too. However, the way they do so is different from that in China. In the West, students would normally expect to speak directly with the instructor. If students went to a teacher's supervisor, their actions would be seen as a statement that the teacher was not respected or trusted by the students and that they had to "go above his head" to bring down the power of his boss on him. Rather than avoiding discomfort between themselves and Raymond, the students actually embarrassed Raymond. If they had come to him directly, he could have responded directly to their suggestions and thus avoided the embarrassment of being criticized by his superior.

Part Five Knowledge Practice

Translation

I. Translate the following passage into Chinese.

Many English-speaking people in Eastern countries have been heard to complain about being stared at. In fact, a young woman from one of Western countries, and who is a good friend of the author's, decided to leave the Eastern country partly because of this. Although she liked her teaching in the country and had strong feelings of affection towards that country and people in that country, she decided she could no longer stand the constant staring, wherever she went. The fact that she is unusually tall and large explains the behavior of many of the passersby in the Eastern country. When she left the country, it was with some reluctance; nevertheless, she left before she had planned to. The feelings aroused by staring can be that strong!

II. Translate the following passage into English.

中国传统社会价值观念跟西方近代社会价值观相比,有很大不同,第一个特点是"责任先于自由",就是很强调个人对于他人、对社群,甚至对自然所负有的责任,责任意识非常强。我们讲以天下为己任,孟子就讲过了。古人在汉代就明确要以天下为己任,己任就是责任。从古代先秦的"君子"到汉代的士大夫,有一个很突出的责任意识,就是对天下的责任心。

⬤ Case Study

I. Case 1

Different Philosophies

Dr. Richard Lowry, a prominent American engineer, was commissioned by a company in Indonesia to direct a bridge-building project in the interior of the company, working together with a local construction supervisor. Before going to Indonesia, Dr. Lowry studied the Indonesian language and customs of the people that he would be working with. He also studied Islamic religion since the local Indonesian supervisor was a Muslim. Although he adjusted to the local community as possible as he can, there were still aspects of work to which he had difficulties adapting. Material never seemed to meet the demand that their work required. Workers seldom go to work on time, and when they showed up for work on time, they were to get started. The relationship between him and the Indonesian supervisor was far from he expected. They couldn't seem to agree on a schedule for when the goods should be sent. In fact, it seemed that his partner even didn't care about completing the project as planned. During his three-month assignment, Dr. Lowry became so frustrated that he became less productive and frequently thought about returning home. (Wang Fuxiang & Ma Dengge, 1999)

Questions for discussion:

What caused the problem above?

Does it result from their different philosophies on management or different world views?

II. Case 2

American's Work Ethic

Americans have for centuries believed that they were guilty of sin if they did not work as carefully and hard as they could when they did anything. Even as children Americans were taught, "If it's worth doing it, it's worth doing well." But some people have gone beyond the usual sense of diligence. They are especially attracted to the notion of "climbing the ladder" so as to increase their status, financial position, and sense of self-worth. Thus in English a new word has been created to describe people who work compulsively. The word "workabolic" describes an individual who is as addicted to work as an alcoholic is to alcohol.

Questions for discussion:

1. What culture value makes Americans have one characteristic of "work ethic"?
2. Do you agree with the point that workabolics are valuable members of society? And why?

(Wang Dawei, 2011: 41)

III. Case 3

Does Adopting a Businesslike Atmosphere Work in This Situation?

Ronald, an ambitious executive, was sent to take over the Sales Branch of an American company in San Paulo of Brazil. He spent a few weeks learning routine work with the departing manager, and was somewhat disturbed by the informality and lack of discipline that seemed to take place in the office. People seemed to be keen on excessive socializing, and conversations seemed to handle more personal than business matters, and no one seemed to stick to their set schedules. Once Ronald had formally taken over, he tried to do something about this problem, so he called the staff together for a meeting. He told them seriously that work rates and schedules had to be adhered to, and demanded a more businesslike atmosphere. Over the next few months, he focused on the issue of improving office efficiency. High bonuses and incentives were offered for those who worked well, and private warnings were offered to those who did not. By the end of the first quarter, he felt he had considerably improved the situation, but was surprised to find sales figures had dropped since he took over the Sales Branch of the American company. (ibid.)

Questions for discussion:

1. What businesslike atmosphere does Ronald adopt?
2. What do you think should Ronald do to improve sales figures?

Unit 7
Intercultural Communication and Education

Learning Objectives

By the end of this unit, you should be able to:
1. Understand the popularity of intercultural education;
2. Intercultural Communication in Educational Settings;
3. Understand how culture influences teaching and learning styles;
4. Compare differences between Chinese and Western education and analyze the reasons behind them;
5. Understand the significance of building a multicultural school;
6. Explain what a multicultural school is and explain how teaching in a multicultural school can be effective.

Part One Warming Up

Watch the video clip "Kate and Li Hui Talking about University Study Life", and then answer the questions below the script.

Questions for discussion:
1. What are the differences of teaching and learning styles between Chinese and British education in the selected video clip?

2. What can you understand the differences in educational systems between China and Britain?

<table><tr><td>**Part Two**</td><td>**Basic Knowledge of Intercultural Communication and Education**</td></tr></table>

1. The Popularity of Intercultural Education

With globalization, education is no more limited within one's own country. The number of international students keeps increasing. Take China for example, every year, many Chinese students go abroad to the United States, Britain, Japan, Australia, Canada to study. At the same time, international students all over the world come to China to study.

The popularity of intercultural education brings benefits including enhancing communication between cultures and increasing cooperation between countries. But if educators and students don't know cultural differences in the educational context, misunderstanding may occur and teaching and learning efficiency will be affected.

When students enroll at an institution in a foreign country, they need to adapt to a very different teaching style in a different culture. This transition could be a difficult one for both the migrant students and the educators and is likely to influence the performance of students, teachers and administrators in the host country. As Hall stated, educational systems are products of the cultures they are embedded in, so educators need to be aware of the context in which learning is acquired. They need to understand how learning and teaching differ across cultures.

2. Intercultural Communication in Educational Settings

Much of our communication behavior in the classroom is not interpreted in the way we intend it by people from different cultural backgrounds. Education is deeply embedded in culture, and our expectations for the educational process are a part of our culture. The roles that we enact in the classroom are very much a part of culture influences on education.

2.1 Roles for teachers and students

When Tom taught at a university in Belgium, another professor gave him a helpful cultural tip, "In Belgium, students don't answer the professor's questions, even if they know the answer. In the United States, American students answer the professor's questions, even if they don't know the answer." This cultural generalization was helpful to

Tom as he navigated the role of professor in this different context. Although he did ask questions throughout the term, the lack of discussion in the classroom was understandable. Because he was concerned about imposing his own cultural framework on the Belgian students, Tom did not push them to participate in discussions, nor did he demand that they answer his questions. As the term progressed, some of the students began to speak more in class, even as Tom felt that he was moving toward more of a lecture format. The classroom became a site for negotiation of these cultural differences.

These kinds of cultural differences can create confusion in the classroom for students and teachers. The culture clash over learning styles (the different ways that students learn in different cultures) and teaching styles that instructors use to teach is common as students increasingly travel to study in other cultures. Often we are unaware of our cultural assumptions about education until we are confronted with different ways of learning. Think about the assumptions you have concerning how your instructors should behave. Perhaps you think that instructors should set time aside in class for discussion of the material, or that students should be allowed to say what they think about the readings, or that grading should be done "on a curve". In many universities, for example, students are assigned books to read before the end of the term instead of getting a structured reading list and assignments along the way.

2.2　Grading and Power

As in any other social setting, the classroom is embedded with cultural expectations about power relations. While there may always be a power difference in the communication between instructors and students, this difference can be greater or lesser in various cultures. In the United States, for example, the relationships between instructor and students tend to be less formal than in other cultures. Micheal, a students of ours, recalled the following intercultural conflict, which reflects this power difference: While on a study-abroad program in Malaysia, I received what I thought was an unfair grade on a paper. I discussed my unhappiness with my teacher in his office. In the heat of the argument, I was threatening to report him to the school's governing board, and he was threatening to get me kicked out of the school! Obviously, this conflict spiraled way out of control … Several red flags were telling me that intercultural differences were at play. In his culture, students are disrespectful when they question teachers' decisions. In my culture, questions show that you are paying attention. I chose to explain my actions to the teacher, and we were able to put out the fire. We refocused on communication behaviors and ended in a win-win situation: I got a better grade, and he received more respect.

Michael's experience highlights the role that culture plays in the educational process. Actually, it is the culture influence that the teaching and learning between East and West are quite different.

2.3 Culture Influence on Learning and Teaching

2.3.1 Learning Through Memorizing or Understanding

In some Asian countries, memorization is considered not only a legitimate way of learning, but also that the process of learning inevitably involves committing to memory things that are not totally understood. So students in those countries are required to recall some knowledge of texts instead of analyzing them. So teaching in some East Asian countries mainly focuses on helping students memorizing knowledge effectively. While in some western countries, memorization is considered rote learning, which may affect students' thorough understanding of knowledge. So they emphasize that understanding of knowledge should be done before the memory of information.

2.3.2 Skills First or Creativity First

Education in some Asian countries attaches great importance to basic knowledge and skills, and therefore teachers in those countries hold the view that basic knowledge should be taught to students in school time, and skills should be acquired by students in their early school learning, otherwise, skills may never be acquired. They believe that the idea of creativity can be taught to students in later school learning like in the process of college or university study.

Quite different from those in Asian countries, educators in some Western countries believe that creativity should be acquired by students in their early school learning, otherwise, students' ability of creativity may never emerge or develop. They think that skills can be picked up later.

⊙ Glossary

1. **foster** *vt*. develop (a feeling or idea) in oneself 培养,助长(感情、观念)
2. **merely** *adv*. just; only 仅仅,只不过,纯粹是
3. **echoing** *n*. 回声(波)现象,反照现象
4. **multicultural** *adj*. of, relating to, or constituting several cultural or ethnic groups within a society (与)多种文化(有关)的,融合多种文化的
5. **fusion** *n*. the process or result of joining two or more things together to form a single entity 联合,合并
6. **qualification** *n*. a pass of an examination or an official completion of a course, especially one conferring status as a recognized practitioner of a profession or activity 资格证明,合格证书
7. **sensitive** *adj*. quick to detect or respond to slight changes, signals, or influences 敏感的,灵敏的
8. **ideology** *n*. the ideas and manner of thinking characteristic of a group, social class,

or individual　（团体、社会阶层或个人的）思维方式，意识形态
9. **standardize**　*vt*. cause（something）to conform to a standard　使合标准，使标准化

● Comprehension Check

I. Decide whether the following statements are true (T)or false (F).

1. (　) Culture and education are inseparable from each other.
2. (　) The popularity of intercultural education brings benefits including enhancing communication between cultures，increasing cooperation between countries.
3. (　) When students enroll at an institution in a foreign country，they need not to adapt to a very different teaching style in a different culture.
4. (　) In the United States，for example，the relationships between instructor and students tend to be less formal than in other cultures.
5. (　) It is the culture influence that the teaching and learning between East and West are quite different.
6. (　) The basic notions of concept of education in Asian countries is similar to that of Western countries.
7. (　) The increasingly academic exchanges and a loose environment contribute to the formation of diversity of school culture.
8. (　) With globalization，education is no more limited within one's own country.

II. Answer the following questions.

1. Why does intercultural education become popular in the world?
2. What are the differences between idea of Eastern teaching and that of Western teaching?
3. What is valuable to effective teaching in multicultural school?

III. Fill in each of the blanks in the following passage with an appropriate word from those listed below, and you will learn more about communication.

A. modeled	B. achieved	C. slot	D. exploring
E. accomplish	F. self-reliance	G. likely	H. frustrated
I. displayed	J. desired		

With a few exceptions my Chinese colleagues ___1___ the same attitude as the staff at the Jinling Hotel. Since adults know how to place the key in the key ___2___, which is the ultimate purpose of approaching the slot, and since the child is neither old enough nor clever enough to realize the ___3___ action on his own, what possible gain is ___4___ by having him struggle?

Benjamin may well get ___5___ and angry — certainly not a desirable outcome. Why not show him what to do? He will be happy，he will learn how to ___6___ the task sooner, and then he can proceed to more complex activities, like opening the door or asking for the key — both of which accomplishments can (and should) in due course be ___7___ for him as well.

We listened to such explanations sympathetically and explained that, first of all, we did not much care whether Benjamin succeeded in inserting the key into the slot. He was having a good time and was ___8___, two activities that did matter to us. But the critical point was that, in the process, we were trying to teach Benjamin that one can solve a problem effectively by oneself.

Such ___9___ is a principal value of child rearing in middle-class America. So long as the child is shown exactly how to do something — whether it be placing a key in a key slot, drawing a hen or making up for a misdeed — he is less likely to figure out himself how to accomplish such a task. And, more generally, he is less ___10___ to view life — as Americans do — as a series of situations in which one has to learn to think for oneself, to solve problems on one's own and even to discover new problems for which creative solutions are wanted.

(Li Yinhua, 2003)

IV. Group Discussion.

1. What problems exist in both Chines and Western learning styles? Can the problems be solved through effort?

2. Do you think Chinese culture only has negative influence on Chinese students' second language learning? If not, can you give some examples to support your opinion?

3. Do you think it's better for Chinese students to adapt themselves to foreign teachers' way of teaching or foreign teachers should make their teaching style more acceptable for Chinese students' learning style? Give your reasons.

4. What assessment style can best display students' performance in your mind?

Part Three   Knowledge Expansion

Reading 1

Identity and Social Categorisation: Otherisation and Occidentalism in Encountering "the West"

While identity can furnish us with group membership and a sense of belonging, it can also serve as the basis for negative perceptions and reactions to people who differ from us and our perceived group (s). The similarity-attraction hypothesis posits that human beings are naturally drawn to people who share a similar language and ways of being, and individuals may unconsciously or consciously shy away from those who do not belong to their in-group. Rigid social categorisation (e.g., stereotyping, otherisation) and ethnocentricism, the roots of identity biases, can create barriers to successful, equitable intercultural interactions and hinder intercultural/second language learning.

Social categorisation refers to the way individuals group people into conceptual categories in order to make sense of our complex world. Simply put, people are placed into groups and categories according to current understandings, perceptions and experience. This can easily lead to stereotypes and otherisation. Stereotyping entails "the automatic application of information we have about a country or culture group, both positive and negative, to every individual in it". Closely related to this phenomenon is otherisation or othering, a form of social representation which involves "the objectification of another person or group". In this process, culture is used to account for all of the views and behaviours of "the Other" (e.g., Asians, Westerners), largely ignoring the complexity and diversity of individual acts and attributes (e.g., emotions, ideas, behaviours). Instead of seeing people from different cultural and linguistic backgrounds as individuals, in the eyes of an ethnocentric person, they are merely representatives of a particular cultural or national group, and tied to a fixed set of characteristics and behaviours. Thus, essentialism entails the act of reductionism, whereby diversity within groups is ignored in favour of a simpler, unitary representation.

Since the publication of Said's seminal work in 1978, much has been written about the negative consequences of Orientalism, Neo-Orientalism and the stereotyping of people from "the East" (e.g., Asians); this is giving rise to advances in critical postcolonial studies and intercultural education. While a few studies have been conducted to critique new and old forms of Orientalism, it is worthwhile to study otherisation and Occidentalism, which means that "the construction of the West" (e.g., Europe and English-speaking countries) and "images of Westerners" from the perspective of "non-Westerners".

Occidentalism encompasses ideologies or visions of "the West" developed in either the West or non-west, and includes political attitudes and dehumanized, stereotyped depictions. Outside the Western world, images of "the West" are largely derived from various forms of mass communication (e. g., television, radio, newspapers, the Internet), via entertainment programmes (e.g., American TV sitcoms and soap operas), documentaries, movies and news reports (local and international), as well as government propaganda and published historical accounts (e. g., school textbooks written from particular viewpoints). Pictures of "the West" that have been constructed in Asia (and elsewhere) may be altered or reinforced through direct personal experience, such as education abroad.

(Regis Machart, Fred Dervin, Minghui Gao, 2016: 19 – 20)

Comprehension Check

I. Answer the following questions.

1. What does social categorisation refer to?

2. What does otherisation mean?

3. What does Occidentalism mean?

II. Translate into Chinese the following passage in the above text.

While identity can furnish us with group membership and a sense of belonging, it can also serve as the basis for negative perceptions and reactions to people who differ from us and our perceived group (s). The similarity-attraction hypothesis posits that human beings are naturally drawn to people who share a similar language and ways of being, and individuals may unconsciously or consciously shy away from those who do not belong to their in-group. Rigid social categorisation (e. g., stereotyping, otherisation) and ethnocentricism, the roots of identity biases, can create barriers to successful, equitable intercultural interactions and hinder intercultural/second language learning.

Reading 2

Language and Culture in Intercultural Communication Through English

A recurring theme in many accounts of culture and language has been a view of language as the primary semiotic means of both representing and creating culture. Combined with language socialisation and sociocultural-based theories of learning the relationship between language use and learning and sociocultural contexts is seen as densely interwoven. However, this should not be confused with an advocacy of the strongest interpretations of linguistic relativity or essentialist positions on language and culture, in which our language controls our world view. Language certainly influences our perception of the world but it does not restrict it. In other words, we are all capable of perceiving the world in different ways to those suggested by any one particular language or a variety of languages.

This is most clearly demonstrated in the use of English for intercultural communication in global contexts. In such settings it is overly simplistic to correlate a language and a culture in national terms, for example, English and the UK or US. Conceptions of English as a lingua franca（ELF，通用语，共同语），and Global Englishes，while not denying the influence of the so-called "inner circle, native speaker countries", reject any idea of an inevitable link between English and these countries and cultures. The multitude of users of English and the huge diversity of contexts in which English occurs underscore that in global settings there will be many varieties of English and that correspondingly there can be no one culture of English. Thus，statements proposing that the English language somehow "contains" English culture, for example, "the English language … carries with it values and beliefs which are hidden in linguistic codes but control from the depths the process of meaning making during human interactions", must be rejected as essentialist when we examine English used as a lingua franca in intercultural communication.

Yet，it is equally important to point out that English used as a lingua franca in intercultural communication is not a culturally neutral language as has been suggested by some. Phipps and Guilherme stress that languages in intercultural communication "are never just neutral". Communication is always embedded in and constitutive of social situations and involves speakers with purposes and positions，none of which are neutral. It is crucial that this ideological dimension to intercultural communication is not ignored particularly as regards cultural identity and identification. How we conceive of and make use of culture is always an ideological process. Thus，while it would be naïve to assume that cultures，languages and nations correlate in intercultural communication，the influence of such powerful "myths" and the tensions they may create with the more fluid associations we might expect in ELF communication need to be recognized.

Critical postmodernist perspectives are most relevant to an understanding of intercultural communication through ELF，where definitions of culture and language are approached as emergent and dynamic and the boundaries between one language and culture and another are less clearly delineated. Such an understanding of communication refutes the essentialist idea of a specific language and "national" conception of culture as having the type of unbreakable bond described in linguistic relativity. Rather languages are adapted and shaped to the needs of the individual users and contexts in which communication takes place. Languages such as English are therefore in constant tension between individual，local，regional and global contexts，all of which need to be approached as dynamic and changeable.

Key notions include viewing language and cultural practices as part of a "global flow" which is influenced by and in turn influences more localised linguistic practices. Pennycook underscores the tensions in these flows between the centrifugal forces of "fluidity" and the centripetal forces of "fixity". The commensurable idea of liminality also aids in an understanding of the way in which cultural and linguistic practices can take on new forms and meanings in intercultural communication that are not attributable to any one culture；

although, with the caveat that ELF users are not seen as borrowing the resources of a particular community or in-between "target" languages and cultures. Furthermore, viewing culture as a discourse community or system adds to a characterisation of culture as being one of many interrelated discourse systems which can be utilised and referred to in communication. Again though with the caveat in which discourse is approached from the more dynamic positions taken by writers such as Kramsch and Pennycook rather than structuralist perspectives. Thus, cultures need to be seen as dynamic and fluid resources in intercultural communication that emerge in-situ as more or less relevant to creating understanding. Such is the dynamic nature of culture that Roberts, Byram, Barro, Jordan, and Street, drawing on Street, recommend using culture as a verb and discuss "doing culture" in an attempt to rid culture of the static connotations given to nouns.

In sum, intercultural communication needs to be viewed as a sociocultural process in which the cultural dimension is crucial. Therefore, just as learning and using a language involves an understanding of grammar, vocabulary and phonology, it will also entail an understanding of the role of sociocultural contexts. However, for languages such as English in global lingua franca settings the connections between language and sociocultural forms, practices and references are likely to be diverse, complex, and emergent. This would suggest that there is no clear "target culture" to which English can be assigned. Alongside a knowledge of the more formal features of language, knowledge of culture is needed, but not of only one specific target culture. Language users need to be equipped with a general knowledge of the relationships between language, culture and communication and an ability to apply this to diverse situations.

(Will Baker, 2011: 198 – 200)

Comprehension Check

I. Answer the following questions.

1. What role does English language play in intercultural communication in global contexts?

2. Why is English language used as the lingua franca in intercultural communication?

II. Translate into Chinese the following passage in the above text.

In sum, intercultural communication needs to be viewed as a sociocultural process in which the cultural dimension is crucial. Therefore, just as learning and using a language involves an understanding of grammar, vocabulary and phonology, it will also entail an understanding of the role of sociocultural contexts. However, for languages such as English in global lingua franca settings the connections between language and sociocultural forms, practices and references are likely to be diverse, complex, and emergent. This would suggest that there is no clear "target culture" to which English can be assigned.

Alongside a knowledge of the more formal features of language, knowledge of culture is needed, but not of only one specific target culture. Language users need to be equipped with a general knowledge of the relationships between language, culture and communication and an ability to apply this to diverse situations.

Part Four   Knowledge Application

Case Analysis

I. Case 1

Two Different Teaching Ideas Towards Children Education

For a month in the spring of 1987, Russell Baker, an American educator, and his wife Ellen lived in the bustling eastern Chinese city of Nanjing with their 18-month-old son Benjamin while studying arts education in Chinese kindergartens and elementary schools. But one of the most telling lessons the couple got in the difference between Chinese and American ideas of education came not in the classroom but in the lobby of the Jinling Hotel where they stayed in Nanjing.

The key to their room was attached to a large plastic block with the room number on it. When leaving the hotel, a guest was encouraged to turn in the key, either by handing it to an attendant or by dropping it through a slot into a box. Because the key slot was narrow, the key had to be positioned carefully to fit into it.

Benjamin loved to carry the key around, shaking it vigorously. He also liked to try to place it into the slot. Because of his tender age and incomplete understanding of the need to position the key just so, he would usually fail. Benjamin was not bothered in the least. He probably got as much pleasure out of the sounds the key made as he did those few times when the key actually found its way into the slot.

During the time Benjamin was trying to put the key into the slot, the couple were perfectly happy to allow Benjamin to bang the key near the key slot. His exploratory behavior seemed harmless enough. But Russell Baker soon observed an interesting phenomenon. Any Chinese staff member nearby would come over to watch Benjamin and, noting his lack of initial success, attempt to assist. Any one of the Chinese staff members would hold onto Benjamin's hand and, gently but firmly, guide it directly toward the slot, reposition it as necessary, and help him to insert it. The "teacher" would then smile somewhat expectantly at Russell Baker and his wife Ellen, as if awaiting a thank you — and on occasion would frown slightly, as if considering the couple to be neglecting their parental duties.

Analysis:

This case reflects the different ideas of Chinese and Western education. Chinese people hold the teaching idea that learning should take place by continual careful shaping and molding, which reflects the best Chinese traditional education method: ba zhe shou jiao — "teaching by holding his hand", which focuses on skill teaching, because Chinese people are fearful that if skills are not acquired early, children may never acquired them. Therefore, when those well-intentioned Chinese observers working in Jingling Hotel in Nanjing came to Benjamin's rescue, they did not simply push his hand down clumsily or uncertainly, as Russell Baker might have done. Instead, they guided Benjamin with extreme facility and gentleness in precisely the desired direction. While westerners pay special attention on developing their children's creativity ability because they think creativity is the priority over skill. Such self-reliance is a principal value of child rearing in middle-class America. Therefore, when Jingling failed to put the key into the slot in Jingling hotel in Nanjing, the American couple were perfectly happy to allow Benjamin to bang the key near the key slot. The couple think their son's exploratory behavior seemed harmless enough, and it is good for their son to develop ability to solve problems on his own and even to discover new problems for which creative solutions are wanted in his future life.

(LI, Yinhua, 2003)

II. Case 2

Different Ways of Family Education

I am an English teacher at Changshu Institute of Technology. During my stay in the UK as a visiting scholar, I once went to visit a couple in York. They came to the railway station to pick me up together with their five-year old son. As soon as he saw me, the host took my backpack over and gave it to his son, and he said, "Be a gentleman, Mick." Then, the little stout child followed me all the way. I felt embarrassed, so I said, "I can carry it myself." However, the hostess insisted, "It's OK. We feel proud of him, being able to do something for a lady!"

Analysis:

This case reflects the different focuses of Chinese and Western family education. Chinese people tend to spoil their children by relieving them of housework so that they can focus on their studies, while Westerners pay special attention to developing their children's independence.

Part Five　Knowledge Practice

Translation

I. Translate the following passage into Chinese.

In terms of attitudes to creativity there seems to be a reversal of priorities: young Westerners making their boldest departures first and then gradually mastering the tradition; and young Chinese being almost inseparable from the tradition, but, over time, possibly evolving to a point equally original.

However, I do not want to overstate my case. There is enormous creativity to be found in Chinese scientific, technological and artistic innovations past and present. And there is a danger of exaggerating creative breakthroughs in the West. When any innovation is examined closely, its reliance on previous achievements is all too apparent (the "standing on the shoulders of giants" phenomenon).

II. Translate the following passage into English.

那些善意的中国旁观者前来帮助本杰明时,他们不是简单地像我可能会做的那样,笨拙地或是犹犹豫豫地把他的手往下推。相反,他们极其熟练地轻轻地把他引向所要到达的确切方向。我逐渐认识到,这些中国人不是简单地以一种陈旧的方式塑造、引导本杰明的行为,他们是在恪守中国传统,手把手教,教得本杰明自己会愉快地要求再来一次。

学习应通过不间断的精心塑造与引导而得以实现,这一观念同样适用于艺术。我们观看了孩子们在教室里学习艺术的情景,他们的娴熟技艺令我们惊讶。年仅五六岁的孩子就带着成人的那种技巧与自信在画花、画鱼和动物;九十岁的小书法家写出的作品足以在博物馆展示。有一次我们去两位小艺术家的家里参观,从孩子的父母处得知,他们每天练习数小时以完善他们的技艺。

Case Study

I. Case 1

Why is He Angry with Me?

Peter Zhang had just started working for the foreign owned company. He was sitting at his workstation but had not been given assignment that he should be doing at this moment. He was relaxing and waiting and then thought he would take the opportunity to have a look around. He poked his head into several offices just to see what there was to be seen.

Suddenly Mr. Green came up to him and angrily asked him what he was doing. Peter Zhang was embarrassed. He laughed and quickly started to move back toward his workstation. This did not seem to satisfy Mr. Green who started to talk rapidly and angrily. Hoping to calm him down, Mr. Zhang smiled and apologized, trying to explain that he was trying to learn more about the department. However, Mr. Green got even angrier. Finally, another worker came by and calmed him down. Mr. Green left, but still looked angry. Mr. Zhang sighed; he knew he had made a bad start but still didn't understand why.

Questions for discussion:

1. Why was Mr Green angry with Mr. Zhang?
2. What was wrong with Peter Zhang's behavior in the company?
3. What do you think Peter Zhang should do to avoid making Mr. Green angry?

II. Case 2

Maintaining the Quality or Increasing the Intake?

Interviewee: It's a really difficult balance to strike, actually maintaining the quality but making sure as many young people as possible and older people as well — there's been a surge in the number of over 25s applying, and we take many people who are over 25. But we've got to get that balance right. It's going to be terribly difficult for us next year.

Hostess: Given the cuts that the government announced a couple of weeks ago, and the numbers that we know in terms of applications, where are you going to draw that line? Are you going to have a look at cutting intake in order to maintain the quality of the courses?

Interviewee: We're trying not to cut intake at the moment. But what it means is that we're going to have to be extra-cautious in the number of offers we take, because we simply cannot afford to go over our quota of the number of offers. Because if we do, it means that we could be fined, or we just simply haven't got enough money to make sure the students' experience is right. So it means that maybe last year we would allow a few more people to have an offer. This year is going to be tougher.

Hostess: Do you lay some of the blame for the situation at the door of government?

Interviewee: If you look to France. Sarkozy is actually increasing the budget for higher education. Obama in the U. S. has done the same thing. So we're just slightly puzzled as to why the government seems to be cutting back on higher education rather than pumping more money into what we think is a service that is absolutely vital for the economy.

Questions for discussion:

1. What educational cultures are reflected in the above interview?
2. What are the differences of the French and American educational systems from the Britain's in terms of budget?
3. Do you think China should increase its educational budget? Why?
   (Wang Dawei, 2011)

Unit 8

Culture Shock and Intercultural Adaptation

By the end of this unit, you should be able to:

1. Know what culture shock is;
2. Identify the symptoms of culture shock;
3. Explain the effects of culture shock;
4. Know the ways to alleviating culture shock;
5. Know what adaptive cultural transformation competence is;
6. Learn to behave toward intercultural personhood.

Part One Warming Up

Watch video clip 1 "Feeling depressed in a new cultural environment" and video clip 2 "Going to see the doctor in Britain", and then answer the questions below the script respectively.

Video clip 1: Feeling depressed in a new cultural environment

Questions for discussion:

1. What are Janet's main symptoms of her illness?
2. What cultural reasons cause her illness?

Video clip 2: Going to see the doctor
Question for discussion:
1. What are the differences in daily food between Chinese culture and British culture?
2. What should Janet do to reduce her depression?

| Part Two | **Basic Knowledge of Culture Shock and Intercultural Adaptation** |

1. Definition of Culture Shock

Culture shock is a multifaceted experience resulting from numerous stressors occurring in contact with a different culture. Culture shock occurs for immigrant groups (e.g., foreign students and refugees; businessmen on overseas assignments) as well as for Euro-Americans in their own culture and society (e.g., business institutions undergoing reorganization; populations undergoing massive technological and social change; and staff, clients, and public in schools, hospitals, and other institutions).

(Yong Chen, 2010: 189)

2. Symptoms and Effects of Culture Shock

2.1　Symptoms of Culture Shock

It differs greatly from person to person about the reaction to culture shock. It may take only a few weeks for some to overcome the psychological distress in adaptation caused by the cultural difference they experience; but it may take a long period of time for others to get rid of the frustration of culture shock. For some severe cases, only when they return to their familiar cultural surroundings can they eliminate the problem caused by culture shock.

According to Thomas (1985), people who encounter culture shock display the following symptoms: depression, helplessness, hostility to the host country, feelings of anxiety, overidentification with the home country, feelings of withdrawal, homesickness, loneliness, paranoid feelings, preoccupation with cleanliness, irritability, confusion, disorientation, isolation, tension, need to establish continuity, defensiveness, intolerance of ambiguity, and impatience. Researches show that the symptoms of culture shock are as follows: excessive hand washing; concern over drinking water, food, dishes, and bedding excessively; fear of physical contact with attendants or servants; an absentminded, faraway stare; a feeling of helplessness and a desire for dependence on long-term residents of one's own nationality; fits of anger over delays and other minor frustration; delay and outright refusal to learn the language of the host country; excessive fear of being cheated, robbed, or injured; great concern over minor pains and eruptions of the skin; and finally, a longing to be back home, to be able to have a good cup of coffee and a piece of apple pie, to walk into a fast-food restaurant, to visit one's relatives, and in general, to talk to people who really make sense.

2.2 Effects of Culture Shock

Culture shock is a temporary experience, it can be considered as a transitional process of the sojourners' gradual awareness of and adjustment to the different cultures in a new environment. This process may evolve into two directions, depending on individual personality.

On one hand, culture shock may bring positive effects on individual growth. Studies show that culture shock may contribute several beneficial outcomes for sojourners. Firstly, culture shock may provide a learning opportunity for sojourners to learn how to deal with a constantly changing cultural environment. Secondly, culture shock may provide an environment of motivational force for us to move to new levels of self-realization, for almost everybody tends to pursue a unique and special goal. Thirdly, sojourners can get a sense of achievement from culture shock as they succeed in dealing with people from different cultural backgrounds. Fourthly, to a certain degree, some personal anxiety can increase the amount of learning. In other words, culture shock offers most of us a high but not excessive degree of anxiety that would arouse our desire to learn about a new culture and about ourselves. Fourthly, the experience both positive and negative accumulated from culture shock can give rise to new ideas that would be helpful to deal with future unfamiliar situations. Finally, during our sojourn, we are probably inspired of new ideas and thinking modes, which mostly derive from cultural comparisons and contrasts. This practice will also be of some help dealing with cultures that we are not familiar with.

On the other hand, there's also negative consequences caused by culture shock. First, culture shock may cause a feeling of being disoriented. On one moment, we may feel excited, while, on another, we may experience feelings of hysteria, confusion, anxiety, and depression. This uncertainty may be harmful and even damaging to the sojourners' psychological growth. Second, a set of behaviors considered respectable or proper in one culture may be viewed as bizarre or weird in another. Moreover, it may take a long time for some sojourners to sort through feelings about cultural differences and even may turn out to be impossible for other sojourners. What's worse, this may cause a tendency of judging the unfamiliar cultures more harshly.

(Guo-Ming Chen & W.J. Starosta, 2007)

3. Alleviating Culture Shock

Generally speaking, culture shock can be alleviated, some multinational firms try to minimize culture shock by selecting employees for overseas assignments who possess certain personal and professional qualifications. In addition, it is advisable that the company conduct training programs for employees prior to overseas assignments.

Culture shock is an unfortunate side effect of going abroad, but people need to know that it will pass. If they have prepared themselves by learning about potential problems and differences, developing their language skills, and making a plan to get involved in the new community, they will be able to effectively deal with the challenges of acculturation, alleviate or minimize culture shock. Actually, there are many ways for people to take for reducing cultural clashes. What follows are some suggestions for enhancing the international business experience by reducing clashes with the local culture.

3.1 Learning Throughout Your Stay

You should understand that learning about the host culture is a process that continues throughout your stay in the host culture, and beyond. For more learning will occur after your arrival in the host country. Make certain that you use a wide variety of information sources to learn about the host culture, including local people, newspaper, tourist information, libraries, and your own observation. Find a friend or colleague (either a local resident or an experienced expatriate) to serve a guide and mentor to help you learn as quickly as possible.

3.2 Get Involved

Soon after arrival, become familiar with your immediate physical surroundings. Armed with a good map of the vicinity, leave your hotel and walk in a number of different directions, exploring the city or town on foot. Identify local buildings, what they are used for, where they are in relation to one another, the pattern, if any, of how streets are configured, and where people seem to congregate. A familiarity with the "lay of the land" will provide an excellent base for learning about other aspects of the culture.

3.3 Master Simple Tasks

Within the first several days of arrival, work on familiarizing yourself with some of the basic, everyday survival skills that your hosts take for granted. These include such capacities as using the local currency, using the public transportation system, buying stamps, using the telephone system, and ordering from a menu. By mastering these seemly simple tasks, you will minimize frustrations and embarrassment quickly, as well as gain the self-confidence to master some of the more subtle aspects of the host culture.

3.4 Try to Understand

As difficult as it may be, try to understand your hosts in terms of their culture rather than your own. When you encounter a behavior or an attitude that appears strange or even offensive, try to make sense of it in terms of their cultural assumptions rather than your own. This is not to suggest that you should adopt their attitudes or behaviors, or even like them, but you will better understand them when views from their proper cultural perspective.

3.5　Learn to Live with Ambiguity

Particularly in the beginning, learn to live with the ambiguity of not having all the answers. Trying to operate in a new culture is, to a great extent, a highly ambiguous situation. The person who insists on having immediate and clear-cut answers for everything is likely to be frustrated. It is important for the cultural neophyte to know that there will be many unanswered questions. By being patient and learning to live with ambiguity, the new arrivals will preserve their mental health and buy time to learn more answers, reduce the ambiguity, and thus eventually adjust to the new culture.

3.6　Be Empathetic

As a way of enhancing your relationships with your hosts, make a conscious effort to be empathetic, for example, put yourself in the others' shoes. It is only natural for people to be attracted to those individuals who can see things from their point of view. Empathy can be practiced by becoming an active listener. First try to understand, and then try to be understood.

3.7　Be Flexible and Resourceful

Understand that flexibility and resourcefulness are key elements of adapting to a new culture. When living and working in a different culture, the best-laid plans often are not realized. When plans do not work out as expected, you need to make and execute new plans quickly and efficiently without becoming overstated. Resourceful people are familiar with what is available in the host culture, are comfortable with calling on others for help, and know how to take advantage of available opportunities.

3.8　Be Humorous

Don't lose your sense of humor. People in any situation, either at home or abroad, tend to get themselves in trouble if they take themselves too seriously. When struggling to learn a new culture, everyone makes mistakes that may be discouraging, embarrassing, or downright laughable. In most situations, your hosts will disarmingly forgive your social faux pas. The ability to laugh at your own mistakes (or at least not lose sight of the humorous side) may be the ultimate defense against embarrassment.

To be certain, no bottled remedies for culture shock are to be found at the pharmacy. But, simply knowing that culture shock exists, that it happens to everyone to some extent, and that it is not permanent, is likely to reduce the severity of the symptoms and speed the recovery. Don't think you are pathological or inadequate if you experience some culture shock. The anxiety resulting from trying to operate in a different environment is normal. Give yourself permission to feel frustration, homesickness, or irritability. Eventually, you will work through these symptoms and come up with a much richer appreciation of the host culture. But it is also important to remain realistic. There may be others who, for purely personal reasons, you will not like and **vice versa**. And there are things that may never be understood. But once you understand that these problems are perfectly normal reactions for anyone in the same situation, you can begin to search for solutions.

(Wang Weibo, Che Lijuan, 2008: 107 - 110)

4. Adaptive Cultural Transformation Competence

Adaptive cultural transformation refers to a process in which one constantly adjusts one's own cultural beliefs, values, and behaviors to those in the target culture, and gradually develops multiple identities necessary to operate in different intercultural communication settings with appropriate, effective, and meaningful communicative performance.

Adaptive cultural transformation competence encompasses a wide array of competencies. It not only addresses what competencies one needs in successful communication, but also why and how such competencies can mark one's identities in different social settings. Adaptive cultural transformation competence can be referred to as the ability that enables an individual to communicate appropriately and effectively in the target culture by expanding his or her social identity to one that blends the new set of values, habits, and social norms in the target culture with those in the home country. It consists of a set of skills that are needed in appropriate, effective, and satisfactory cultural adaptation. Therefore, the adaptive cultural transformation competence model consists of three major components: social identity negotiation skills, culture-sensitive knowledge and mindful reflexivity, and communicative competence. (Gao Yongchen, 2010: 246 - 247)

5. Ways to Adapting to a New Culture

In order to adapt to a new cultural society, some effective ways to adapting to a new cultural society should be taken.

5.1　Acquire Knowledge about the Host Culture

We begin with the most obvious, yet most overlooked, suggestion regarding adaptation. Simply put, adaptation is greatly facilitated if you are aware of the characteristics of the culture with which you will be interacting. Chen and Starosta note: "Cultural awareness refers to an understanding of one's own and others' cultures that affect how people think and behave. This includes understanding commonalities of human behavior and differences in cultural patterns." As you have learned throughout this book, gathering a fund of knowledge about another culture takes a variety of forms, ranging from the apparent to the subtle. For example, it is rather clear that learning the language of the host culture produces positive results. In addition, there is ample research that supports the notion that insufficient language skills may result in negative consequences in that it reduces interpersonal interactions. If you cannot learn the language of the host culture, you can at least try to master some of the basics that you can use for exchanging greetings and shopping. (Gao Yongchen, 2010: 252 – 253)

5.2 Learn to Be Open and Flexible

According to Kim, learning how to be open and flexible helps "facilitate strangers adaptation by enabling them to endure stressful challenges and maximize learning." Openness does not mean you talk to every stranger you encounter; rather it implies that you are willing to accept change and are not closed to new ideas. Flexibility also means that competent communicators must develop a repertoire of interpersonal tactics, which is also called "a willingness to use various ways to communicate". You need to be flexible and adapt your communication style to each culture and situation that confronts you. (Gao Yongchen, 2010: 253-254)

5.3 Increase Contact with the Host Culture

As you would suspect, direct contact with the host culture promotes successful adaptation to a new culture. Hence, you should try to follow the advice of Harris and Moran: "Immerse yourself in the host culture. Join in, whenever feasible, the artistic and community functions, the carnivals, the rites, the international and fraternal or professional organizations." (Gao Yongchen, 2010: 254)

6. Behaving Toward Intercultural Personhood

The movement from a cultural to an intercultural perspective with our individual and collective consciousness presents one of the most important and exciting challenges of our time. Toffler (1980) once said, "Today, there are numerous indications of the need for us to pursue a new personhood and a culture that integrates Eastern and Western world views." Gebser's "integral consciousness" presents an emerging mode of consciousness which is integrated.

If we are to actively participate in this evolutionary process, the dualism inherent in our thinking process, which puts materialism against spiritualism, West against East, must be changed. The traditional Western focus on the intellect and material progress need not be considered as "wrong" or "bad". Instead, the Western orientation is a necessary part of an evolutionary stage, out of which yet another birth of higher consciousness, an integration of East and West, might subsequently evolve. We need to realize that both rational and intuitive modes of experiencing life should be fully cultivated. When we realize that both the Eastern and Western types of concepts are real, ultimate, and meaningful, we will realize that Eastern and Western cultures have only given expression to something in part true. The two seemingly incompatible perspectives of East and West can be reconciled without contradictions in a new, higher-level, intercultural perspective—one that more closely approximates the expression of the whole truth of life.

Life, especially human life appears as a process of self-realization. With openness toward change, a willingness to revise our own cultural assumption, and the enthusiasm to work it through, we are on the way to cultivating our human potentialities and to contributing our share in this enormous process of cultural change. Together, the East and the West are showing each other the way.

(Kim, 1994b)

Glossary

1. **multifaceted**   *adj*. having many facets   多方面的
2. **psychological**   *adj*. of, affecting, or arising in the mind; related to the mental and emotional state of a person   心理的,精神的
3. **frustration**   *n*. the feeling of being upset or annoyed, especially because of inability to change or achieve something   (尤指因无能为力而引起的)痛苦;恼怒
4. **eliminate**   *vt*. completely remove or get rid of (something)   消除,根除,除去
5. **symptom**   *n*. (medicine) a physical or mental feature which is regarded as indicating a condition of disease, particularly such a feature that is apparent to the patient: dental problems may be a symptom of other illness   (医)症状
6. **depression**   *n*. severe despondency and dejection, typically felt over a period of time and accompanied by feelings of hopelessness and inadequacy   沮丧,抑郁
7. **hostility**   *n*. hostile behaviour; unfriendliness or opposition   敌对行为,不友善,反对
8. **identify**   *v*. (-ies, -ied) (常作 be identified) recognize or distinguish (especially something considered worthy of attention)   认出,辨别出(尤指值得注意的事物)
9. **paranoid**   *adj*. of, characterized by, or suffering from the mental condition of paranoia   类偏执(或妄想)狂的,有偏执狂特征的
10. **preoccupation**   *n*. the state or condition of being preoccupied or engrossed with something   全神贯注,入神
11. **disorient**   *vt*. make (someone) lose their sense of direction   使迷失方向
12. **isolation**   *n*. the process or fact of isolating or being isolated   隔离;孤立;脱离;分离

13. **ambiguity**   *n.* uncertainty or inexactness of meaning in language   （语言）意义不明确,含糊

14. **excessive**   *adj.* more than is necessary, normal, or desirable; immoderate   过多的,过分的

15. **outright**   *adv.* altogether   全部地,彻底地

16. **eruption**   *n.* an appearance of a rash or blemish on the skin   （发）疹

17. **transitional**   *adj.* relating to or characteristic of a process or period of transition   转变的,变革的;转型期的,过渡期的

18. **sojourn**   *v.* stay somewhere temporarily   短暂地停留,旅居

19. **outcome**   *n.* the way a thing turns out; a consequence   结果,结局;后果

20. **constant**   *adj.* occurring continuously over a period of time   不断的,连续的

21. **consequence**   *n.* a result or effect of an action or condition   结果,后果;影响

22. **disorient**   *v.* (often as adjective disoriented) make（someone）lose their sense of direction.   使（某人）迷失方向

23. **bizarre**   *adj.* very strange or unusual, especially so as to cause interest or amusement   怪诞的,古怪的,奇形怪状的

24. **weird**   *adj.* suggesting something supernatural; uncanny   超自然的,怪异的

25. **harsh**   *adj.* cruel or severe   残酷的,严厉的

26. **alleviate**   *vt.* make（suffering, deficiency, or a problem）less severe   减轻,缓和

27. **acculturation**   *v.* assimilate or cause to assimilate a different culture, typically the dominant one   （使）适应新文化（尤指主流文化）,（使）被同化

28. **enhance**   *v.* intensify, increase, or further improve the quality, value, or extent of [as *adj.*]（enhanced）   提高……的质量（或价值、程度）

29. **vicinity**   *n.* the area near or surrounding a particular place   邻近地区,周围地区,附近

30. **congregate**   *vi.* gather into a crowd or mass   集合,聚集

31. **empathy**   *n.* the ability to understand and share the feelings of another   同感,共鸣;同情

32. **overstate**   *vt.* express or state too strongly; exaggerate   把……讲得过分;夸大

33. **pharmacy**   *n.* a shop or hospital dispensary where medicinal drugs are provided or sold   药店,药房

34. **permanent**   *adj.* lasting or intended to last or remain unchanged indefinitely   永久的,永恒的,持久的

35. **pathological**   *adj.* involving, caused by, or of the nature of a physical or mental disease   由疾病引起的;疾病的

36. **transformation**   *n.* a thorough or dramatic change in form or appearance   （形状、外貌方面）彻底的改变,巨变,改观

37. **encompass**   *vt.* surround and have or hold within   环绕,围绕

38. **array**   *n.* an impressive display or range of a particular type of thing   显眼的一系列,展示,陈列

39. **reflexive**   *adj.* (logic)(of a relation) always holding between a term and itself (逻)(关系)自反的

40. **apparent**   *adj.* clearly visible or understood;obvious   清晰可见的,清晰明了的,明显的

41. **subtle**   *adj.* (especially of a change or distinction) so delicate or precise as to be difficult to analyse or describe   (尤指变化或差别)微妙的,细微的,难以描述的

42. **fraternal**   *adj.* of or like a brother or brothers   兄弟的,兄弟般的

43. **potential**   *adj.* having or showing the capacity to become or develop into something in the future   潜在的,可能的

44. **outcome**   *n.* the way a thing turns out;a consequence   结果,结局;后果

45. **countryman**   *n.* (*pl.*-men) a person from the same country or district as someone else   同乡;同胞

46. **evolutionary**   *n.* the process by which different kinds of living organism are thought to have developed and diversified from earlier forms during the history of the earth   进化,演化

47. **dualism**   *n.* the division of something conceptually into two opposed or contrasted aspects,or the state of being so divided   二元性

48. **materialism**   *n.* a tendency to consider material possessions and physical comfort as more important than spiritual values   实利主义,物质主义

49. **spiritualism**   *n.* (Philosophy) the doctrine that the spirit exists as distinct from matter,or that spirit is the only reality   (哲)唯灵论(主张精神独立于物质之外而存在,精神是唯一的实体),唯心论

50. **evolve**   *v.* develop gradually,especially from a simple to a more complex form   逐步发展,演变

51. **intuitive**   *adj.* using or based on what one feels to be true even without conscious reasoning;instinctive   直觉的,凭直觉感知的

52. **incompatible**   *adj.* (of two things) so opposed in character as to be incapable of existing together   (两物)不能共存的

53. **reconcile**   *vt.* restore friendly relations between   使和解,使和好;把……争取过来

● Comprehension Check

I. Decide whether the following statements are true (T) or false (F).

1. (   ) The longer one lives in a foreign culture,the quicker he or she reaches the

adaptation state.

2. ( ) Recovery stage is a stage of culture shock, in which the new arrivals may feel euphoric and be pleased by all of the new things encountered.

3. ( ) People of different cultural backgrounds usually behave and respond in different ways in the same context.

4. ( ) For some multinational firms, they can alleviate culture shock by selecting employees for overseas assignments who possess certain personal and professional qualifications.

5. ( ) The easier it is to adjust to a new culture, the easier it is to readjust to home culture.

6. ( ) A and B are taking an exam. A cheats in the exam, and B looks down upon such deeds. So we can draw the conclusion that A and B have interest conflicts.

7. ( ) The longer one lives in a foreign culture, the more cultural competence he or she will have.

8. ( ) Knowing yourself is crucial to improving intercultural communication.

9. ( ) Learning a foreign language is sufficient for intercultural understanding.

10. ( ) Intercultural communication competence is contextual.

II. Answer the following questions.

1. What are the symptoms of culture shock?

2. What do you think are the effective ways to alleviate culture shock?

III. Fill in each of the blanks in the following passage with an appropriate word from those listed below, and you will learn more about communication.

A. aware   B. personality   C. challenge   D. individual

E. styles   F. identify   G. ignored   H. impossible

I. Practically   J. means

Any discussion of culture, however fascinating it might be, is not without some problems. Of course one issue is in the defining of culture, as we have seen. In embracing one aspect of culture, another could be __1__. Focusing on religious traditions, for example, can obscure the political practices that may govern and attempt to regulate such traditions. This __2__ that the point of focus might mask or hide, to some extent, the realities occurring under the surface of the issue in question.

Further, although it is probably __3__ to account for every single detail of a dynamic, discursive, meaningful analysis of culture, the important point is to be __4__ that no person or social entity ever operates in isolation, but rather in sync with a host of other incoming variables or influences. __5__ speaking, this means that when we talk about such notions as time and what time means for different groups, we must not forget that time operates in conjunction with speed, context, and in some cases, spatial requirements.

A third problem we face when analyzing intercultural interaction is that not everyone agrees on what constitutes a cultural variable as opposed to ___6___ or character traits. Related to this problem is the fact that cultures are not completely homogeneous, which means that not everyone in a given culture practices the same behavior consistently! The point is this: just as there is no universally accepted definition of culture, so there are also no perfect boundaries for localizing social action, or separating social acts as a symbol of group membership from ___7___ acts. As a general rule, however, we will focus on the larger social practices, rather than on individuality and all its complexity.

Of course another ___8___ is the fact that whenever we make claims about culture, we will no doubt find exceptions to those claims! Any cultural characterization brings with it the high probability of exceptions; in fact, sometimes the exceptions are what help ___9___ the norm. Social linguists often characterize Germans, for example, as being highly direct in their conversational ___10___. It would be wrong, however, to state that all Germans are direct, since obviously other discourse styles exist and some Germans prefer non-confrontational approaches. A well-documented business example describes upper management as using more indirect conversational styles, quite possibly because they no longer feel the need to compete in a direct, confrontational way with their colleagues.

(Melanie Moll, 2012: 8)

Part Three　Knowledge Expansion

Reading 1

Culture Clash

Culture is indefinable in a single sentence. Culture is understood in many different aspects of life by different people. One part of commonly accepted definitions of culture includes the presence of a distinct system of belief and views among the constituents of the society. Many view culture as the actions and behaviors of a society while others view culture as what it produces, including everything from the society's art to its institutions. Cultures differ from each other in their distinctly different systems of belief, value, behavior, etc.. This causes clashes and misunderstandings due to lack of tolerance, patience, and even knowledge of the world of society.

To put it simple, although culture cannot be easily defined, people know it when they see it and are quick to recognize the differences that distinguish a newly encountered culture from their own. Indeed, cultural differences often command much more attention than similarities. Ignorance or lack of patience often causes these differences to appear insurmountable or even lead to intolerable "culture clash".

This clash and lack of patience is very evident in the movie Pushing Hands by director Ang Lee. A white mainstream American woman, Martha, marries a first generation Chinese American, Alex Chu, and has a son. The family grows until one day the father of Alex Chu comes from the Chinese mainland to live with them. He speaks no English. Immediately conflict arises between the American wife and Chinese father-in-law. Martha and Master Chu's cultures are distinctly different. They both have distinct beliefs concerning how people should act or behave in a society. The first spoken sound in the movie comes from Martha when she yells at Master Chu for placing metal in the microwave. Master Chu has probably never worked with a microwave and cannot communicate to ask about the proper procedure. This is the first main example of the cultural differences, lack of understanding, and lack of knowledge. Martha also does not understand the lack of space in her home. Her husband again explains the Asian culture. He says that ten families would live in a home of their size in China.

New cultures force themselves upon Master Chu. He is forced to conform to the new culture around him in order to survive and be happy. He is forced to give up the idea in his Chinese culture that the elders are supposed to be cared for by their children. He finds his way to Chinatown to escape further clashes between his daughter-in-law and himself in his son's home. There he finds even in Chinatown the Asian culture has been forced to conform to mainstream American culture. Respect for elders has been disregarded. Everything has become a business.

New culture forces people to conform in order to survive. Master Chu has no choice but to become American in many ways. He must learn to use microwaves, learn new ways of behaving, and must understand this new American culture.

(Wang Weibo, Che Lijuan, 2008)

Comprehension Check

I. Answer the following questions.

1. What cultural differences between China and American are indicated in the passage?
2. Do you agree that cultural differences often command much more attention than similarities?
3. What do you think of Master Chu's conformity to American culture in order to survive?

II. Translate into Chinese the following passage in the essay.

Culture is indefinable in a single sentence. Culture is understood in many different aspects of life by different people. One part of commonly accepted definitions of culture includes the presence of a distinct system of belief and views among the constituents of the society. Many view culture as the actions and behaviors of a society while others view culture as what it produces, including everything from the society's art to its institutions. Cultures differ from each other in their distinctly different systems of belief, value, behavior, etc.. This causes clash and misunderstandings due to lack of tolerance, patience, and even knowledge of the world of society.

Reading 2

My Successful Experience of Constructing Adaptive Cultural Transformation Competence

Adaptive cultural transformation means a process in which one constantly adjusts one's own cultural beliefs, values, behaviors to those in the target culture, and gradually develops multiple identities that are necessary for him/her to communicate in different intercultural communication settings appropriately, effectively and meaningfully.

Adaptive cultural transformation competence contains a wide range of competencies. It not only stresses what competencies one needs in successful and smooth communication, but also why and how such competencies can show one's identities in different social settings. Adaptive cultural transformation competence can be viewed as the ability which enables a person to communicate appropriately and effectively in the target culture by expanding his or her social identity to one that blends the new cultural elements including values, habits, and social norms in the target culture with those in his/her own home country.

Adaptive cultural transformation competence comprises a set of skills needed in appropriate, effective and satisfactory cultural adaptation. Therefore, it consists of the following main components, that is, social identity negotiation skills, culture-sensitive knowledge and reflexivity, and communicative competence.

My adaptive cultural transformation in the United States did not come easily. The biggest challenge I ever encountered in this process was how to make a balance between my Asian cultural background and the American cultural environment I was living in, and between my identity in Chinese communities and in American ones. I was highly motivated to adapt myself to the American culture — to obtain new cultural experiences so as to understand and appreciate the target culture. But my Chinese-self, which is characterized by Asian beliefs, values, habits, and customs often caused conflicts in the process of my adaptive cultural transformation, which required my strong determination and willingness to recognize my own culture, and at the same time, to understand and respect the target culture.

In North America, I was viewed as a visible minority due to my typical Asian appearance. In order to maintain my L2 social identity, that is to say, to be accepted as a member of the target culture, which was a very important factor contributing to the success of my professional career. I spared no efforts to improve my communication skills and mannerisms in new cultural communication settings. Due to my cultural adaptation, I was often taken for a Chinese American. Although being identified as a Chinese American could be a symbol of my successful cultural adaptation, it was not necessarily so within the Chinese community. I found it hard to be Americanized when being with my Chinese friends. For example, in an only-Chinese group, speaking English would be viewed as showing off; similarly, dressing like Americans would be regarded as being alienated from the Chinese inner group.

At times, I preferred to show my Chinese ethnic identity among American friends, or mixed groups when talking about something that I was very proud of, such as Chinese ethnic foods that I knew how to cook at home, and China's long history with numerous dynasties. Sometimes, I preferred to hide my Chinese ethnic identity when the topic under discussion was something for which China was often being criticized.

While I believed that personal preference of social identity was dependent on the particular social context, I strongly believed that my social identity had multiple dimensions. Each had its function when performed in the right context. I behaved myself as a different person in different social groups and communities. I was very quiet in class when I was in China as a sign to show my respect to teachers, but I was very outspoken in class at Ohio State University as a sign of my cooperation with teachers. I was not very talkative in Chinese communities in the United States, because I did not want to show off, but I was very passionate when talking about China and Chinese people among American friends in that I thought myself as a cultural informant. I seldom wrote Chinese letters to my relatives and friends in China, without being afraid of losing my Chinese, but I wrote almost every day in English because I still found there were some weaknesses in my English writing. Therefore, I had to present different identities in different contexts, and to change my communication styles when speaking to people from different cultural backgrounds in culturally different communication settings on particular occasions.

I also found that social identity sometimes requires mutual acceptance. Even if I wanted to be admitted as a member of an ethnic group, I might be rejected.

For understanding American culture, I would spend Christmas Eve at my American friends' houses for years even though I was invited again and again by my Chinese friends to go to their Chinese Christmas parties. One Christmas, when I wanted to spend the Christmas Eve with my Chinese friends for a change, I was unfortunately not invited. Later I was told by my Chinese friends that they thought I would have declined their invitation if they had asked me again. I felt miserable about this experience. But perhaps my friends were right; blending to a certain ethnic group needs reciprocal action from both sides. What you want to be identified as is not enough without considering what others might think of you.

In my journey of adaptive cultural transformation, I gradually perceived my Chinese culture boundaries as permeable and flexible. Although my Chinese culture and my well-established first language social identity was sometimes like a shield blocking me from constructing my second language identity in American culture, I managed to become open-minded, and found every chance to participate in various social activities to take every opportunity to experience and understand the target culture. I was considered a fluent English speaker by many native English speakers in the United States. But in my first quarter at OSU, I was so afraid of speaking up in the courses I attended. I was overwhelmed by the various teaching styles professors adopted in different courses, the intensity of information given in each class, the amount of reading required before each class, the weekly testing-format, and the straightforwardness of my American classmates. As a result, I kept quiet, trying to figure out what I should do to carve a niche for myself in the new classroom culture. I conducted numerous "experiments" on myself in getting accustomed to this special social setting — the academic content classroom. I tried to speak up when I was pretty sure of something, but failed the first few times, as I was anxious about making grammar mistakes. Then I tried several times to concentrate on the basic concepts in the readings and gave my interpretations of the concepts when they were discussed in class. Undoubtedly, my purposeful preparation somewhat helped my participation, but I still felt nervous to speak up in class as I would pay attention to slightly unnatural tones in my voice. However, I kept trying and reflecting on my own experiences in participation and interaction with classmates. A couple of quarters later I was aware that my participation in classes had become instantaneous, improvised, and effortless.

Learning some of the "normal" behaviors in classroom communication in the target culture, and unlearning some of the "normal" classroom behaviors in my own culture gradually led to an internal transformation in me. In time, I kept far away from the accepted patterns of my original culture in classrooms and acquired the new patterns of the target classroom culture. This brought about an increased functional fitness, a greater congruence and compatibility between my internal state and the conditions of the American classroom environment. As a consequence, my increased oral participation in content courses gradually made me aware of my existence in class. I could voice my opinion in discussion, and I had a sense of belonging. This increased confidence in myself also gradually enabled me to attain a level of communicative success beyond the classroom setting to satisfy my own social needs in such things as dealing with people from different cultural backgrounds, and seeking graduate research and teaching assistants across campus; achieve psychological balance in terms of having high self-confidence, low level of stress and anxiety, and high self-esteem; as well as philosophical drives in terms of being more creative in work and study, and achieving a sense of personal fulfillment.

While my increased classroom participation strengthened my functional fitness and the potential effectiveness of my communicative competence and performance in the target culture outside the classrooms, it had also affected my personality and self-identification, which transformed from being mono-cultural to being increasingly intercultural. Instead of being confined to the Chinese culture, I have taken a more fluid intercultural identity by observing and practicing different sets of social values, beliefs, and norms in different cultural communities. Such an intercultural identity allows me to adjust to the situation and to creatively manage or avoid conflicts that occur frequently in intercultural communication settings. Through this dynamic and continuous process of cultural adaptive transformation, my internal condition has gradually moved toward becoming increasingly intercultural.

(Liu Jun, 2003)

Comprehension Check

I. Answer the following questions.

1. Do you think that social identity is dependent on the social context?
2. Why was it difficult for the author to fit in American culture?
3. In which way was a traditional Chinese classroom different from a typical American one?
4. How can Chinese students adjust themselves to an American classroom setting?

II. Translate into Chinese the following passage in the above text.

Adaptive cultural transformation competence contains a wide range of competencies. It not only stresses what competencies one needs in successful and smooth communication, but also why and how such competencies can show one's identities in different social settings. Adaptive cultural transformation competence can be viewed as the ability which enables a person to communicate appropriately and effectively in the target culture by expanding his or her social identity to one that blends the new cultural elements including values, habits, and social norms in the target culture with those in his/her own home country.

Adaptive cultural transformation competence comprises a set of skills needed in appropriate, effective and satisfactory cultural adaptation. Therefore, it consists of the following main components, that is, social identity negotiation skills, culture-sensitive knowledge and reflexivity, and communicative competence.

Part Four Knowledge Application

Case Analysis

I. Case 1

Home Sick

Huang was the first born son of a well-to-do family in Hong Kong. He had done well in his undergraduate studies at the University of Hong Kong and had been accepted for graduate studies at a prestigious American university. He made his initial adjustment fairly well, finding housing and joining a support group made up of other students from Hong Kong who lived near his university. After a time, however, he began to be disappointed in his work and was unhappy with life in America. He liked an American woman, but the relationship broke up because of their differences in personality. While not failing any of his classes, he was by no means among the top students in his department, as shown by both test scores and participation in class seminars. Not wanting his friends from Hong Kong to learn about his problems, Huang went to the student health center with complaints about an upset stomach, severe headaches, and lower back pain. The doctor at the health center prescribed acetaminophen with codeine. Huang began to take the pills, but the problem persisted.

Analysis:

This case shows the negative effects of culture shock imposed on Huang, an outstanding Hong Kong graduate student who is now studying in the United States. In the process of adjusting to a new culture, some symptoms triggered by culture shock have become detrimental to his psychological wellbeing. Sojourners, depending on their individual personality, may suffer from varying degrees of culture shock. In the case of Huang, he reported to the doctor many symptoms, for which medicine could not provide relief. His disorder is psychological, not physical. The uneasiness, anxiety and alienation induced by assimilating with an entirely different cultural or social environment are the causes of his psychological distress.

II. Case 2

Public and Private

Mark was a native of Britain. As a teacher of English, he had opportunities to work in Asian countries such as Singapore and Japan. In 2001, he was offered a job in Shanghai as a senior trainer. He was glad to accept the offer and was fully confident of the potential in this huge market. He left for Shanghai with the expectation that he would start a brand new life, for he believed that he had understood a lot about oriental culture to communicate with the local people.

Just as he expected, Mark received a warm welcome from his Chinese colleagues when he arrived in Shanghai. With their help, he was able to open three new training centers downtown during the first several months. When he received a large bonus, he treated his coworkers to show his gratitude for their cooperation and hard work. At the dinner, he was thrilled with excitement and future ambitions.

Helpful and hardworking as they were, the Chinese colleagues annoyed Mark in several ways. First, they seemed to care too much about his private life. Several days after they met, they began to ask private questions during casual conversations, including questions about age, family and marriage. When they knew that he was still single, they began to introduce potential girl friends to him despite his clear disapproval. He was quite embarrassed on these occasions.

Another source of irritation was the unexpected arrangement of off-work entertainment. His Chinese colleagues seemed to arrange things on impulse and informed him at the last minute that they were going to sing Karaoke or on an outing. At such moments, he was at the edge of breaking down his composure. Seeing as there was no hope for them to respect his personal schedule, Mark would refuse these unexpected invitations.

Mark sensed that the relationship between them had undergone a subtle change, for his Chinese colleagues began to treat him in a deliberately polite way. When he entered the office, they nodded with an assuming smile. They did not invite him to dinner or Karaoke any longer, and at office they gathered together and whispered in Chinese. Mark sometimes felt lonely at the office and intended to break the ice between them but he did not know how to start. (Dou Weilin, 2011)

Analysis:

There are two major conflicts in this case. The first is that Mark was embarrassed by his Chinese colleagues' over enthusiasm towards his personal life, like family and marriage. People from a Western cultural background don't want their colleagues intruding into their private lives. However, to the Chinese, showing great concern for someone's private life, including introducing a potential girlfriend, indicates a friendly and healthy relationship between colleagues.

Secondly，the spontaneous after-work outing annoyed Mark，who preferred a regular and predictable schedule. His Chinese colleagues believed that they could decide what to do after work even at last minute in the office. Thinking his Chinese colleagues had no consideration for his personal schedule，Mark refused their invitations，which further isolated him from them.

The last straw for Mark was the issue of the medical examination. It is common for Chinese personnel to leave the reports on a table in the conference room，and make it public knowledge in the office. However，Mark thought it a great violation of his privacy to let everybody know about his health status. Their advice and commentary on his health did not improve their image in his eyes which led to his outburst.

Mark decided to leave the office because he felt his colleagues continually violated his sense of privacy. To his Chinese colleagues，Mark was demanding and difficult to please.

Part Five Knowledge Practice

Translation

I. Translate the following passage into Chinese.

Do you think studying in a different country is something that sounds very exciting? Like many young people who leave home to study in another country, do you think you would have lots of desirable fun? Certainly, it is a new experience, which brings the opportunity of discovering fascinating things and a feeling of freedom. In spite of these advantages, however, there are also some challenges you will encounter. Because your views may clash with the different beliefs, norms, values, and traditions that exist in different countries, you may have difficulty adjusting to a new culture and to those parts of the culture not familiar to you.

II. Translate the following passage into English.

很明显，文化冲击是一种生活在异国他乡的人们无法避免的东西。当你经历文化冲击的这四个阶段时，它似乎并不是一件有益的事。然而，当你完全适应了某一种新的文化时，你会更加充分地喜爱这种文化。你学会了如何和他人交流，而且你还了解了大量与自己不同文化背景的人们的生活情况。此外，了解其他各种文化以及当你生活在其中时懂得如何去适应所受到的冲击，可以帮助你更好地了解你自己。

Case Study

I. Case 1

Taking a Taxi

Jun is a Chinese student who has just arrived in New York to begin his graduate studies. After a long and annoying wait with all his luggage, he finally succeeds in hailing a taxi. But the driver asks him to sit in the back seat while the passenger seat in the front is available. Although somewhat confused and agitated, he obeys. The taxi is comfortable, so he is able to relax a little during the long drive to his school. When he arrives, the taxi's meter reads $30.30, so Jun proceeds to take the amount out of his wallet. But the driver turns around and says he should give him $45!

Questions for Discussion:

1. Why does the driver ask Jun to sit in the back seat?
2. Why do you think the taxi driver is asking for $45 instead of $30.30?

II. Case 2

What's Wrong With Training?

This is a Sino-German joint venture. According to the newly signed contract, VW is responsible to train engineers' designing skills, so every year a group of Chinese engineers will be sent to the VW Company in Germany technology.

For the first year, a group of ten engineers were sent to the VW Company, where some worked in two workshops; some worked on some projects with German engineers.

For the first week, they found themselves busy with everything they did and felt they learned a lot from their introduction of each workshop or each project they would join in.

Later, they discovered that German colleagues turned out to be cold to them, leaving them alone. These Chinese colleagues were not responsible for any part of the projects although German colleagues were busy all the time. Therefore, they began to feel that German colleagues did not trust them.

After the whole day's work, they came back to their apartment and began to complain to themselves, thinking about why each project leader or manager didn't assign any part of the work to them.

Half a year later, they are back home, feeling that they have not learned anything there, but wonder why the German engineers didn't welcome their training there.

What's wrong with them?

(Zhuang Enping, 2011:309)

Questions for Discussion:

1. What made the Chinese engineers feel that their German colleagues seemed cold to them?

2. Why did the Chinese engineers complain that they did not learn anything in German after they came back?

3. What suggestions would you give to the Chinese engineers on how to show their concern and take more initiative in doing things?

References

[1]   SAMOVAR L A, PORTER R E, STEFANI L A. Communication Between Cultures [M]. 3rd ed. Beijing: Foreign Language Teaching and Research Press, 2000.

[2]   SAMOVAR L A, PORTER R E, MCDANIEL E D. Communication Between Cultures [M]. 6th ed. Boston: Wadsworth, 2007.

[3]   LERMAN. Antony "Guardian.co.uk" [M]. London: Guardian. Retrieved, 2010.

[4]   MELANIE MOLL. The Quintessence of Intercultural Business Communication [M]. Berlin Springer-Verlag Berlin and Heidelberg, 2012.

[5]   DESHUN LI. On Chinese Culture[M]. Heilongjiang: Heilongjiang Education Press, 2016: 31 - 34.

[6]   GHENADIE ANGHEL. Doomed to Internationalization and Modernization of Corporate Culture[M]. Gabler Verlag: Springer Fachmedien Wiesbaden GmbH, 2012: 24 - 27.

[7]   YIJIE TANG. Confucianism, Buddhism, Daoism, Christianity and Chinese Culture [M]. Beijing: Foreign Language Teaching and Research Publishing Co., Ltd., 2015: 17 - 18.

[8]   HALL ET. Beyond Culture [M]. New York: Anchor Books, 1977.

[9]   JUNE OCK YUM. Confucianism and Communication: Jen, Li and Ubuntu [J]. China Media Research, 2007, 3(4).

[10]   HALL, EDWARD. The Silent Language [M]. New York: Doubleday & Company, 1959.

[11]   VARNER I, BEAMER L. Intercultural Communication in the Global Workplace [M]. Beijing: Tsinghua University Press, 2003.

[12]   DAVIS L. Doing Culture: Cross-Cultural Communication in Action [M]. Beijing: Foreign Language Teaching and research Press, 2004.

[13]   DRESSLER D, CARNS D. Sociology: The Study of Human Interaction [M]. New York: Alfred A. Knopf, 1969.

[14]   HOFSTEDE, GEERT. Culture and Organization: Software of the Mind [M]. New York:

McGraw Hill, 1997.

[15] GUDYKUNST W B. Bridging Differences: Effective Intergroup Communication [M]. Thousand Oaks, CA: Sage Publications Inc., 1998.

[16] MEHRABIAN A, WIENER M. Decoding of Inconsistent Communications [J]. Journal of Personality and Social Psychology, 1967.

[17] MARTIN J, NAKAYAMA T. Experiencing Intercultural Communication: An Introduction [M]. 2nd ed. New York: McGraw-Hill Companies, Inc., 2005.

[18] AXTELL R E. Gesture [M]. New York: JohnWiley & Sons, Inc., 1991.

[19] KEESING F. Cultural Anthropology: The Science of Custom [M]. New York: Hot, Rinehart, & Winston, 1965.

[20] HALL E T. Beyond Culture [M]. New York: Doubleday, 1976.

[21] DAVIS L. Doing Culture: Cross-Cultural Communication in Action [M]. Beijing: Foreign Language Teaching and Research Press, 2001.

[22] STORTI C. Figuring Foreigners Out: A Practical Guide [M]. Yarmouth, Maine: Intercultural Press, Inc., 1999.

[23] OATEY H. The Customs and Language of Social Interaction [M]. Shanghai: Shanghai Education Press, 1988.

[24] NOVINGER, TRACY. Intercultural Communication: A Practical Guide [M]. Press: University of Texas Press, 2011.

[25] WILL BAKER. Intercultural Awareness: Modelling an Understanding of Cultures in Intercultural Communication Through English as a Lingua Franca [J]. Language and Intercultural Communication, 2011,8(3): 198 - 200.

[26] REGIS MACHART, FRED DERVIN, MINGHUI GAO. Intercultural Masquerade [M]. Beijing: Higher Education Press, 2016: 19 - 20.

[27] CHAIKA E. Language: The Social Mirror [M]. New York: Newbury House Publishers, 1989.

[28] VARNER I, BEAMER L. Intercultural Communication in the Global Workplace [M]. 3rd ed. Shanghai: Shanghai Foreign Language Education Press, 2006.

[29] DODD C H. Dynamics of Intercultural Communication [M]. 5th ed. New York: Mc-Graw Hill Companies. Inc., 1998.

[30] HALL E T. The Silent Language [M]. New York: Anchor Books Editions, 1990a.

[31] HOFSTEDE G. Culture's consequences: Comparing values, behaviors, institutions, and organizations across nations [M]. 2nd ed. Thousand Oaks: Sage Publications, 2001.

[32] HU WENZHONG, CORNELIUS N, ZHUANG ENPING. Encountering the Chinese: A Modern Country, An Ancient Culture [M]. 3rd ed. London: Intercultural Press, 2010.

[33] DAVID SOLOMON, P.C. Lo: The Common Good: Chinese and American Perspectives [M]. London: Springer Dordrecht Heidelberg, 2013: 97 - 100.

[34] WANG DAWEI. New Horizon College English — Speaking, Listening, Viewing (3) [M]. 2nd ed. Beijing: Foreign Language Teaching and Research Press, 2011.

［35］ LI YINHUA. College English-Integrated Course （2）［M］. Shanghai：Shanghai Foreign Language Education Press，2003.

［36］ CHEN GUOMING，WILLIAM J S. Foundations of Intercultural Communication ［M］. Shanghai：Shanghai Foreign Language Education Press，2007.

［37］ KIM YY. Intercultural Personhood：An Integration of Eastern and Western Perspectives ［M］//In L.A. Samovar & R.E. Porter（eds.）Intercultural Communication：A Reader ［M］. 7th ed. Belmont，Calif.：Wadsworth Publishing Co.，1994b.

［38］ LIU JUN. From an EFL Learner to an ESL Leader：Reflections in a Nonnative Voice. Featured Speech at 2003 TESOL Convention in Baltimore ［C］. Maryland，USA，2003.

［39］ ZHUANG ENPING. Intercultural Business Communication ［M］. Beijing：Capital University of Economics and Business Press，2011：309.

［40］ Snowball JD. Measuring the Value of Culture ［M］. Berlin：Capital Springer-Verlag，2008：20‐21.

［41］ 贾玉新.跨文化交际学[M].上海：上海外语教育出版社,1997.

［42］ 胡文仲.跨越文化的屏障[M].北京：外语教学与研究出版社,2004.

［43］ 胡超.跨文化交际实用教程[M].北京：外语教学与研究出版社,2006.

［44］ 陈文娟,嫣小凤.跨文化交际叙事研究[M].北京：国防工业出版社,2012.

［45］ 窦卫霖.跨文化交际基础[M].北京：对外经济贸易大学出版社,2007.

［46］ 许力生.跨文化交流入门[M].杭州：浙江大学出版社,2004.

［47］ 许力生.跨文化交际英语教程[M].上海：上海外语教育出版社,2004.

［48］ 汪福祥,马登阁. 文化撞击——案例评析[M].北京：石油工业出版社,1999.

［49］ 杜瑞清,田德新,李本现.跨文化交际学选读[M].西安：西安交通大学出版社,2004.

［50］ 高永晨.跨文化交际与地球村民[M].苏州：苏州大学出版社,2009.

［51］ 邓炎昌,刘润清.语言和文化[M].北京：外语教学与研究出版社,1989.

［52］ 余卫华.跨文化研究读本[M].武汉：武汉大学出版社,2006.

［53］ 王维波,车丽娟.跨文化商务交际[M].北京：外语教学与研究出版社,2008.

［54］ 窦卫霖.跨文化商务交际[M].北京：高等教育出版社,2011.